Alcoholism, Family and Social Work Practice

Alcoholism, Family and Social Work Practice

C.P. Singh

RAWAT PUBLICATIONS
Jaipur • New Delhi • Bangalore • Hyderabad • Guwahati • Kolkata

ISBN 978-81-316-0696-4

Published by
Prem Rawat for **Rawat Publications**
Satyam Apts, Sector 3, Jawahar Nagar, Jaipur 302 004 (India)
Phone: 0141 265 1748 / 7006 Fax: 0141 265 1748
E-mail: info@rawatbooks.com
Website: www.rawatbooks.com

New Delhi Office
4858/24, Ansari Road, Daryaganj, New Delhi 110 002
Phone: 011 2326 3290

Also at *Bangalore, Hyderabad, Guwahati* and *Kolkata*

Typeset by Rawat Computers, Jaipur
Printed at Nice Printing Press, New Delhi

Dedicated to

alcohol affected families, professional social workers and all those concerned with fighting alcoholism

Contents

List of Tables and Figures

Tables

Figures

Acknowledgement

My association with professional social work is more than three decades old as a student, social worker, teacher, researcher, and practitioner. During this period I learnt to study and understand society, people and their problems in a different perspective which is more mature, scientific and different in approach. During my interaction with people in field work, in research and practice, I found that the problem of alcohol use, abuse, and problem drinking is a very serious problem but neither the suffering population nor the governing and controlling authorities are taking it seriously. The sufferings of the effected people and disintegrating family relations prompted me to study this problem with a different angle.

While writing acknowledgement, as a normal human being, I was struck by emotions and the feeling of elation and cheering as something is done by me in the area of social work education and practice. The feeling of elation because I realized that my association with such an interesting and complex work is now in the shape of a book for which I spent my days and nights as feeling concerned about the suffering families, individuals, about the seriousness of the problem and its effects. Cheering because I felt that the readers may find that the complex nature and magnitude of the problem of alcohol addiction needs that there is still so much to be done, so much to be discovered, so much to meliorate and improved upon. It may work as a source to encourage others to find out some ways and means to fight with the myths and misconceptions prevailing in the society about the use and abuse of alcohol and be able to present a realistic and correct view.

This work has been made possible by the support, encouragement and guidance of many well-wishers. I would like to express my debt and gratitude to all those who co-operated with me by sparing their valuable time and wisdom while interacting with me and my team and provided the desired information.

I am specially grateful to all the respondent families who confided in me and answered all my queries and participated in discussions patiently. My thanks are due to Professor R.K. Upadhyay for his feedback which encouraged me to work with more zeal and enthusiasm. I would also like to express my gratitude to all the faculty members of the Department of Social Work, Kurukshetra University, Kurukshetra.

At this important movement of my life, I wish to remember my mother late Smt. Sudha Rani Tanwar who has always been an eternal source of inspiration and guidance to me. I also offer my deepest regards to my revered father Chaudhry Pritam Singh Tanwar who imbibed in me the qualities of hard work, honesty and dedication.

Finally my thanks to Mrs. Santosh Tanwar my wife the best friend and a sincere companion of my life and Swati and Siddhartha my talented children and Ishashish Raghava my beloved son-in-law who bear with me in all my anxieties and frustrations and kept me occupied with pen and paper.

C.P. Singh

Prologue

On the basis of continuous media coverage, reports of experts, national and international research findings it is obvious that many problems are increasing in society because of alcohol consumption. It has also diverted the attention of all concerned toward the menace of alcohol abuse and problem drinking. Criminal incidences associated with alcohol intake such as theft, property disputes, kidnapping, drug trafficking, rape, murder etc. are the extreme whereas the abuse of alcohol is primarily responsible for the break-up of the family structure. Fast changing modern society, increasing industrialization and modernization are mainly considered responsible for stress, tension and frustration among people and who also struggle to cope up with an adverse environment in family, neighbourhood, community and work place where they live and work. The use and abuse of alcohol is precipitated by the prevailing myths and misconceptions in the society. Ignorant, illiterate and unaware common persons could not understand that alcohol has been accepted as status symbol, helpful in reducing tension, gives soothing effect in tiredness and a means of enjoyment, is responsible for total destruction and has ruined the personal, family, professional and social life of the person.

According to Word Health Organization, alcohol has been identified as fifth largest risk factor for the global burden of injury and diseases. It is the third largest risk factor in industrialized countries and now the highest risk factor in developing countries. It means that millions of children growing up in families, are impaired by parental alcohol problems, and a large number of families are affected by alcohol abuse resulting in increase in divorce, family breakup, child-neglect and abuse, financial crises and other family problems. It is also a main cause of road accidents and liver diseases. Information from enforcement agencies about the increase in production and marketing of alcohol reveals that day by day a large number of people are involved in drinking at high risk level, which is not only the problem of individual health and well-being, but also poses a serious threat to society as well as to the family.

Alcoholism is a progressive disease responsible for major physical and mental health problems which leads to individual disorganization and ending to hospitalization (if arranged timely), mental and physical deterioration and even causing death. In the developing countries like India it is seriously affecting all the sections of population resulting to serious family problems. But neither at the individual nor at the government level thoughtful efforts are done to deal with this problem which is affecting large number of people for which the exact figures are not available but can be estimated by calculating that one alcoholic at least affects four other key individuals such as the spouse, children, relatives and employer directly and many more indirectly such as neighbours, friends, co-workers, co-passengers etc. Various dimensions of these problems require different types of interventions which broadly include control on supply of alcohol, reducing demand of alcohol and followed by scientific and professional treatment of those whose problems are associated with alcohol use.

The Plan of the Book

In this book an attempt has been made to study, discuss and analyse the problem of alcohol abuse based on the study of 800 families in the state of Haryana, India affected with this problem and practical experience of the author in dealing with this problem during his practice for the last two and a half decades.

The first chapter gives an over all perspective of the problem, production, availability of alcoholic beverages, level of alcohol consumption in Haryana and alcohol related problems, status and effects of alcohol abuse in the light of researches and the methodology used to study the problem.

The second chapter discusses the socio-economic condition of the affected families, marital status, educational level, technical know-how, family composition and number of family members using alcohol, duration, frequency, time, place and company of use, income and income consumption pattern of families and use of alcohol among children are some major areas covered to find out the effects of alcohol use and problem drinking in the family.

The third chapter covers some facts about marital and domestic life, domestic violence, child abuse and neglect, school performance of the children, sufferings and emotional problems of children, sexual abuse of children, financial problems of the family and information about family's assets, loan and problems of indebtedness among the families suffering from the alcohol abuse.

The chapter four presents the health status of person/persons using alcohol, the health problems of spouse and children including mental health problems of the family members and efforts of the family for the treatment of the alcoholic or problem drinker.

The chapter five discusses the social implications of alcohol use in family and tries to analyse the social position and relationships with neighbours, friends, relatives, celebrations of social and religious functions in such families, behaviour of problem drinkers, violence outside home and confrontation with police, accidents and injuries. Major sufferings of alcohol affected families due to social ostracism are also discussed in the chapter.

The chapter six provides the guidelines for the treatment of alcoholics with an emphasis on social work intervention through family. How family counseling and if required use of family therapy by the social workers could help the families affected by the problem of alcohol abuse and problem drinking. A practical approach is presented to deal with the problem by discussing the real examples as experienced by the author while dealing such cases during practice and research work.

The chapter seven present some case studies discussing the real life situations of the suffering families and finally chapter eight concludes with presenting recommendations for further policy strategies, steps for education and public awareness, health and the treatment provisions, intervention and assistance for families affected by alcohol abuse and problem drinking.

The overall purpose of this book is to:

- dispel myths about alcohol and alcohol abuse, its effects and beliefs.
- evaluate the realities and doubts regarding its effects on individuals and family members with the empirical data.
- provide correct information about the use, abuse of alcohol and its effects based on sufferings, observation and present state of knowledge of the affected population.
- discuss physical, psycho-social, health and financial aspects of the victim families due to alcohol abuse and problem drinking.
- contribute to better informed public opinions.
- provide update and contemporary treatment methodology and strategies to over come/minimize the problem.
- encourage the sufferers specially women and children to face this problem more realistically and try to find out solutions through professional approaches.
- give an open platform for further research in this area.

At the end, it would not be out of place to mention that the present work is only a moderate attempt to study a very complex problem. It will not only point out significantly the problems faced by families because of alcohol abuse/dependence and problem drinking but will also help the government in framing public friendly alcohol policy and to incorporate changes time to time in it. The study will also provide guidelines to NGOs and civil society groups, students, teachers and researchers working in the field of alcohol abuse/dependence and problem drinking.

C.P. Singh

1

The Problem of Alcohol Abuse in India

The history of mankind reveals that there have always been those who for a variety of reasons have resorted to substances, which have capacity to alter sensations, mood, and consciousness and produce euphoric effects. Alcohol use has been the part of man's behaviour since times immemorial but its effect on the person as individual, on family and on the community had been experienced in many ways. It has been observed that in the present world of competition, modernity and show off, the normative and controlled drinking behaviour, a feature of ancient drinking is severely affected. The social customs and community surveys reveal that now throughout the world a large number of people use alcoholic beverages in different forms and to varying extents. People drink alcohol in moderate quantity on most occasions; some indulge in drinking at high-risk levels.

The use of alcohol in India has long traditional and social roots dating back to 2000 BC to early Indo-Aryan civilization (Dube, 1972). Aryans would drink a liquid known as *somras* derived from the *sarcostemma vimivale* plant on all occasions of festivities and sacred rites. The *Rig Veda*, the most accepted and respected religious, literature, explains 120 hymns to *somras*. In these hymns many qualities of *somras* are explained as *amrita* (draught of immorality), *gods' drink*, etc. It recognized *somras* as life prolonging and strength giving substance (*Rig Veda*).

In the *Veda*, there are references to the drinking of *sura* another form of intoxicating liquid. As the explanations reveal it appears to have been used by the common folk which gives a vulgar intoxication and it is perhaps, for this reason that a certain degree of odium is attached to it 'दुर्मदासो न सुरायाम्' – Just like the persons badly intoxicated with 'sura' (liquor) – (*Rig Veda*, viii, 2,12).

Sura, a beverage distilled from rice meal, was popular among warriors (*Kshatriyas*) and the peasant population. This description in the ancient Indian literature verifies that, the use of alcohol was present in ancient society in one or the other way also. There are evidences to show that in the age of *Ramayana* and *Mahabharata* *Somras* was used by kings and their courtiers.

There is no agency to record any statistics about the use of alcohol and total number of alcoholics in India, but it is evident that like other parts of the world a large number of people drink alcohol in India also. Since the Vedic period (1500 to 700 BCE), the Islamic invasions (1100 to 1800 CE), the period of British rule (1800 to 1947) and the period of post-independent India, the consumption of alcoholic beverages has changed considerably. Hazardous and excessive drinking is common in India. Various researches have indicated that moderate social drinking is a minority practice (Bryan, 2010). The World Health Organization (WHO) estimates that there are about 2 billion people worldwide consuming alcohol beverages (Global Status Report on Alcohol, WHO, 2004). In India, the recorded per capita consumption of pure alcohol per adult (15 years+) in 1996 was 0.99 litres (WHO, 2002). This consumption seems to be low as compared to other countries such as Slovenia (15.15 litres), Republic of Korea (14.40 litres), Australia (9.55 litres), United Kingdom (9.41 litres), United States of America (8.90 litres), Russian Federation (8.08 litres), Canada (7.52 litres) but the trend in per capita consumption in India is alarming. While the per capita consumption of alcohol beverages in 1970–72 was 0.45 litres, it increased to 0.93 litres in 1994–96. The 106.67 per cent increase in consumption of alcohol is the leading risk factor for disease burden in developing countries like India and also responsible for many psychological, social and psycho-social problems in society.

Alcohol does significant harm to the physical, psychological and social health of individuals, families and communities throughout the world (WHO, 1995). Alcohol is a dependence producing drug and this dependence is associated with an increased risk of illness and death which has serious social effects on the society.

In other words, alcohol abuse damages health. Death rates are much higher in alcohol abusers than non-abusers, i.e. two to four times higher in the case of men, and three to seven times higher in the case of women (Edward, 1989). The higher death rate for women reflect a difference in the way women and men metabolise alcohol. Women tend to begin drinking heavily at an older age, when their organ systems are more vulnerable (Schuckit, 1995). These situations may not be apparent in traditional communities of Asian and African countries where women are culturally and socially bound. In tribal communities where drinking alcohol among women is common the death rate among women may be higher than men.

Production and Availability of Alcoholic Beverages

In India, alcoholic beverages are produced in many settings such as licensed industrialized sector and illicit home brew. The industrialized sector is a rapidly growing industry in which maximum share is of beer industry while wine industry is new and still in its initial stage of growth. The spirits industry is divided into two parts (i) Indian Made Foreign Liquor (IMFL), (ii) Country Liquor. Large industrial houses make IMFL and the country liquor is made by small manufacturers from locally available raw materials (mostly molasses) marketed locally in different names (in India) such as *desi sharab, tari, areack, tharra, anguri,* etc. These are cheap and legally available alcoholic drinks, so, much popular among masses and consumed in large quantities all over the country. Besides, the above-mentioned categories of IMFL and country liquor, illicit liquor are also produced in small and domestic distilleries all over the country. No tax or excise duty is paid on these illegally produced alcoholic beverages. Therefore, they are cheaper than even country liquor hence extremely popular in rural and tribal areas.

Table 1.1 shows that there is a constant increase in the production of alcoholic beverages in India except in 1986–87, 1992–93 and 1993–94 for which no explanations are given. This increase in the production of alcohol exposed the people to an increased and easy availability of alcoholic beverages. Information regarding the years 1989–90 and 1990–91 are not available. There is a decrease in the production from 1992–93 to 1993–94 for which the reasons are not clear. Perhaps, it is because of the non-availability of complete information from some states rather than actual decrease in production. The data on the production of beer and wine is not included in this table.

Table 1.1 Estimated alcohol production in India 1982–2007 (in million litres)

Year	*Production*
1982–83	286.3
1983–84	310.5
1984–85	331.1
1985–86	340.7
1986–87	320.5
1987–88	343.2
1988–89	419.0
1989–90	No Data
1990–91	No Data
1991–92	489.5
1992–93	346.7
1993–94	362.6
1994–95	605.6
1995–96	No Data
1996–97	No Data
1997–98	No Data
1998–99	1411.8
1999–2000	1654.0
2000–01	1685.9
2001–02	1775.2
2002–03	1869.7
2003–04	1969.2
2004–05	2074.5
2005–06	2187.0
2006–07	2300.4

Source: Prevention of harm from alcohol use, WHO, 2003 and 10th five year plan.

The rapid economic and socio-cultural changes accompanied by the easy availability of alcohol puts a serious dent in the normative drinking behaviour in Indian society. In ancient societies drinking was controlled by religious edicts, prospective norms and social controls on the availability of alcohol, which is now losing its control because of changes in the administrative structure, economic and technological development, socio-cultural changes. The reports of World Health Organization show that there is 106.67 per cent increase in the consumption of alcohol in adult population in India (Global Status Report on Alcohol, WHO, 1999). The figures given in Table 1.2 explain the per capita consumption of alcohol in India.

Table 1.2 Estimated production and per capita consumption of alcohol in India – 1995–96 (in litres)

Total population	936 million
Adult population	606 million
Licit absolute alcohol production	788.8 million
Illicit absolute alcohol production	394.4 million
Total absolute alcoholic production	1183.2 million
Per capita total population consumption	1.26
Per capita adult consumption	1.95
Per capita adult male consumption (Female consumption 5%)	3.56
Per capita adult male drinker consumption (Drinking among 40% adult males)	8.90

Source: Prevention of harm from alcohol use, WHO, 2003.

The alcohol use in India is very uneven among different regions, population groups and socio-economic strata. The estimates given in Table 1.2, explain that though the per capita consumption for India is low, the figures are rising considerably for all adults, adult males and adult male drinkers. If the figures of unrecorded illicit alcohol consumption are included, the per capita consumption will be much higher.

Alcohol Consumption in Haryana

The figures of alcohol consumption in Haryana indicate that this state is not an exception to the worldwide increase in alcohol use. The figures show that in 1990, 13 to 14 crore bottles of liquor were consumed, of which legal liquor (both country made and Indian made foreign liquor) constituted 8.17 crore bottles and rest was *'desi-daru'* (illicit liquor). The revenue records also confirm that in November 1966 when the state of Haryana was created out of Punjab, it was getting only ₹ 3.53 crore from all types of excise revenue and the earnings from alcohol were just a little less than ₹ 3 crore. But in the year 1990–91, the state earned about ₹ 117 crore from liquor excise alone (*The Hindustan Times*, 1 May 1990). The government expects to collect ₹ 2,200 crore revenue from excise in 2010–11 as against anticipated collection of ₹ 2,000 crore in the financial year 2009–10. As outlined in the current year's policy the government has decided to renew the needs of both country liquor and Indian made foreign liquor at a reasonable increase of 10 per cent and 5 per cent (expect L-2 vends of Gurgoan, Faridabad, Palwal, Mewat, Rewari, and Narnaul which would be renewed at an increase of 8 per cent respectively. This increase in the excise from the sale of liquor confirms the phenomenal increase in the consumption of liquor.

Table 1.3 Consumption of alcohol in Haryana

Year	*Country Liquor (proof litres)*	*IMFL (proof litres)*	*Beer (bulk litres)*
1966–67	1,420,345	50,785	146,994
1970–71	41,46,157	170,546	567,526
1975–75	5,496,374	1,513,180	1,551,665
1980–81	49,93,664	44,43,067	57,21,755
1981–82	72,32,976	50,49,768	71,39,032
1982–83	80,05,330	54,32,743	62,61,948
1983–84	1,00,81,749	81,51,318	64,32,728
1984–85	1,19,97,430	77,84,723	82,44,445
1985–86	1,29,16,338	94,31,469	1,01,59,798
1986–87	1,34,85,708	1,12,44,918	86,86,941
1987–88	1,66,19,187	1,34,12,104	1,01,66,464
1988–89	1,87,52,696	1,36,72,159	1,96,88,826
1989–90	2,12,17,271	1,59,72,335	1,31,06,187
1990–91	2,38,54,788	1,79,82,875	1,59,00,936
1991–92	2,66,36,938	1,63,30,489	1,11,91,069

Cont'd...

...Cont'd

1992–93	2,87,03,526	1,83,71,962	1,26,02,363
1993–94	3,00,84,612	1,79,56,761	91,92,873
1994–95	3,10,73,144	1,84,97,378	97,87,197
1995–96	3,14,25,065	1,89,04,517	1,06,09,851
1996–97	Enforced Prohibition w.e.f. 01–07–1996		
1997–98	Prohibition (Full year)		
1998–99	3,11,87,000	2,13,93,244	1,70,75,375
1999–2000	3,70,00,000	2,02,57,525	1,75,97,216
2000–01	4,29,90,000	1,76,88,000	1,70,41,875
2001–02	4,50,00,000	1,91,31,000	1,43,64,000
2003–04	4,27,39,000	1,78,06,000	1,39,17,361
2004–05	43,97,86,000	2,02,27,000	1,58,24,510
2005–06	4,15,70,000	2,33,21,000	1,55,95,750
2006–07	5,75,40,753	3,61,33,675	5,79,29,513
2007–08	6,80,95,531	4,65,27,197	70,156,104
2008–09	7,16,64,405	4,17,14,714	53,109,094
2009–10	9,60,64,711	5,06,57,544	63,244,149

Source: Excise and Taxation Department, Haryana (2010–11).

The increase in the consumption of alcohol especially in rural areas posed a major socio-economic problem, which effected community and family life of every village and household. A large part of family income was siphoned off to the licensed liquor shops or liquor traders, resulting to a lot of sufferings especially for women and children (Singh, 2000). The health of the person using alcohol regularly was severely affected and the women and children were regularly beaten up. This resulted into widespread agitations against the distribution, sale and use of alcohol in the state, and women took a leading role in these agitations. The government was forced to review its policy on liquor sale, and all the licensed shops in rural areas were closed in 1993–94. After the change of government in Haryana the total prohibition was introduced from 1 July 1996. This abrupt promulgation of prohibition in the state was a political decision, not based on scientific and rational steps. This resulted into serious administrative, financial and law and order problems in the state. The government had to review its decision and the prohibition was removed in April 1998.

The consumption of alcohol in Haryana has increased and it affects all sections of society in the state. Hence, it becomes essential to study the effects of alcohol abuse on the 'family', the basic unit of society. Therefore, an attempt has been made to study the problem of alcohol use and its effect on family in Haryana where time-to-time efforts were made to restrict consumption of alcohol by curbing illicit distillation of alcohol, imposing local tax on sale of alcohol (in rural areas) and introducing prohibition as political and administrative measures.

Alcohol Related Problems

The customs of drinking alcohol and the problems related to alcohol abuse are very complex and diverse in nature. The diversity in the forms of alcohol as stated earlier and the reasons for their use have also meant widely differing patterns of drinking, and widely ranging consequences. At one side, alcohol is useful for medical purposes and is widely used in pharmaceutical compositions, where as on the other side, its use for pleasure brings many problems. Heavy and inappropriate drinking leads to very serious individual, family, community, and social problems.

Drinking alcohol may never have been problem-free for traditional societies, but in the modern world problems from drinking have taken on new dimensions. Economic and political changes throughout the world bring technology at the doorstep of a common man. The fast and competitive life has changed the life style and thinking of the man. Thus, drinking alcohol today cannot be understood simply in terms of traditional problems, but it has entered into the new forms resulting into the changing social circumstances, which may lead to an escalation of alcohol related physical and social problems. Alcohol related problems may occur in many realms of human life. Practically no organ in the body is immune from alcohol related harm (Bower, 1992). Drinking can bring in its wake emotional and mental disorders. Alcohol is casually implicated in many casualties, both to drinker and to others. Many social, economic and health problems are due to use of alcohol and the pattern of drinking can adversely affect family life, community life, occupational and work life and performance of social roles.

The drinking of alcohol, which has been the part of our social life, mostly starts with the light to moderate quantities on various occasions. This light to moderate drinking of alcohol doesn't have serious adverse consequences; rather it is experienced as a means of enjoyment, relief and relaxing agent in the stress and troublesome situations of life. In developing countries like India where illiteracy and ignorance are the major characteristics of the population such type of myths and beliefs about alcohol are common. But the realities about the effects of use of alcohol in any quantity are different from these prevailing beliefs. The international evidences indicate that light to intermediate levels of alcohol consumption may have a protective effect upon rates of premature mortality (Gronbeek et al., 1994; Plant, 1994) but in spite of this, some of those who drink, do so in ways that lead to adverse consequences, either to themselves or to others. Most of this harm is attributed to acute, periodic heavy and inappropriate drinking; which is the result of light and occasional use of alcohol.

Drinking can impair performance as a parent, as a spouse, and as a contributor to household functioning. In many families where drinking alcohol is very common it is the major cause of their financial and domestic problems. Wife battering, child neglect and violence are common. It was observed while visiting the family counseling centres that most of the family problems are because of alcohol abuse. The spouse specially wife is either deserted or sometimes lives willingly separately or with parents, when the habit of drinking alcohol by husband becomes intolerable for her. In such situations the entire burden of family shifts to the wife. It becomes more serious when the wife is illiterate (which is common in the developing countries like India) and there is no source of income. In rural areas the problem of drinking is responsible for disturbing the source of earning of agriculture based families to the extent that many drinkers have sold their agriculture land and left their families bare hand.

The problem is very serious in labour families where the major part of income is spent on alcohol. In these families the daily budget of the family depends on the daily earnings. The earning hand of the family comes intoxicated in the evening having hardly anything left out of his day's earning for the daily needs of family members. Thus the drinking habit of the sole earning hand consumes his hard earned money and depletes resources of a poor family, leaving family members in distress.

The negative impact of alcohol on society is clearly visible in report by WHO which shows that alcohol is responsible for an estimated 7,74,000 deaths per year, and also for an estimated 3.5 per cent of the total burden of diseases (Global Status Report on Alcohol, WHO, 1999). The family is the direct sufferer because this damages not only the economy of family but also destroys this basic unit of society. The damage can be immediate, such as violence associated with intoxication or long term problems for example financial problems, discard and breakdown of family and ill health. Child neglect is a very common problem in such families. In a survey by European Union it was found that at least 4.5 million children in Europe are living in families suffering from the effects of alcohol. The child may experience various forms of dereliction and feel abandoned by parents. The female family members are the worst victims of verbal or physical aggression. They also witness violent conflicts between parents, which is a serious threat for the development of a healthy personality.

It has been observed that social life is often severely disturbed by the use of alcohol in the family. It is contrary to the thinking of people that alcohol leads to enhance the enjoyment and status in the society. In reality it has been observed that when the pattern of drinking changes from light and moderate drinking to regular and heavy drinking the activities particularly social and recreational within the family are likely to be restricted as the drinker becomes unwilling or unable to participate. In many situations the other family members themselves choose to avoid activities out of fear of the behaviour of the drinker.

The prolonged and excessive use of alcohol affects the individual, his psyche, his physique and interpersonal relations. Marital, parent-child and inter-family relations often become tense. The family members and in many cases individuals who have been experiencing the effects of alcohol use, and abuse want to get rid of this problem. The hospital records (where available) show that people come there for treatment but the patients discontinue treatment or even if they are well treated and go to their homes, relapse after sometime. Recently many studies have been conducted on alcohol and drug abuse, reporting it the cause of road accidents, crime and abuse among youth etc. but no efforts have been made to

Figure 1.1 Coverage of alcohol trading, trafficking and other related news in local newspapers in Haryana, India shows the magnitude and level of the problem

दैनिक जागरण सोमवार, 4 जुलाई, 2005

नकली शराब की फैक्टरी का भंडाफोड़, एक काबू

जागरण संवाददाता, हिसार

जिला पुलिस के आबकारी स्टाफ ने नकली शराब की फैक्टरी का भंडाफोड़ करते हुए नकली शराब बनाते हुए एक व्यक्ति को काबू किया है। भारी पुलिस दल के साथ मारे गए इस छापे में नकली शराब बनाने का सामान व भरी बोतलें बरामद की है। बड़े ही सुनियोजित तरीके से मारे गए इस छापे में पुलिस ने नकली शराब बनाने वाला पेशेवर तस्कर गिरफ्तार किया है।

पिछले एक सप्ताह में जिला पुलिस ने नकली शराब की तीसरी फैक्टरी काबू कर यह साबित कर दिया है कि जिले में इस जहरीली शराब का गोरखधंधा काफी बड़े स्तर पर चल रहा है। रविवार को पुलिस ने मिलगेट क्षेत्र में सुंदर नगर फेस-2 के एक मकान को चारों ओर से घेर कर भीतर छापा मारा तो देसी शराब

■ भारी मात्रा में सामान बरामद, कंपनी के नाम पर माल बेचकर कूटी चांदी

की कंपनी के लेबल लगाकर नकली शराब तैयार करते हुए दीपनगर निवासी अनिल उर्फ दारा को दबोच लिया गया।

जानकारी अनुसार अनिल ने इस क्षेत्र के निवासी प्रतापसिंह का मकान किराए पर लिया हुआ था। पिछले काफी समय से इस मकान में नकली शराब की फैक्टरी चलाते हुए शहर में शराब सप्लाई कर रहा था। जिला पुलिस प्रमुख की रणनीति अनुसार जिले में नकली शराब बनाने वालों पर शिकंजा कसते हुए पुलिस लगातार छापे मार रही है। इसी अभियान के चलते आज पुलिस को गुप्त सूचना मिली कि मिलगेट के सुंदरनगर क्षेत्र में भी यह गोरखधंधा चल रहा है। पुलिस उपनिरीक्षक विनोद शंकर ने एक दल तैयार कर तुरंत मौके पर छापा मारने की योजना बनाई। इस दल में एएसआई सतनाम सिंह व पंजाब सिंह, हवलदार राजेंद्र सिपाही रविंद्र, प्रदीप, संजय, विरेंद्र व महिला सिपाही सुमन साथ थे।

ठेके पर डीसी का छापा

जागरण संवाद केंद्र, कुरुक्षेत्र

जिला उपायुक्त टीके शर्मा ने पुलिस बल के साथ पुराने बस अड्डे के नजदीक शराब के ठेके पर छापा मारा। इस कार्रवाई में पंद्रह पेटी शराब मौके से बरामद हुई है। हालांकि ठेकेदार का कोई कारिंदा गिरफ्तार नहीं किया जा सका है। इससे शहर में अवैध तरीके से शराब का कारोबार करने वाले लोगों में हड़कंप मच गया है। शीघ्र ही कुछ और ठिकानों पर भी कार्रवाई हो सकती है। गौरतलब है कि कुरुक्षेत्र नगर परिषद की सीमा में शराब बेचने पर प्रतिबंध है। बावजूद इसके कुछ लोग धड़ल्ले से शहर में शराब बेच रहे थे। इसकी शिकायत लगातार मिल रही थी। कई संगठनों ने पहले भी इस शराब के अवैध कारोबार के खिलाफ मोर्चा खोला था व शराब माफिया के खिलाफ कार्रवाई करने की मांग की थी। कुंभकरण की नींद सो रहे पुलिस प्रशासन ने इस संगठनों की (शेष पृष्ठ 12 पर)

■ पर छापे के दौरान मौजूद उपायुक्त टीके शर्मा।

▶ पंद्रह पेटियां शराब बरामद ठेकेदार के कारिंदे फरार

■ अवैध शराब की पेटियों की गिनती करते पुलिसकर्मी। जागरण

छापा मारकर पंद्रह पेटियां शराब बरामद की। जिसमें देशी शराब की बजाय अंग्रेजी शराब की पेटियों की संख्या अधिक थी। एक्साइज विभाग के सहायक उप निरीक्षक ओम पाल, भीम सिंह व कांस्टेबल धर्म सिंह समेत अन्य कर्मचारियों इस टीम में शामिल थे। उपायुक्त टी.के. शर्मा ने कहा कि यह कार्रवाई शिकायत के आधार की गई है। उन्होंने यह भी कहा शिकायतों के आधार पर आगे भी इस तरह की कार्रवाई की जाएगी। इन छापों के चलते शराब माफियों में हड़कंप का माहौल बन हुआ है।

जहरीली शराब से दो लोगों की मौत

भादसों/करनाल। गांव बैरसाल में जहरीली शराब पीने से 2 लोगों की मौत हो गई व एक की हालत गंभीर है। मृतकों में से एक का अंतिम संस्कार कर दिया गया, जबकि दूसरे का पोस्टमार्टम नहीं हो सका था। गांव सरपंच के पति हरबंस सिंह, शंटी, दयाल सिंह व जसविंद्र सिंह ने बताया कि सोमवार की रात को बलबीर सिंह पुत्र ज्योति राम, बख्शा राम व पंजाब निवासी एक अन्य व्यक्ति ने शराब पी। पंजाब निवासी इंद्री में रिश्तेदारी में आया था। ज्यादा नशा होने पर तीनों लोग सो गए। सुबह बलबीर सिंह जागा को उठने पर उल्टियां शुरू हो गई। हालत बिगड़ने पर घर वालों ने उसे करनाल के एक निजी अस्पताल में भर्ती कराया, जहां देर रात उसकी हालत ज्यादा बिगड़ गई और वह अंधा हो गया।

study the problems faced by the family because of alcohol abuse/dependence. This area of problem is relatively unexplored. Therefore, it needs more careful attention. The present study will be an attempt to cover this gap and to help the government in framing public friendly alcohol policy and also help government departments and NGOs, to strengthen and improve their services for the betterment of the people and families suffering from this menace.

Problem in the Light of Research

Practically all-human knowledge, discovered so far, can be found in libraries. Unlike other animals, which start from beginning with each generation, man builds upon the accumulated and recorded knowledge of the past. Man is the only animal that does not need to begin from scratch in every generation, but can take advantage of the knowledge, which has been accumulated through centuries. This fact is of particular importance in research (Mouly, 1968).

In past few years, literature regarding drug abuse has considerably grown simply because in the recent years drug abuse and misuse have received the attention of social scientists by dint of its disastrous impact on the different segments of population. But the studies focusing on alcohol use, abuse and its effect are still limited particularly to India.

One of the most important results that came out of recently conducted problem-drinking surveys betrayed that people can have a whole series of debilitating alcohol problems but still they continue with a family and work life. Alcoholics are not just those shambling outcasts who gather under railway arches, slum corners, or at a village common place: they live in your street, they build your houses, they drive your trains and buses, they make your laws, they teach your children and they treat your ailments. Culturally, alcohol has always been considered with love and hate. Alcoholism is reported to be very high among Irish people, Spanish Americans, American Indians, and Czechoslovaks. Alcoholism among Muslims, Jews, Brahmins (in Hindus) is much lower due to religious taboos and social restrictions. But now the reality about alcohol consumption is that the per capita consumption of alcohol has fallen in developed countries and increased in the developing countries (Jernigan, 2000). The situation in India is in no way different from the other parts of the world and alcoholism is showing a rising trend everywhere. We do not have statistics about India in regard to the use of alcohol and total number of alcoholics but it is evident that large number of people drinks in India and drinking alcohol from moderate to severe levels is prevalent among both elite as well as poor (Figure 1.1).

While studying road accidents in India N. Balakrishna (1967) (quoted by Tek Chand,1972) reported that, death rate in India is 6.6 times more than that of other countries and alcohol has been found to be the most important responsible factor for this.

Certain regional and area wise information confirms that not only a large number of people drink but do so without developing signs of addiction or alcoholism or physical ill health. In a study conducted by Indian Council of Medical Research (ICMR) it has been estimated that in India 0.4 to 4.8 per 1000 person abuse alcohol (ICMR, 1977). While studying the problem in and around Agra city (UP). Dube and Handa (1969) found that 1.24 per cent of population were abusing alcohol and cannabis. In a survey of four villages in Punjab, it was found that 78.38 per cent of population used alcohol (Deb and Jindal, 1974). In another study conducted by Singh and Lal (1978) 29.3 per cent of surveyed population abused alcohol in Punjab, while the rate of drinking in male in age group above 15 was nearly 50 per cent. Mohan and others (1977) reported 52.4 per cent as prevalence rate of alcohol use in Punjab. Sethi and Trivedi (1979) surveyed 2010 general population adults from northern India and discovered that 21.4 per cent had abused at least one drug or other usually either alcohol or cannabis.

While studying rural and urban areas of northern India, Verma et al. (1980) questioned 1031 people and reported that 60.3 per cent of these had never drunk alcohol. The prevalence of drinking in the previous years (1977 and 1978) was 23.7 per cent (current users) and records of past show it was 16 per cent. In case of adult male the prevalence rate was 41.0 per cent while only 2.0 per cent was reported in the females. In his study of rural general population, Mohan et al. (1980) found that 58.3 per cent of adult males drink, while only 1.5 per cent of adult females did so. Probable dependence among current male drinkers was 3.9 per cent and per capita consumption was estimated at 6.62 litres of absolute alcohol.

In a study of rural areas of Ajmer district in Rajasthan, Advani, et al. (1980) observed that there was a positive predilection for drug abuse on the basis of caste system. Alcohol consumption was found more in the communities like Rajputs, Gujjars and Scheduled Castes; the use of cannabis (*bhang*) was more in Brahmins, sadhus and the trading communities like Maheshwaris. In the Jat community the use of opium was high. In the Rajputs and Jats, alcohol and opium is used on festivals like *Holi, Diwali, Shivratri* and on certain social ceremonies as an essential offering, which is called as *Manwar* in their local dialect. While analysing the effects they also observed that due to this custom, children are socialized in culturally established attitudes of the consumption of alcohol and other drugs.

In another scientific study of general population in western India, Sundaram et al. (1984) reported, population above 15 years of age contributed to 3 per cent of the drug abusers. The abuse was mostly among married and illiterate Hindus, probably due to increasing, permissiveness of the society. The rate for males was found 36.1 per cent and 13.4 per cent for females. While studying the drinking behaviour in rural population of South India, Mathrubootham in 1989 found 33 per cent of the men to be active drinkers. The drinking of alcohol was higher among those of lower socio-economic strata. In his study about the prevalence of alcohol use in South India, Chakravarthy (1990) reported alcohol use varying from 26 per cent to 50 per cent among rural South Indian males, and the prevalence was higher among those who were illiterate. Similarly in another study Pomudurai et al. (1991) used the Michigan Alcohol Screening Test (MAST) to estimate problem of drinking in a large city of South India and found a prevalence of 16.7 per cent among males. While studying the community participation in research and action against alcoholism in another large community Bang and Bang (1991) reported that about 25 per cent of the sample were alcohol drinkers, this study was carried out approximately on four lakh people.

In a study on the impact of alcohol in Latin American countries Marva Dixon (2000) reported that alcohol is the drug that registers the largest number of active consumers. While analysing the drug use and drug behaviour of drug addicts he found that along with tobacco, alcohol is the drug which individuals consume to make their entrance for using other drugs. In a study conducted by Institute of Alcoholism and Drug Dependence in 1987 in Costa Rica on a sample of 2083, 3.5 per cent (n=73) had used illegal drugs. Of this number, 81 per cent (n=59) had also used alcohol. In contrast to non-consumers of illegal drugs (n=2010) only 34.2 per cent (n=687) used alcohol Pan-American Health Organization (PAHO), special report 1990.

While studying the increase in heavy drinking and alcohol dependence among young people Bejarano et al. (1996) found that in 1995, 14.3 per cent of those aged 12 to 20 years reported having at least one instance of drinking to intoxication over a period of two days or more. Between the age group of 15 and 24 years, 8 per cent were alcoholic in 1990, but this rose to 22.2 per cent by 1995. Among alcoholics of all ages, 55 per cent had begun drinking prior to the age 15 years (61.5 per cent males, 22.7 per cent females), while among moderate drinkers, only 31 per cent had begun drinking at such a young age. It concludes that in Costa Rica the drinking alcohol excessively starts at the age of 15 years, alcohol addiction begins to manifest at the age of 20 and reaches its peak among those aged 30 to 34 years, the most productive age of the person.

In an analysis of alcohol related crime and violence it was reported that in Latin American countries reports about alcohol related traffic accidents varies from 3.4 per cent to 55 per cent. It is because of the lack of established criteria, such types of deaths are difficult to document, mainly because many deaths occur long after the incident (Rosovosky and Borges, 1992). In Bolivia, traffic accidents involving a positive Blood Alcohol Concentration (BAC) compromised 19 per cent of all accidents. In Brazil, 25 per cent of vehicle operators involved in traffic accidents had some degree of alcohol in their blood (Madrigal). In Costa Rica 15.4 per cent of those who committed suicide had some amount of alcohol in their blood (quoted by Dixon, 2000).

While studying the involvement of youth in drugs and alcohol and its impact Richard (quoted by Dixon) reported that there are numerous factors, both psychosocial and socioeconomic responsible and entangled in alcohol and drug related violence and crime. He found that youths who sold cocaine in 1999 year before the study were three to four times more likely to report having attacked someone with the intention of seriously killing or hurting him or her than the youths who did not sell cocaine. This puts us at a point where the closeness of drug and alcohol is the condition of survival, where poverty plays an important role in the life of a family. Young people run the risk of getting involved in the activities of this phenomenon (production, trade, consumption) as a way to fulfill their economic aspirations. In Latin American countries, on the Atlantic cost of Central America, families face many problems that propitiate the consumption of alcohol and thence lead to the use of other drugs. Many farmers lost their property and had to work as labourers for the new owners of what was theirs in the past (Dixon, 2000).

In a review of the available literature on alcohol problems, Orme and Rimmer in 1981 pointed out that there was no proper indication of any association between parental alcohol problems and the perpetration of childhood violence by the parents, it may be because of methodological ineptitude. In a later review, West and Prinze (1987) indicated that the link between parental alcoholism and perpetration of child abuse, if any, may be due to third variables such as socioeconomic status. Researches were conducted with the use of more sophisticated studies like Conflict Tactics Scale and improved sampling techniques. Based on these, the association between parental alcohol problems and experiences of violence for their children was established (Kantor and Straus, 1990; Radomosky, 1991; Famularo et al., 1992a, 1992b; Kantor, 1992,).

Downs and Miller (1996) in a study entitled 'Inter-generational links between childhood abuse and alcohol related problems proposed' various hypotheses to study the link between alcohol use and violence. First the disinhibition hypothesis posits a direct pharmacological link between alcohol use and aggression and thus is largely physiological in nature. This hypothesis has received little empirical support. According to the second hypothesis cognitive disorganization, alcohol use alters perception of environmental threat, and an increased likelihood of violence (Richardson, 1981). The study pointed out that while drinking, already stressed individuals may misinterpret interpersonal cues and is more likely to restore to violence than other individuals. Third, in the deviance disavowal/expectancy hypothesis, drinking allows the perpetrator to 'construct a story' that acknowledges the violence but allow him or her to continue to believe that it is 'normal' by attributing the violence to the use of alcohol. Thus alcohol does not act pharmacologically to increase violence but due to cultural expectancies about the effects of alcohol, functions as a rationale for violence. Therefore, interpersonal violence is conceptualized and is a function of the alcohol itself; the physical setting of the norms about violence in that setting, and cultural expectations about violence (Fagan, 1993). Fourth, while studying the pattern of drinking may be a contributing factor to parental violence. Kantor and Straus (1990) found parents with highest levels of abuse to be mothers with drinking patterns and fathers with high daily alcohol consumption patterns.

Harrison and Luck (1996) studied the problem of drinking and homelessness in UK. In this study it was pointed out that the problem of drinking has now entered into more areas of persons' life. The attention had shifted from alcohol dependence to a wider focus on a range of alcohol related problems from drunk driving to soccer violence. There were increasing challenges to stereotypical representations of problem drinkers and to what many felt was an unhelpful pre-occupation with the homeless Skid Row 'alcoholic'. The study reported that the levels of alcohol consumption are known to be raised significantly among homeless people seeking health care. A primary health care and service aimed at the single homeless in East London (Balas) found 49 per cent of men (N=2, 101) and 15 per cent of women (N=485) drinking at high risk levels. Problem rates among women are generally much lower, but UK based estimates of the prevalence of current alcoholic-related problems among single homeless men range from 16.5 to 25 at present.

In order to provide services to the homeless problem drinkers in UK the case management approach has been introduced which involves advocacy and the integration of care from a variety of formal and informal networks. Case management for homeless people involves stabilizing client's lives by acting as a 'service broker' in basic support areas such as financial aid and housing. In this approach the emphasis was laid on proper and immediate use of community resources and statutory entitlements rather than attempting to provide an all-inclusive package of care, case management (Detrick and Stiepock, 1992; Cox et al., 1993; Homan et al., 1993).

While studying the drinking problems among women Waterson (1996) in a study 'Gender divisions and drinking problems' points in terms of other possible indicators of alcohol-related problems of women that women are only responsible for 5 per cent of all drinking and driving offences, but between 1975 and 1989 the number of offences committed by females per one lakh drivers increased by 65 per cent – at a time when the proportion of male offences was decreasing. Similarly rates for liver cirrhosis have been increasing amongst women. Sex differences in alcohol drinking were also studied by Waterson (1996) in the same paper and quoted various studies such as Office of Population Censuses and Surveys (OPCS) (1992) in a General Household survey in 1990 reported that the recent national data shows that rates of drinkers as compared with non-drinkers are converging between the sexes. The General Household Survey (GHS), 1990 indicates that women are twice as likely as men to be non-drinkers (12% to 6%) and are much less likely to drink above sensible levels (11% to 28%). The current sensible drinking level advocated for women is less than fourteen units per week. Consumption in excess of this is deemed to be potentially harmful. Women drinking 35 units or more a week are very likely to suffer from liver damage or other physical problems (Royal College of General Practitioners, 1986). Office of Population Consensuses and Surveys (OPCS) (1992) also reported that amongst women heavy drinking is associated with socio-economic status. In 1990, 14 per cent of professional women were drinking more than sensible limits, where only 6 per cent of the women were drinking at these levels in unskilled manual group.

So far as the pharmological composition and characteristics of alcohol are concerned it has sedative properties and whether, it really helps to reduce tension or not is debatable (De Boer et al., 1993). Nevertheless, it is a very common assumption and very strong feeling among people that it does. Harz et al. (1990) reported that in a study of 1,008 executives in UK, when asked of ways of reducing stress, 54 per cent said that they had an alcoholic drink. In a study of industrial workers in the Haryana State of India, C.P. Singh (2000) reported that 27.33 per cent workers (N=300) accepted that they initiated to use the drugs continuously (large number use alcohol) because of stress. Reasons of stress were given as economic loss, dispute within family, disappointment in love, divorce/separation from spouse, indebtedness and sexual problems etc. Further, analysing the reasons for continuing to take the drug to very heavy levels it was found that 33.67 per cent workers use drugs continuously (large number use alcohol) because of stress and strain at work. They feel relaxed after the use of the drug of their choice, firstly alcohol and then they go for some other drug or drugs. General stress, both social and psychological is frequently cited as a cause of heavy drinking. While discussing about the causes of stress, Breeze (1985) found that heavier drinkers complained more that things were getting on top of them, of losing confidence, that nobody understood them, that life had no purpose, and of feeling miserable or depressed. Feeling shy in company, anxious or nervy, irritable, touchy or worried about the future were also more commonly reported by them.

Some of the studies conducted to find out the problems of alcohol use among women and its effect on them and their families reported that women who were subject to any difficulties in their life started using alcohol and then became regular users. Johnson (1982) reported that women drink to increase self-confidence, to aid interpersonal contact, decision-making or in executing some particularly demanding action. Cooke and Allan (1984) in their study 'Stressful Life Events and Alcohol Abuse in Women: A General Population Study' found that female alcoholics are often depressed. North American studies of pregnant women carried out in deprived inner-city areas found that the heaviest drinkers had multiple social problems (Stephens, 1985).

All alcohol problems are subject to some stigma. Some studies conducted from time to time found that though the use of alcohol is increasing and is a regular practice in some societies but still it is not free from stigma, particularly when it is among women. British community surveys repeatedly illustrate that the term alcoholic is used in a pejorative sense to refer to a person physically, psychologically and socially deteriorated member of a deviant minority group, or somebody who is essentially tainted (Breeze, 1985). In a research based evaluation of alcohol problems Mills-Hopper (1992) reported that women with alcohol problems always receive more disapprobation than men. Such distorted but powerful stereotypical view of female drinking remains in our society. Its influence is pervasive because it encourages to hold more negative views of women with alcohol problems. Even in the educated societies, the professionals continue to hold distorted pictures in their thinking about the women with alcohol problems than of men with similar problems (Smith, 1992). Therefore, it can be concluded that in much of the literature, female drinking till yet, has been stigmatized and viewed as essentially unfeminine. Women with alcohol problems and specially who are heavy drinkers experience difficulties in their role performance and lead to serious family problems.

Recent research studies conducted in Europe about the nature of alcohol problems and its effect on family indicate the scale of the problem. In a study conducted by Eurocare and Coface (Confederation of Family Organization in the European Union), 'Alcohol Problems in the Family: A Report to the European Union' (1998) reported that large majority of European adults consume alcohol, at least occasionally. In the European Union as whole non-drinkers comprise around one in ten men and one in five women. In a study of heavy drinking and alcohol dependence it was reported that substantial proportions of adult Europeans regularly consume excessive amount of alcohol, which substantially increases the risk of experiencing health or social problems. Smaller but still substantial proportions of Europeans experience its signs and symptoms of alcohol dependence. The study estimated that the entire European Union shows that 14 per cent of men and 4 per cent of women report lifetime experience of alcohol abuse or dependence. It means that 42 million Europeans have experienced alcohol problems for some period of their lives. If we estimate that even if each of these drinkers adversely effected only one other person, that means there are 84 million people in Europe either suffering from alcohol problems or afflicted by another's drinking. If we try to look into the problems of children, the study found that at least 4.5 million children in the European Union are living in families suffering from the effects of alcohol. The study points out that the actual figures may be much higher, possibly as great as 7.7 million. While analysing the effect of alcohol use in the family in European countries this study found that alcohol abuse and dependence in some countries might often result in the breakup of the family. Countries where divorce/separation is less socially acceptable, people maintain their marital relations even with alcoholics and problem drinkers. For example in Portugal about 70 per cent of people treated for alcohol dependence are married. In Spain 66 per cent of the population suffering from alcohol related problems are married, and 80 per cent of them have an average of 2.5 children, which is higher than the average of the general population (Eurocare and Coface, 1998).

In the study conducted in some other countries in Europe the problem is serious and the family is severe sufferer. In France, it was found that 29.5 per cent of men and 11.1 per cent of women seen and examined by general medical practitioners are excessive drinkers who are at risk of alcohol related diseases or are already ill. The study estimated that over five million French adults fall into this category and two million French adults are alcohol dependents (Health in France, 1994; French High Committee on Public Health, 1996). In Germany, around 16 per cent of 18–59 year olds are drinking at dangerous level and 6.6 million problem drinkers. In Portugal, there are an estimated 1,70,000 alcoholics and problem drinkers which comprise of about 21 per cent of the adult population.

In some other small countries of Europe the problem of alcohol use is very serious. A study conducted in Ireland in 1997, reported that around 23 per cent of men and 5 per cent of women exceed the recommended 'sensible limits' of regular consumption of alcohol and 8 per cent of men and 2 per cent of women report signs of alcohol dependence. In Norway, about 10 per cent of the adult population experienced alcohol problems or suffer from alcohol dependence. In Sweden, 10 per cent of adult men and 3 to 6 per cent of adult women are heavy drinkers and in UK 7 per cent of men and 2 per cent of women reported the symptoms of alcohol dependence.

Jerzy Mellibruda (2001) reported in his study of alcohol related problems in Poland, that these problems are treated as a serious challenge. Youth drinking and alcoholism were the third and fourth most important social problems in Poland (public opinion poll). The study reported that the following were the main kind of alcohol related problems in Poland:

- Suicide of alcoholics (6,00,000–7,00,000 people)
- Health problems of abusers (1–1.2 million people)
- Youth drinking (high risk group is 20–25 per cent for teen age population)
- Alcohol; threat to family life (2–3 million children and co-dependent adults, domestic violence)
- Alcohol threat to work place
- Alcohol threat for public safety (drunk drivers, delinquency)
- Illegal activity of producers and sellers of alcohol (20 per cent of vodka in gray zone and violation of advertisement ban)

The study found that there are more than 1.5 million young children of alcoholics in Poland and the majority of them have serious health and personal problems. It suggested that the development of effective treatment programme for their parents is important but will not create a solution for majority. The local communities must actively participate for the solution of such problems. Establishment of prevention clubs and common rooms for the children of alcoholics is an important task, with some other steps such as controlling the alcohol market, psycho-social and substantial aid for families and the counteraction of violence.

A study carried out by Gunasekera (2000) in the Asian region found that the problem of alcohol in the Asian region is very serious specially its effect on the socio-economic and health consequences of increased consumption of alcohol. A micro study conducted in one district of Sri Lanka showed that there is a close correlation between alcohol and tobacco use and continued poverty. The study showed that the beneficiary families had spent more on alcohol and tobacco annually than the total loans granted to them during a period of six years. There are greater incidences of malnourishment, illness, disease and morbidity in families with alcohol problems as compared to families having no alcohol problems. Statistics available in certain countries show that health costs have risen considerably due to increase in alcohol-related disease such as cancer, cirrhosis of liver, alcohol psychoses, dependence and withdrawal symptoms. According to random studies made in Nepal and Sri Lanka 25–30 per cent of hospital beds are occupied by persons suffering from one or the other alcohol related disease. The study reported that there is an upward trend in the number of broken homes due to feuds and family violence. Crimes, including rape, road or work place accidents and loss of manpower working days are increasing because of increase in alcohol use.

The above studies explain that the problem of alcohol consumption is increasing alarmingly throughout the Asian region and South Asian region. A summary of this regional profile given below (WHO) clearly indicates the situation:

- The region has seen a rapidly growing market for alcoholic preparations over the last decade.
- The licensed production of foreign liquor such as whisky, rum, wine, gin, brandies, vodka, beer etc. is common in many countries in the region.
- In some countries illicit production is as high as over 50 per cent of licit production.
- All countries realize significant revenue from alcohol production and sale, constituting between 4–10 per cent of government revenue, especially in the large countries.
- There has been a substantial increase in alcohol consumption in almost all countries of the region. It is estimated that 45 per cent of men and 5 per cent of women use alcohol, regionally.
- Average per capita consumption of alcohol among male drinkers is 9.2 litres.
- Despite their high socio-economic and health implications, alcohol related control measures are the least supported programmes in the region.

The problem in India is also very serious. The use of alcohol and addiction to alcohol among various sections of society and illicit production and trade of alcohol is increasing alarmingly. There is no national prevalence study available in India. But the increase in alcohol production, trade and sale indicate towards the increasing levels of consumption. The Global Status Report on Alcohol reported that the Indian beer industry currently produces 4.32 million hectolitres of beer per year, and is growing at a rate of 17 per cent annually. Spirits industry is divided into two segments: Indian made foreign liquor (whisky, gin, rum, vodka etc.), and Indian made country liquor (licensed distilled spirits made locally). Common varieties of country liquor are *Anguri, Jagadhri No. 1, arrack, desi sharab, tari* etc. The distillation of illicit liquor is also very common and it is produced clandestinely mainly in rural and slum areas in small production units. Home production for self-consumption is also common in some parts of India with popular names such as *desi daru, toddy, chhang, tharra* etc. These names are given according to their local dialect for easy language communication.

The consumption of all brands of alcohol has increased in India. Both beer and spirits consumption have been rising recently, possibly due to the liberalization of the Indian market. The consumption of illicit liquor which is unrecorded is estimated at 50 per cent of recorded consumption. The total adult consumption of alcohol in 1996 was approximately two litres of pure alcohol (WHO, 1999). While analysing the use of alcohol and age patterns, study by WHO (1999) reported that, studies from the late 1970s and early 1980s found that 12.7 per cent of high school students, 32.6 per cent of university students, and 31.6 per cent of non-student young people were consuming alcohol.

While explaining the alcohol related problems, Saxena (1999) reported that developing countries like India faces many alcohol related problems such as health problems, economic deprivation, accidents on road and industry, domestic violence. The rapid increase in the consumption of alcohol has also increased the likelihood of further growth of these problems. Explaining the effects on family, he further enumerated that excessive drinking by one or more family member(s) results in several negative consequences for others in the family, especially for the wife and children of a male drinker. In the case of economically weaker sections these effects are more serious. The large amount of their family income may be used for alcohol, in many cases loss of job and work is reported and in such situations wife and children have to work for their survival. Family violence such as wife battering, physical and mental abuse of children is very common.

Alcohol Problems in the Family: A Study

The use and abuse of alcohol and the problems faced by the family has been studied in context of Haryana. I would like to incorporate this study as one of the attempt to examine the agony of the families in which alcohol is very common. The increase in use of alcohol and its effect on the social fabric is one of the several forms of individual disorganization, which is the result of extra-ordinary complex interaction between man and his environment. The motivating factors for initiating use of alcohol such as peer group pressure, enjoying life in high, relief from problems, social status seems to be same for all but plays a differing and important role in determining the seriousness of the problem, which varies from individual to individual and family to family. The nature and severity of the problem, though varying to a great extent in the different parts of the world, have emerged in the recent years as one of the serious social problems that needs an in depth study so as to enable the experts to suggest suitable preventive and curative measures. From time to time different approaches were used by the expert researchers to assess the problem of alcohol abuse, alcoholism and effects of alcohol on different sections of population. They have confirmed certain types of research approaches (methods) such as descriptive studies, analytical studies and cohort studies for this purpose (Sundaram, 1981). The present work based on the research study, 'Alcohol Problems in the Family: An Exploratory Study in Haryana' (Singh, 2007) is an attempt to explore the problem of alcohol use and its effect on family and to focus on various factors such as continuous increase in use of alcohol, problems faced by the suffering families, economic cost of alcohol, domestic violence and marital conflicts, child abuse and health hazards of the alcoholics and their family members.

The research study was conducted in Haryana in 2003–2007. Though Haryana is ranked at top in agriculture, it is also very fast emerging as an industrial state. At one hand, the development in agriculture and industrial production helped the farmers and others of this state in increasing their economic status on the other hand urbanization, industrialization and modernization played a significant role in the increase of alcohol consumption. The records of counseling and de-addiction centres, media reports show that in this state a good number of unemployed and self-employed youths, university and college students, industrial and transport works, farmers and agricultural workers, rickshaw pullers, landless labourers use alcohol which includes illicit liquor known as *desi-daru* (illegally brewed liquor).

The specific objectives of the research were to study the nature, types, composition and socio-economic status of the families in which alcohol is abused; to examine and locate the social, psychological, cultural and other factors contributing to alcohol use and abuse in families; to study the effects of alcohol abuse on the family and psychosocial problems faced by the family of alcoholics; to find out and highlight the social and economic cost of alcohol use borne by the family and society; to study the role of alcohol in domestic violence and marital conflicts and the nature of domestic violence in the families with alcohol problems; to record the effect of parental alcohol abuse on the growth and development of children in family and effects of alcohol abuse on the role performance of the family members; to study the impact of alcohol consumption/sale policy of the government on family and suggest approaches for formulation of effective and people friendly alcohol policy; and to suggest treatment modalities and strategies of social work intervention with the people having alcohol problems and approaches to help their families;

Keeping in view the above objectives some questions were posed to answer the problem:

- What are the reasons for the use of alcohol and persistence of alcohol abuse in the family?
- What are the socio-economic characteristics of alcohol using people?
- Do the families recognize use of alcohol as a potential social problem, which disrupt family relationship?
- What are the effects of alcohol use on the family?

- Does the use of alcohol affect the normal social functioning of the user?
- What are the various problems suffered by the families because of alcohol abuse?
- Do the family members recognize and understand the needs and problems of alcoholics?
- Does alcohol promote domestic violence?
- Does alcohol abuse affect the status of the family in society?
- Does alcohol consumption in family affect the children?
- Does the use of alcohol in family effect the socialization of children in family?
- Does the alcohol in family responsible for behavioural problems in children?
- Does the alcohol abuse in family affect the role performance of family members?
- Does the alcohol abuse effect the social life of family?
- What are the economic and financial effects of alcohol abuse on the family?
- Does the alcohol abuse effect the marital relations and encourage marital violence?
- Does the alcohol responsible for divorce, separation and family break-up?
- Does the alcohol abuse effect the interfamily and intra-family relations?
- What are the specific problems of women in the families with alcohol problems?
- What is the role of government policy on alcohol in promoting the family alcohol problems?
- What are the effects of alcohol abuse on the health of family members?
- What is the effect of deterioration in work performance of the alcoholic on his family life?
- What are the psychological and psychosocial effects on the family members of the alcoholics?
- How a participation of family is recognized in the treatment of the problem?

- Does the family understand the social and economic cost of alcohol use?
- Does the problem of alcohol use in family promote its use in next generation?
- How do the family and family members cope up with the problems because of alcohol use?

In this exploratory study multi-stage sampling has been adopted for selection of families suffering from alcohol problems. Haryana is divided into four divisions with eighteen districts (at the time of taking information the number of districts was eighteen, one more district was declared out of Mewat region named Satyamev Puram in 2004 which is the part of Gurgaon and Faridabad districts), now it is again renamed as district Mewat. In the first stage, two districts with highest alcohol use were selected from each of the four divisions. The information about the consumption of alcohol was obtained from the Excise and Taxation Department of the Government of Haryana for the years 2002 and 2011 (Table 1.4). In the second stage a list of alcoholics and effected families was prepared for each selected district from drug de-addiction centres, counseling centres for drug addicts and alcoholics, family counseling centres, hospitals, PHCs, sub-centres, doctors practicing in the village/mohalla. At this stage a 'network sampling technique' (i.e. starting with a few known users, other alcohol users and alcoholics were traced and contacted with their help) helpcd a lot in collecting the required information.

Table 1.4 District-wise consumption of alcohol in Haryana

Division	*District*	*Total alcohol consumption (in proof litres)*	
		2002	*2011*
AMBALA	Ambala	64,71,375	68,32,399
	Panchkula	21,35,000	33,28,643
	Yamuna Nagar	29,95,000	72,52,869
	Kaithal	32,48,000	65,88,194
ROHTAK	Karnal	48,90,000	69,19,000
	Panipat	33,33,000	68,22,834
	Sonepat	99,03,625	74,33,156

Cont'd...

...Cont'd

	Rohtak	25,99,000	55,77,653
	Jhajjar	38,58,000	63,43,251
GURGAON	Faridabad	80,19,750	1,71,11,734
	Gurgaon	47,08,500	1,77,81,000
	Rewari	49,80,750	53,97,753
	Mohindergarh	16,70,000	31,23,510
HISSAR	Bhiwani	34,45,000	72,11,988
	Jind	35,60,000	67,78,430
	Hissar	45,83,000	97,52,619
	Fatehabad	26,05,000	46,61,326
	Sirsa	32,85,000	79,11,643

Source: Excise and Taxation Department, Haryana (2010–11).

There are many definitions and criteria regarding alcohol dependence. In International Classification of Diseases-10 (ICD-10) (WHO, 1993), dependence syndrome is defined as 'a cluster of physiological, behavioural and cognitive phenomena in which the use of a substance or a class of substances takes on a much higher priority for a given individual than together behaviours that once had greater value. A central descriptive characteristic of the dependence syndrome is the desire (often strong, sometimes overpowering) to take psychoactive drugs (which may or may not have been medically prescribed), a alcohol, or tobacco'.

While selecting the families suffering from alcohol abuse the diagnostic guidelines for dependence syndrome due to alcohol or other substances of abuse in ICD-10 is that if three or more of the following have been experienced or exhibited during the year or should have occurred together repeatedly within a twelve month period:

- A strong desire or sense of compulsion to take the substance;
- Difficulties in controlling substance-taking behaviour in terms of its onset, termination, or levels of use;
- A physiological withdrawal state when substance use has ceased or been reduced, as evidenced by: the characteristic withdrawal syndrome for the substance; or use of the same (or a closely related) substance with the intention of relieving or avoiding withdrawal symptoms;

- Evidence of tolerance, such that increased doses of the psychoactive substance are required in order to achieve effects originally produced by lower doses;
- Progressive neglect of alternative pleasures or interests because of psychoactive substance use, increased amount of time necessary to obtain or take the substance or to recover from its effects;
- Persisting with substance use despite clear evidence of overtly harmful consequences, such as harm to the liver through excessive drinking, depressive mood states consequent to periods of heavy substance use, or drug-related impairment of cognitive functioning; efforts should be made to determine that the user was actually, or could be expected to be, aware of the nature and extent of the harm (ibid.).

The third stage constitutes of the process of selection of the families (subjects) for the collection of data for the study. At this stage a sample of 20 per cent of the listed alcohol affected families was drawn randomly from the selected districts and a list of 1,048 families was prepared. Out of the 1,048 families 248 respondent families were rejected because of various reasons, such as non-availability, insufficient information, rejecting our request for interview, reluctant to be interviewed, non-cooperation and unreliable information given during interview etc. Therefore, such cases were either deleted from the list or rejected when found insufficient for analysis and from the selected districts best suitable 100 families, 70 from rural areas and 30 from urban areas were selected for collecting the data. For convenient analysis the proportion of families was taken in round figures. Hence the study was finally based on a sample of 800 families.

Table 1.5 District-wise number of families and size of sample

District	*No. of families listed*	*No. of families selected*	*No. of families rejected*	*No. of families interviewed*	*Total no. of families*
Ambala	580	116	16	70+30	100
Kaithal	540	108	08	70+30	100
Karnal	660	132	32	70+30	100

Cont'd...

...Cont'd

Sonepat	690	138	38	70+30	100
Jind	640	128	28	70+30	100
Hissar	710	142	42	70+30	100
Faridabad	780	156	56	70+30	100
Rewari	640	128	28	70+30	100
Total	5240	1048	248	560+240	800

Source: Alcohol Problems in Family: An Exploratory Study in Haryana (Singh, 2007).

Sociological studies generally use three methods of data collection: observation, interview and questionnaire (Harlambos, 1989). In this study (i) interview (ii) interview schedule, (iii) observation and (iv) verbal reports of the significant persons were used for collecting the relevant information.

Interview involves eliciting information from the subjects of the study through questioning. Obviously, this method is useful to study human beings when their opinion, feelings, situation, traits etc. are to be recorded and other forms of communication are considered to be unsuitable, and do not yield the required information.

In this exploratory investigation, the problem of the families effected by alcohol use, their living conditions, causes of initiating the use of alcohol and reasons for continuing its use, effects on health, economic condition of family, effect on spouse (specially wife) and on children, personal and social life etc. were to be investigated for which interview was considered to be most suitable. Since the nature of questions to be asked were of specific type and seek to explore the depth of subject's personal, family, social as well as financial and occupational life. The non-verbal methods available were not found suitable to elicit the required details. Moreover, the interviewing was best suited to study the uneducated/partially educated, ignorant and psychologically disturbed members of the alcohol effected families. Interview also gave an opportunity to observe the reactions of the subjects and check the contradictions in their responses to the questions put to them. It is only because of these reasons that interview method along with observation was adopted to study the families suffering with the alcohol problems. Interview was structured with the help of interview schedule, containing a set of questions in a particular order. Thus, a structured interview helped in eliciting objective and subjective facts by providing appropriate opportunity to probe into the subject matter.

Interview Schedule, the main research tool used for the study (containing nine parts) was prepared on the basis of the existing literature on alcohol use, alcohol problems, field experiences and opinion of experts in this area. The major areas included in this schedule were:

PART-I GENERAL INFORMATION
- Information about the alcoholic
- Information about the family
- Family history and details
- Occupation and source of income
- Income consumption pattern

PART-II INFORMATION ABOUT USE OF ALCOHOL
- Reasons for first use
- Frequency of use
- Time of use
- Company
- Quality/Brand
- Source of getting alcohol
- Number of family members using alcohol

PART-III HEALTH PROBLEMS
- Health problems of alcoholic
- Health problems of spouse
- Health problems of other family members
- Affect of alcohol on the health of other family members

PART-IV MARITAL AND DOMESTIC LIFE
- Domestic responsibilities
- Relationship with spouse
- Misbehaviour or fighting with spouse
- Violence after drinking alcohol
- Misbehaviour or fighting with other family members
- Ostracism because of alcohol use

PART-V CHILD ABUSE AND NEGLECT
- Schooling of children
- Affect on children
- Violence after drinking
- Child Abuse

PART-VI SOCIAL LIFE
- Social status of family
- Relationships with neighbours
- Relations with relatives
- Relations with friends
- Social and cultural celebrations in family and effect of alcohol
- Police case/Jail/punishment

PART-VII FINANCIAL POSITION OF FAMILY
- Affect of alcohol use and needs of family
- Family assets
- Sale of asserts/property due to alcohol use
- Loan and indebtedness
- Loss of job/occupation
- Working efficiency

PART-VIII INTERVIEW SCHEDULE FOR SPOUSE

PART-IX INTERVIEW SCHEDULE FOR CHILD

Observation as a method of data collection was also used to supplement and corroborate the replies of the respondents. This was helpful in corroborating their replies to the questions about alcohol use and relations with the spouse, reactions of children, family disputes, and relationship with neighbours/relatives/friends, sale of property etc. Questions in these areas were not answered properly and adequately by many of the respondents, therefore, observation was used to ascertain the facts. Since the researcher and his team had experience of home visits in problem cases, it posed no problem to him and his team in recording these observations or confronting and seeking clarifications from them.

Definitions of the Terms Used

Alcohol

There are many types of alcohol-amyl, butyl, isopropyl, isobutyl, methyl, ethyl alcohol etc. Ethanol is the type of alcohol which is contained in all ingested alcoholic beverages and commonly consumed. It is a clear, thin, highly volatile liquid with a harsh burning taste. In this study we are going to talk only about Ethanol or Ethyl alcohol therefore, when 'Alcohol' is mentioned it will refer to Ethanol or Ethyl alcohol.

Alcohol is a dependence producing, habit forming, highly addictive drug. Even though many people are not aware of it, it is an undisputed fact that alcohol is a potent drug. Ethyl alcohol (C_2H_2OH) the intoxicating substance in alcoholic beverages produces physical and psychological changes.

Alcoholic

An alcoholic is one whose drinking causes continuous problem in every aspect of his life (family relationship, health, financial position, occupation and work life etc.). In spite of these problems he keeps on drinking, 'Continuing' is the key word that differentiates him from a social drinker (Mann, 1952).

Alcoholism

Alcoholism is a chronic illness, psychic, somatic or psychosomatic which manifests itself as a disorder of behaviours. It is characterized by the repeated drinking of alcoholic beverages, to an extent that exceeds customary dietary use or compliance with the social customs of the community and that interferes with the drinker's health or the social or economic functioning (Keller and Effron quoted in Ranganathan, 1989).

Drug

Drug is a substance having capacity to alter sensation, mood, consciousness, and other psychological and behavioural functions. Alcohol, having the capacity to alter the sensation, mood, consciousness and psychological and behavioural functions is also considered as a drug in this study.

Alcohol Dependence

Alcohol dependence is a cluster of physiological, behavioural and cognitive phenomenon in which the use of alcohol takes on a much higher priority for a given individual than other behaviours that once had greater value. Thus, the central feature of alcohol dependence is the overpowering desire to consume alcohol (WHO, 1993).

Regular Use

Taking one or more substances (types/brand of alcohol) at least once a week or more often to daily (Ranganathan, 1989).

Alcohol and Drug Abuse

Abuse is the repeated or episodic self-administration of alcohol or drugs to the extent of experiencing harm from their effects or from the social or economic consequences of their use.

Prevalence

The ratio of the number of individuals, using one or more substances of a specific category of drug (alcohol in this study) at a particular period of time.

Frequency of Use

Refers to the degree of dependence a person has and is thus quantified in terms of how often he consumes a drug (alcohol in this study).

Psychological Dependence

A state characterized by emotional and mental pre-occupation with the effects of the drug (alcohol in this study) and by a persistent craving for it. When psychological dependence develops the user gets mentally 'hooked on' to the drug/alcohol.

Physical Dependence

A state when the user's body becomes totally dependent on the drug (alcohol) and with prolonged use, the body becomes so used to functioning under the influence of the drug (alcohol) that it is able to function normally only if the drug (alcohol) is present.

Tolerance

'Tolerance' refers to a condition where the user needs more and more of the drug (alcohol) to experience the same effect. Smaller quantities, which were sufficient earlier, are no longer effective and the user is forced to increase the amount of drug (alcohol) intake.

Withdrawal Symptoms

After the user becomes dependent, if the intake of drugs (alcohol) is abruptly stopped, the body becomes confused and protests against the absence of the drug (alcohol) that is called withdrawal symptom. The withdrawal symptoms may range from mild discomfort to convulsions depending on the type of drug abused.

Family

'A family is a group of persons united by the ties of marriage, blood or adoption, constituting a single household interacting and inter communicating with each other in their respective social role of husband and wife, mother and father, son and daughter, brother and sister, and creating and maintaining a common culture' (Burgess and Locke, 1945).

Field Realities

Family is the basic unit of society, which provides the natural frame work for the emotional, economic and material support essential for the growth, development and well-being of its members. A person in his/her family feels more secure and caring in all the developmental stages of his/her life. But when the very nature of the family is disturbed by the drinking of alcohol by one or more family members it results in several negative consequences, for others in the family. The relationship of faith, security and caring is disturbed. The first difficulty encountered in the field was that the family was not ready to accept the fact that somebody in their family is an alcoholic, all peremptorily refused to talk on this issue. The research team discussed it with some experts, consulted the relevant literature and on the basis of their earlier experience, used some new persuasive methods and social resources. Project Associate and other volunteers associated with the team were also oriented and prepared to counter such situations through tactful handling. Consequently, they were able to overcome this problem gradually.

In many cases, the family members were not much helpful and they felt bad and reluctant to discuss with a stranger about this problem of their family, which is natural. Therefore, to contact and interview the family members (specially wife) the research team had to spend much time in explaining the need and objectives of this exercise. The female members who are the sufferers in many cases accepted it, but there was a feeling of doubt among the male members. There was a hesitation in sharing some personal maters related to personal health, husband-wife relationship, sexual problems which could not be discussed with male members. In such situations help of educated girls and women available in the community was taken. Some volunteers of N.S.S. from nearby colleges and girl students of MSW (Master of Social Work) were also included in the research team (though informally). This helped a lot, and the women who were reluctant and hesitant in first attempt gave very important and clear responses to these girls. This was a very important limitation with the research team because the socio-cultural limitations of Indian society where women are not supposed to freely and frantically interact with out-siders. But this problem was solved with the experience of the field-work settings when such problems were frequently encountered and solved with the use of skills in human behaviour and social work practice.

Even after agreeing to give the interview, some respondents created problems in replying to some questions specially the ones related to time, frequency and company, family break-up, encounter with law and police, street brawls, relationship with neighbours and relatives and sometimes even gave wrong information on many of these questions. The research team had to check such type of doubtful answers from other resources, which was again time consuming. Interestingly, during visits many alcoholics were found under the influence of alcohol, therefore, some time adjustments were made with the family members and interview had to be postponed for next visit.

Another difficulty, which was faced, was the non-availability of the subjects during crop sowing and harvesting seasons in the villages. The research team had to wait long and make repeated visits to interview the family. In some cases the team had to go to the agriculture farm of the subjects where the urgency of the work was to be explained. This exercise was also time consuming and expensive. The fieldwork was to be suspended during the Parliament elections and the elections of State Legislative Assembly and after these local bodies' elections of rural and urban areas. Being a very sensitive issue the political party workers raised objections and the research team had to face many difficulties during this period, therefore, during election period the fieldwork was not possible.

The continuous and excessive use of alcohol affects individuals and their families to the extent that inter-family and intra-family relations become tense. At one point of time the family members and the person affected want to get rid of the problem. Many studies, conducted recently on alcohol and drug abuse, reported of road accidents, crime, abuse among youth etc. But no heed is paid to the problems faced by a family owing to alcohol abuse/dependence. Records of hospitals shows that patients go for treatment of alcohol abuse but discontinue it before stipulated duration. Even if, they're well treated and sent back to their houses, it relapses after some time and create lot of problem for the family – ultimately the family is the worst sufferer. This area of problem is relatively uncharted-unexplored and needs careful attention. The present study is an attempt to fulfill this gap and help the government in framing public friendly alcohol policies. It'll also stand NGOs in good stead by strengthening and improving their services. Hence this attempt will be an aid to rejuvenate ailing society by helping it to put a check on the menace of alcoholism.

2

The Suffering Families Under Socio-Economic Scanner

In the Chapter 1 a comprehensive understanding of the problem of alcohol abuse in India had been explored with this background now an attempt will be made to discuss the socio-economic profile of the respondent families. The characteristics covered include religion, caste, occupation, residential status, type of family, number of family members, age, marital status, education qualification, type of accommodation and ownership of house, family income, alcohol use in family, etc.

Religion is considered as one of the most important methods of social control. According to Arnold W. Green, 'It is a system of beliefs and symbolic practices and objects governed by faith rather than by knowledge, which relates man to an unseen supernatural realm beyond the known and beyond the controllable.' It is generally observed that a man who is dominated by his sexual and aggressive derives can be controlled by the pressure of Religiosity. 'Religion', according to Taylor (1930) is the belief in superior beings. Frazer (1950) explains it as a method of reconciliation of powers superior to man, which are believed to direct or control the course of nature and of human life. Many authors highlighted the negative relationship between religiosity and belief in religion and drug abuse. Coleman (1969) observed that the incidence of alcoholism varies with religions' affiliations. It is low among Jews, Mormons and Muslims whose religious values prohibit the use of alcohol. While discussing belief in religion and its relationship with drug abuse, Mc Glothlin (1975) explained that religious people are less likely to be the users of drugs.

India is a multi-religious society with religions such as Buddhism, Christianity, Hinduism, Islam, Sikhism and many more. Every religion has its own attitude towards the use of alcohol and psychotropic drugs. Manu, the ancient sage, who contributed important practices to be followed in his life by a person through literature named *Manu Smriti,* strictly forbade drinking by Brahmins, and learned people in the society. The use of alcohol was allowed to the people belonging to other castes, only on certain occasions such as religious ceremonies and social wars. In Hindu religion abstinence was considered virtuous for the common people, but alcohol consumption by specific groups in a society-approved manner is common and was tolerated (Tek Chand, 1972). Buddhist writers do not directly mention of prohibiting or permitting the use of drugs and alcohol but they strictly prohibit the use of alcohol by monks and in monasteries. However, they do not favour drugs, intoxicants, and alcohol for the mankind. Christianity is also found to be almost totally silent in this regard.

According to the Islamic religious edicts, there is total prohibition against alcohol use but drinking was common among the Mughal emperors and their subjects (Singh and Lal, 1979). The increasing trends in the consumption of alcoholic beverages in Islamic countries like Pakistan, Bangladesh shows the ambivalence of the Muslim society about the use of alcohol (WHO, 1999). Sikhism prohibits the use of tobacco, but does not mention any thing with regard to other drugs and alcohol.

Keeping in view all these factors, an attempt has been made to study the problem of alcohol abuse and distribution of sample according to religion. A majority of the respondent families (92.6%) are Hindus, 6 per cent are Sikhs, 1.1 per cent Muslims and 0.3 per cent Christians. From this data one may not be able to reach any conclusion that there is any relationship between religion and use of alcohol. One aspect, observed during fieldwork and discussion with the family members of the alcoholics that the use of alcohol affected the religious atmosphere of the family. Family members explained that how they were regular in worshipping, and visiting the religious places before the regular use of alcohol, but when the person started using alcohol regularly and crossed all limits religious atmosphere in the family was also disturbed. The religious celebrations such as *Navratras, Devi Jagran,* socio-cultural festivals like *Diwali, Gurpurab, Lohri, Id* were very much disturbed because the alcoholic person in their family created problems at one or the other occasion or, there is a fear of any untoward incidence.

The social differentiation on the basis of high and low is the historical heritage of all societies. These social strata and layers, divisions and sub-divisions have over the time been accepted on different basis such as sex and age; status and role; qualification and inefficiency; economic and political positions ritual and ceremony and on many other basis. Caste as the basis of stratification is a unique social institution in India. This stratification of our society, commenced with the *Chatur-Varna* system. Its origin is unknown, however, it gained prominence at the end of the Rig Vedic age. One could choose one's own *varna,* which was determined by his Karma (deeds) and individual characteristics. It was also explained by the *Gita* that a person is recognized by his traits (गुण) and deeds (कर्म), Chapter 4, verse 13 (गुण-कर्म-विभागश: गीता, 4/13) But with the change in time this *Chatur-Verna* system changed its structure presently known as caste system/Jati system, which has come to be homogeneous, endogamous group claiming common origin due to its heredity character. It is the complete perversion of the original *Chatur-Verna* system. It is now determined by the caste at the time of birth (*Janama*). It determines the living pattern, and has an effective say in the development of an individual. It has been one of the most important elements in defining the role and status of the individual and allotment of occupation in the Indian social structure.

Traditionally, the use of intoxicants was linked to some castes like *Kshatriyas,* some tribes and labour class working in strenuous and hazardous occupations. It was also associated with the source of livelihood for some castes such as *Kalal* or *Walias* (a caste of the north-west part of the country) associated with brewing and trading in liquor. At the same time the use of alcohol was not only prohibited in higher castes such as Brahmins but carried a stigma also. In the Northern parts of Madhya Pradesh, some parts of Rajasthan, Andhra Pradesh, tribals brew wine on their own under different names such as *Arhack, Hondia,* etc. from different types of raw materials like *mahua,* rice etc. What is then the association of castes with respect to alcohol abuse in families?

In the present study, the analysis of the data indicates that the majority of the respondent families (43.6%) belong to general castes (i.e. which are not covered under the category schedule of reserved castes) known as Savarna such as Brahmin, Vaish, Rajput, Ror*, Jat*, and Punjabis. Backward and Other Backward Castes (as per the list of state government.) are 33.9 per cent followed by Scheduled Castes, which are 22.5 per cent.

The family is the universally recognized basic biological and social unit. It interprets and transmits social norms and practices to the next generations. In spite of many changes in society that have altered their roles and functions, families continue to provide the natural framework for the emotional and material support essential to the growth and well-being of their members. However, the institution of family is far from being static. It must be viewed as a living, evolving institution, which is affected by socio-economic factors as well as by the changes that shape the social environment in which it functions. Joint family is considered to be a characteristic of the institutional structure of Indian society. Process of industrialization and modernization is said to have adversely affected it, both in structure and function (Goode, 1965). More recently, new types of families have begun to emerge, such as single-parent family, blended family which doesn't fit the traditional types of family such as 'Extended', 'Joint' and 'Nuclear' families.

In Indian context, the assumption is that industrialization and modernization disintegrated the traditional joint family system. The continuous increase in the use of alcohol in the name of modernization is an important factor, which may affect the family, its role and functions. The essential functions of the family are to meet the needs of its members for physical, psychological, social and economic security and well-being and the provision of a satisfactory environment for the support, education and socialization of children. The problematic consumption of alcohol can seriously disturb all these functions. Therefore, it is essential to study the types of family, size of family, of the respondent families. The relationship of all these with the use of alcohol in family will be discussed in the succeeding chapters. The data reveals that majority of the subjects (48.6%)

---

* These castes are included in Backward Castes by the Government of Haryana in 2013. A court case is also pending in Supreme Court of India against the decision of the State Government.

belong to the joint family, very closely followed by nuclear families (47.8%), 3.3 per cent families were extended families while 0.3 per cent were living alone. It was found that still some extended families are found in rural areas. While discussing with the respondents and family members it was observed that the number of nuclear families are increasing day by day. A small difference of less than 1 per cent supports the fact that the number of nuclear families are increasing very fast in both rural as well as urban areas.

It was also observed that many families, which were interviewed, became nuclear because the male member was using alcohol and it was a continuous problem for the joint family. An octogenarian lady explained the present situation, that how her joint family was disturbed by the use of alcohol and problem of drinking of her younger son for last 10–12 years. Other family members tolerated for a long time but it was not possible to continue with this agony hence he (the alcoholic son) was separated from the joint family. This was not the story of one family but many joint or extended families were disturbed because of problem drinking and alcoholism. But after a long tolerance when the problem drinking/alcoholism of any family member starts, and it create problems, the families which were already suffering because of interpersonal problems start breaking into nuclear families.

In rural areas another situation was observed during field-work that some families were living in the same premises (*Haweli*) having their separate kitchen (*Nyara Chulha*) but did not accept or reveal that they were separate from joint or extended family. In an informal discussion with some elderly family members or neighbours it was found that in reality, the family was separated because of alcohol problem. This was probably because in rural Indian society division of family is still not accepted in a positive way, hence they try to hide the realities, which they face in real life situations.

Big size of family had been a characteristic of the traditional Indian Society. It was quite usual for families to comprise three or four generations, to live under the same shelter and to eat from common kitchen. Besides property and work, mainly agriculture and other allied work where more the hands more the income support it, joint worship, celebrations and ritual were important forces that kept the family united. In spite of changes, due to modernization and industrialization there are still large sized families specially in rural areas. In this context an effort was made to study the size of family and it was found that 31 per cent of the families were with five members and 29.5 per cent families had four members. The families with six members were 18.2 per cent and 8.1 per cent families were with three members. As many as 7 per cent families composed of seven members and 2.1 per cent were with eight members. Some families with more than eight members were also found as 1.4 per cent families were with nine members and 0.8 per cent with 10 members and one family was with 11 members. While 1.5 per cent families were with two members and two persons were found living alone.

Housing (accommodation) is the most important basic need of a person. House is a place where a person feels himself safe and secure with a sense of psychological satisfaction. Apart from the place to rest after the day's hard work and its utility for a comfortable living, house, signifies our status in society. It is one of the primary needs of a human family in the present civilized society, but unfortunately growth of housing facilities in the country has not kept pace with the increase in population. Unplanned growth of industrial centres, large number of migration has outstripped almost all available resources including housing accommodation on account of limited space, high value of land and costly material for construction creates hardships for a common man to construct a simple house. Therefore, the nature and type of accommodation of the respondent families was studied in two parts; one is the type of accommodation and another is the nature of accommodation according to the ownership of house. It was found that 90.4 per cent families were having their own houses, while 5.5 per cent living in rented accommodation and 4.1 per cent were living in the houses provided by company or government office in which they are employed.

It was also observed that in what type of accommodation the family was living. The question was asked on the basis of physical nature of house, i.e. *pucca* house, *kacha* house, or *kacha* and *pucca* mixed or living in a hut. A majority, 66 per cent of the families were living in *pucca* houses. Out of this about 9.5 per cent houses were either on rent basis or provided by government or by the company in which the persons were employed. It means about 56 per cent of the families were living in their own and *pucca* houses. And 29.0 per cent families were living in *kacha* and *pucca* mixed houses, in which a large part of the house was *kacha* and old only a small part, i.e. one room was rebuilt as *pucca* and rest remained un constructed, partially repaired by using mud and wood. A small population of the respondent families (0.8%) was also found living in *jhonpri* (hut).

During discussion different situations were observed and many things were explained by the respondents. The condition of the *pucca* houses was not good, many of them needed immediate repair which was not possible because the financial position of the family was disturbed by the problematic alcohol use, some houses were found in semi-constructed conditions. Only one room was completed and the work of construction was stopped because family suffered serious financial crisis as the major part of the income was being drained off in the use of alcohol. One very important fact revealed during discussion was that most of these *pucca* and semi-*pucca* houses were constructed by the parents or grandparents of the respondent families. The present generation has not contributed anything in the house, rather in reality the family could not manage proper repair and maintenance of these houses. Therefore, one can easily conclude that the use of alcohol especially problem drinking by one or more family members disturbed the composition of the family (joint to nuclear) and lead to the division of house which was unplanned and disfigured the original shape of the house. While discussing it during field work one old lady in a village said, 'इस दारू ने तो म्हारा घर ही खत्म कर दिया, यो घर इसके दादा ने बनाया था। और इसने तो इस घर की शक्ल ही बिगाड़ दी।' (The use of alcohol has shattered the original house and disfigured it which was constructed by the grandparent of this person (alcoholic, who was in the drunken state at that time). Another thing, which came into picture during various discussions, was that many houses were either mortgaged or sold by the alcoholic persons, therefore, the ownership of houses was under dispute, but at the time of interview the family was living in the same house, hence it was covered in the category of their own house.

Occupation is the backbone of a family which not only provides financial base to the family but also determines its social status and reflects the person's social standing. The occupational background of the respondent families was studied and it was found that 33.9 per cent families were agriculturists and 31.4 per cent were labourer. As many as 22.5 per cent were in government or private service and 12.2 per cent were involved in their own business. Thus, it was clear that a good number of respondents were related to agriculture and allied occupations. It was found that majority of the labourers were also associated with the agriculture labour. It indicates that majority of the respondents were from agriculture and allied occupations because agriculture is the main occupation of the rural society in India. Business was preferably found in urban areas where trading, shop keeping, small-scale home industry, commission agents etc. were covered as their occupations.

While discussing about occupation, some interesting facts came before the researcher. The complaints were made by the family members specially wife that it is the work (occupation) which made the person alcoholic. A rich folklore exists on the association of drinking problems with certain occupations. There are some occupations, which are traditionally associated with heavy drinking or problem drinking. Therefore, some important questions arouse that how far the occupations are responsible for problem drinking? Which are these occupations? What is the effect of problem drinking on the occupation? The answer to these questions needs an in-depth study of the problem of alcoholism and problem drinking and its relationship with occupation. Some aspects of the problem will be covered in the proceeding chapters of the book.

The distribution of the families on the basis of income (monthly basis) shows that about 55 per cent families had their income between ₹ 2,001–5,000, of these 21.2 per cent were the having between ₹ 2,100–3,000; 18.3 per cent between ₹ 3,001–4,000 and 15.4 per cent between ₹ 4,001–5,000 of the rest, 16.0 per cent were having income between ₹ 1,000–2,000 and 29.1 per cent had income more than ₹ 5,000.

While analysing the level of family income it can be concluded that the income status of the respondents is not bad if we compare it with the latest minimum income level approved by the Haryana Government (which is ₹ 2,000 a month). Only 16 per cent families were found having income below ₹ 2,000 a month. But in many families where the income was good, now the sources of income were found disturbed and depleted. For example in many families with agriculture as their occupation, sold their agriculture land, some with business lost their business, some with skilled labour such as confectioner (Halwai), mason, mechanics, plumbers etc. lost their jobs and did not get work because of irregularity and loss of faith. Those who were doing unskilled labour did not go for it. Thus the source of family income gradually started shrinking and subsequently finished totally in many cases.

Marital Relations of the Respondents (Spouse)

The cultural significance of marriage is universal. It is accepted as a status-giving device in the society; it enlarges social responsibilities and role obligations in the wider kinship and social network. In this context, the marital status might have implications for adjustment patterns with the stresses and strains of social and economic nature generated in the present environment. The marital relations of the respondents are important because of the intimacy and mutual care it provides to its partners. When none cares, it is the spouse who stands by his/her partner in the hour of need and provides succour, and instills a sense of hope and security.

Respondents in the present context mainly the wives of the alcoholics or in some cases their mothers (when wife was not available) were subject to various odds and hazards in their family life. So it was important to study their present marital relations because in Indian culture strong family ties and social disapproval to any form of separation forces the family to remain together. Therefore, the present marital relations were divided into the categories of living together, divorced, separated, wife living with parents, disturbed relations. It was found that in spite of the sufferings a good number (49.7%) of the respondents were living together, while 38.9 per cent of the respondents accepted that they were living with disturbed relations. There were 1.5 per cent divorced, 1.6 per cent living with their parents temporarily and 4.6 per cent are separated for a quite long time (Table 2.1).

Table 2.1 Marital relations of the respondents (Spouse)

Marital relations	*Number of respondents*	*Percentage*
Living together	398	49.7
Divorced	12	01.5
Separated	37	04.6
Wife living with her parents	13	01.6
Disturbed relations	311	38.9
No response	11	01.4
Unmarried	18	02.3
Total	800	100

To study the marital relations is a very personal, sensitive and complex investigation, which needs an intimate relationship with the respondents. In the case of sensitive problems like problem drinking and alcoholism, it becomes more complex because of the morality and stigma attached to it. This issue of sensitivity was clear with the researcher and it was covered with the use of interpersonal skills for which the research team tried its best and worked hard to study it up to maximum possible realities related to such problems. In the case of 49.7 per cent respondents living together it was found that the problems of alcoholic husband were not less serious but the support from other family members like father-in-law, mother-in-law, brother-in-law (*Dewar, Jeth*)* and sister-in-law (*Dewrani, Jethani*)** was the main source for keeping the husband and wife together. These family members narrated numerous incidences and stories when the suffering wife was given full support. It was because of the Indian cultural bindings which work as a means to live together. Some-times it leads to serious implications, as there were some cases of suicide or attempt to suicide by any family member or attempt to suicide by the spouse because of the problems created by the alcoholic. In the case of disturbed relations about 39 per cent respondents (spouses) were living in the family where no support was available but still they were living with the family, in the house of husband and accepted the problem. The alcoholic husband lives with the family, gives no support rather the family gives him support at the time of need, such as, health problems or street brawls etc. In such cases, wife or elder children were the main source of support to the family. In many cases, it was found that the alcoholic person was even not traceable for many days even for months, but occasionally comes back to family and starts living with them. In the case of 4.6 per cent separated cases, the wife was living separately from the husband for more than three years and never allowed him to come and had no concern with him.

Therefore, one may say that discord with the spouse is one of the serious problems in the families suffering with the problem of alcoholism. However, in the conservative Indian society still separation and divorce are not so common.

---

* *Dewar*: Husband's younger brother; *Jeth*: Husbands elder brother

** *Dewarani*: Wife of younger brother of husband; *Jethani*: Wife of elder brother of husband.

Income Consumption Pattern of the Families

The level of income of the families with alcohol problems was not bad. Except some families, in which the levels of income were good, i.e. about 63.8 per cent families were found between the income level of ₹ 3,001 to more than ₹ 5,000 per month (as discussed earlier). This level of income is much above the minimum wage level of ₹ 2,800 per month fixed by the Haryana government in July 2005. Therefore, it can be inferred that because of good income the purchasing power of the families is also good. The studies also reported that after the green revolution in Haryana and Punjab the income levels of the farmers and people linked with agriculture and allied jobs had significantly increased, which resulted in the excessive recreational or regular use of alcohol (Singh et al., 1979).

Therefore, it can be said that because of good income the purchasing power of the families is also good. However, the standard of living and health status of the family members were not found in accordance with their income.

Hence, it was considered important to explore the priorities in the income consumption pattern of the families with problematic alcohol consumption. The income consumption pattern is divided into 10 main heads such as food and food products, milk and milk products, house rent or repair, clothing, electricity and water, education of children, health, entertainment including social ceremonies, alcohol, smoking or use of any other drug. During investigation it was found that 63.75 per cent respondents spend ₹ 100 to ₹ 500 per month on food and food products, 23.75 per cent spend ₹ 501 to ₹ 1,000 and only 11 per cent respondents spend ₹ 1,000 and more on food and food products. Merely, 1.35 per cent did not give any response in this regard. More than three fourth of the respondent families said that they spend ₹ 100 to ₹ 500 per month on milk (the rate of milk varies from ₹ 12 to 18 per litre), 17 per cent respondents spend ₹ 501 to ₹ 1,000 and only 2.5 per cent respondents spend ₹ 1,000 and above on milk and milk products. It means that the average milk purchased by 92 per cent families varies from one litre to two litres per day for one family while the number of family members varies from 5 to 10, which itself speaks of the priorities in the family.

House being one of the basic needs for human beings deserves a careful concern. But in the developing countries the due concern is not shown to this head because of the traditional lifestyle of the majority of population. The researcher and his team observed the same situation during data collection.

It was found that the respondents spend very little amount on house rent or repair. The majority of the respondents in rural areas were having their own houses, therefore, they do not spend any money on this head or spend very little amount whenever need arises. About 26 per cent respondents had not given any response to this question and 62.5 per cent respondents said that they spend ₹ 100 to ₹ 500 on house rent or repair in one month, About 10 per cent respondents spend ₹ 500 to ₹ 1,000 while only 1.75 per cent families spend ₹ 1,000 and above on this head. It means the amount spent for housing either used on rent or on house repair (in case of own house) by the majority was very meagre especially when the rates of house rent and house construction material were very high.

Another important head in the household expenditure is the part of income spent on clothing. The data explains that 72.62 per cent respondents spend up to ₹ 500 per month on the clothing of family members (while the number of family members varies from five to 11). There are 21 per cent families who spend in between ₹ 501 to ₹ 1,000 and about only 2.37 per cent respondents spend about ₹ 1,000 on clothing. It indicates that majority of the respondents were not able to spend much amount on the clothing needs of their family members. It was observed during discussion that the family was not able to meet the proper dressing needs of the members because the increasing cost of the clothes and the disturbed expenditure of the family income due to alcohol use in family, which does not allow to spare enough money for this head. Anyhow, the mothers in the family take care about this part of family need in majority of the cases. How she manages, it depends on her personal ability, help from her parents' house, close relatives such as senior married daughters of the family (sister of her husband) etc.

The next important head for the family is the education of children and it was found that 66 per cent families spend ₹ 100 to ₹ 500 on the educational needs of their children, while only 11.75 per cent families could spend ₹ 1,000 and more per month on education. 7.5 per cent respondents did not respond because they were not clear about it or it was not applicable to them.

Another important head in the household expenditure is the expenditure on health of the family members. The data in Table 2.2

reveals that in more than 71 per cent respondent families' expenditure on health was in between ₹ 100 to ₹ 500, 17.6 per cent families could spend from ₹ 501 to ₹ 1,000 and only 1.12 per cent families spend ₹ 1,000 and above on health. It clearly indicates that respondents were not much concerned about the health needs of their family members. The care about health was also not given much priority in the developing countries like India and it is said that Indians avoid seeking medical help till it becomes unavoidable. In many cases it was also observed by the research team that traditional household treatment methods (घरेलु नुस्खे) were very popular in the treatment of common ailments. Moreover, the increased cost of treatment facilities and carelessness of the government medical institutions and services also obstruct the common man to go for the proper treatment of their ailments. Majority of these families accepted that the large part of the family income was being consumed, in such situation in alcohol so how they could think of going to a qualified doctor where the cost of treatment is very high. The details of the health problems in the alcohol-affected families will be discussed in next chapters.

On the question about entertainment, the family members were not clear about the nature and meaning of entertainment hence not ready to answer. After a crucial exercise they agreed to cooperate and respond. Some of the family members (partially educated) said that 'this entertainment' is responsible for the present situation of their family, they were referring to the alcohol related problems (use of alcohol started as entertainment with friends, relatives etc.). They said 'इस मंनोरंजन, मनबहलाव और अतिथि सत्कार ने ही तो इसे शराबी बना दिया है' (This entertainment, enjoyment and care of guests made him alcoholic). About 23 per cent respondents did not response to this question and 61.25 per cent said that they spend ₹ 100 to ₹ 500 on this head. They also explained that it includes all social and religious ceremonies of the family, visiting relatives and entertains the visited relatives and friends. About 13 per cent spent ₹ 501 to ₹ 1,000 and 2.87 per cent spend ₹ 1,000 and above monthly. In many cases the money spent on gambling and lotteries was also included in this head.

Under the head of alcohol 57.12 per cent respondents said that ₹ 1,000 and above was spent on alcohol in one month, 28.37

Table 2.2 Income consumption pattern of the families

Head of expenditure	*Expenditure per month in Rs*						*No response*	
	100–500		*501–1,000*		*Above 1,000*			
	No. of Respondents	*%age*	*No. of Respondents*	*%age*	*No. of Respondents*	*%age*	*No. of Respondents*	*%age*
Food and food products	510	63.75	190	23.75	89	11.12	11	1.35
Milk and milk products	602	75.25	136	17.00	20	2.50	42	5.25
House rent/repair	502	62.75	79	9.87	14	1.75	205	25.62
Clothing etc.	581	72.62	168	21.00	19	2.37	32	4.00
Electricity/water/telephone etc.	504	63.00	225	28.12	17	2.12	54	6.75
Education of children	528	66.00	174	21.75	38	4.75	60	7.5
Health	572	71.5	141	17.62	9	1.12	78	9.75
Entertainment	490	61.25	103	12.87	23	2.87	184	23.00
Alcohol	116	14.5	227	28.37	457	57.12	0	0
Smoking/any other drug	515	64.37	184	23.00	73	9.12	28	3.5

per cent families spend ₹ 501 to 1,000 and 14.5 per cent respondent families said that the expenditure on alcohol was up to ₹ 500 which means that in the majority of the families a large part of income is spent on alcohol. The data given in Table 2.2 shows that in 85 per cent families more than half of the income is spent on the alcohol. It clearly reveals that all this happens at the cost of basic necessities of family life such as good and balanced food, health, proper housing, education of children etc.

The Alcoholic's Profile

This part of the study deals with the socio-economic characteristics of the person who use alcohol and became alcoholic or problem drinker in the family and was responsible for the problems in the family due to alcohol use.

In the traditional Indian society women population abstain themselves from drinking alcohol. In certain tribal groups and tea plantation workers there are substantial numbers of women drinking alcohol, but generally over 95 per cent of the women population still are abstinent (WHO, 1999). While studying the sex composition of the problematic alcohol drinkers in Haryana the study revealed that 99.7 per cent alcoholics were male and 0.3 per cent (i.e. only two out of 800 families) was female alcoholics. Probably it is because that there is no tribal population in Haryana, but it does not confirm that women do not drink. When it was questioned as to how many women family members use alcohol the data revealed that in 6.3 per cent families women drink alcohol, though it may not be a problem drinking, and 93.7 per cent families said that women members do not use alcohol.

The marital status in the respondent families shows that only 2.3 per cent of the alcoholics were unmarried and most of the persons with problematic alcohol use were married, i.e. 97.7 per cent.

Education qualification indicates the education level of the alcoholics in the sample, which reveals that 18.8 per cent were illiterate. There were 23.9 per cent alcoholics who were educated up to metric level, 19.1 per cent up to middle, 13.8 per cent up to primary. Some alcoholics were also found with the higher education levels such as 10+2/Higher Secondary 12.5 per cent, graduates were 9 per cent, post graduates 2.6 per cent and only 1.1 per cent were technical diploma holder.

How many members in the family use alcohol? The use of alcohol in family is a common feature or a casual one is also important to study. Therefore, how many members in the family use alcohol was enquired and it was found that in majority only, i.e. 71.6 per cent families only one-person use alcohol. In 19.2 per cent families of the sample at least two members in the family use alcohol. There were 5.9 per cent families in which three members use alcohol and in 3.3 per cent families four and more than four members use alcohol.

Drinking and serving alcohol in social functions has been the part of family celebrations and accepted as an indicator of a good host. In many families, alcohol is essentially served to guests for the satisfaction of the guest as well as the host. The families where more than one member uses alcohol, all of them may not be the problem drinkers but use it regularly, in such families usually one member is found as a problem drinker. In some families where more than one member were problem drinkers these families were joint or extended families at one time but now the families are divided and have taken the shape of nuclear families.

Duration of Regular Use

The information about the regular use of alcohol was also obtained. It was found that in majority of families (67.5%) alcohol was being used for more than last four years, in 11.4 per cent families alcohol was used for last four years and in 12.8 per cent for last three years (Figure 2.1). In 8.3 per cent families the alcohol use was for last two years and some families accepted that this duration of regular use was noticed when the person using alcohol started creating problems, otherwise the regular use of alcohol by the person may be of more in time but not taken up seriously by the family.

Table 2.3 Duration of regular use of alcohol

Information about the duration	*No. of respondents*	*Percentage*
For last two years	67	08.3
For last three years	102	12.8
For last four years	91	11.4
For more than last four years	540	67.5
Total	800	100.0

Figure 2.1 Duration of regular use of alcohol

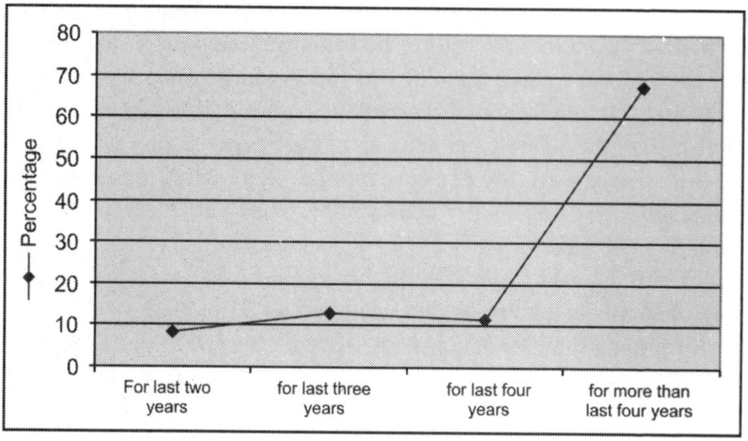

So far as the problems of alcohol use are concerned, it was observed that the family was also not much concerned until the serious problems were not noticed. In many cases, only the alcoholic individual was facing problems and family was ignoring him for a quiet long time. Therefore, the duration of alcohol use may be longer but the period noted for regular use has been considered, when the family members noticed the regular use of alcohol by the person who started creating problems for the family.

Frequency of Alcohol Use

When the respondents (wife or other family members) were asked to state as to how frequently their family member (alcoholic) was consuming alcohol, they were not able to explain properly. Members of the research team helped the respondents to think about it and find out the time of use, the spontaneous response was 'daily'. It was more clearly explained to them through the help of some examples, incidents, etc. and then the response started coming out. They told that in 15.4 per cent families the alcoholics drink several times a day and in 23.5 per cent families many times a week. In 54.0 per cent families the alcoholics take on daily basis while in 7.1 per cent families it has been weekly (Table 2.4).

Table 2.4 Frequency of alcohol use

Frequency	*No. of respondents*	*Percentage*
Once a week	57	7.1
Many times a week	188	23.5
Daily	432	54.0
Several times a day	123	15.4
Total	800	100.0

The data in Table 2.4 clearly reveals that a majority of the families are suffering with the problem of daily use of alcohol by one or more members hence, it is apparent that essentially the users take it regularly almost at the appointed time. The important question is that what is the interval between the intake of alcohol? The data explains and the observation also revealed that it varies from once a week to several times a day. Like other psychotropic drugs alcohol also has withdrawal symptoms and a level of tolerance. Thus, the frequency of use and intake of alcohol depends on these factors also. A careful observation revealed that majority of alcoholics drink on daily basis and the quantity and the frequency of intake is increasing day by day, which is alarming. An attempt was made to study whether the use of alcohol increased during the last one year or not, Table 2.5 explains that in 87.6 per cent families it did not increase but the situation of the alcoholic indicate that the chances of increase were fair.

Table 2.5 Distribution of the families according to increase in alcohol use during last one year

Response	*No. of respondents*	*Percentage*
Yes	701	87.6
No	99	12.4
Total	800	100.0

In a detailed discussion with the family members it was accepted that when a check was imposed there was a fierce and sometimes bestial reaction from the alcoholic person. Some efforts were made to control but gradually the things started going out of their hands. The family faced unhealthy atmosphere, like absence from home, theft, fight, street brawls, violence and other disturbances.

Reasons for First Use of Alcohol

Table 2.6 gives the information as to which factors initiated the alcoholic person to use alcohol for the first time. A variety of reasons were explained by the family members for the first use of alcohol by the alcoholic person. A good number 38.50 per cent families said that peer group pressure was responsible for the first use of alcohol, and 11.10 per cent families said that the person started using it as a fun. In India, especially in rural areas, there is a common practice of using alcohol for enjoyment and recreation. Usually, it is found in the countryside that outside home, at farm or at the cattle shed a group of people come together in the evening and start using alcohol, they build fire, cook meat and drink liquor. Many other reasons were also explained by the family members such as curiosity, to relieve depression, to get relief from tension etc. In 3.80 per cent cases the alcoholics were unknowingly induced to take alcohol, e.g. as a medicine etc. About 6.60 per cent respondents were not able to explain the reasons for the first use of alcohol by their family members (Table 2.6).

Table 2.6 Reasons responsible for first use of alcohol

Reasons for first use	*No. of respondents*	*Percentage*
Curiosity	36	4.50
Peer group pressure	308	38.50
To relieve depression	37	4.60
To relieve pain	33	4.10
To relieve tension	76	9.50
To induce sleep	19	2.40
Just for fun	89	11.10
To solve problem	17	2.10
Unknowingly	30	3.80
Tricked into taking	22	2.80
Took as medicine	11	1.40
To imitate parents/elders or sibling	21	2.60
Financial crises	14	1.80
Family problems	34	4.20
Don't know	53	6.60
Total	800	100.00

The data indicates that peer group pressure is one of the most important reasons for the first use of alcohol. The literature on alcohol use and problem drinking identified two types of motives for drinking alcohol, (i) Social conformity motives; (ii) Enhancement motives (Cooper, 1994). Social conformity motives refer to drinking so as not to be rejected by your peer group and to feel like you are part of the crowd. Enhancement motives are the tendencies reconized and re-established for acceptance and appreciation. The tendency to make the best use of one's potentials and capabilities is impaired by the continuous and excessive use of alcohol. The ability to know one's own capacities and talents and utilize to the maximum is also blocked and further deteriorated by the non-cooperation and negative roles played by the family members. In such situation enhancement motives mediate positive association between mind and body awareness which is linked with drinking of alcohol in social situations and its effect on the alcoholic person's self and family.

So far as the individual's drinking habits are concerned, it has been observed that such habits often change at different stages of the life course. Some young people who start drinking with the peer group pressure, may continue drinking for some time and lead to drinking heavily in a potentially risky way. Some suffer adverse consequences because of this. This may be true for any of the above stated reasons and for many probably for most of such individuals, this is simply a step along a trajectory or 'drinking career'. A common thinking about drinking is that heavy alcohol consumption amongst young, single people is changed in a much lighter consumption later in life, especially following marriage or with other responsibilities. But it is not a case, for example, teenagers who drink heavily will inevitably remain heavy drinkers or move on to develop chronic drinking problems (Plant et al., 1985; Fillmore, 1988). It was observed that the above said reasons for the first use of alcohol proved unsafe and unhealthy because after some time these casual users of alcohol began to drink heavily with increasing irregularity.

Place Where Alcohol is Used

The place where the person uses alcohol is an important aspect to be analysed because directly or indirectly it affects the mode of drinking alcohol. As the patterns of drinking reveals that use of alcohol in all societies is mainly a social activity. It is the important part of social celebrations such as marriage and other marriage related ceremonies, birth of a male child, promotion in job, profit in business, purchase of property, etc. A very interesting and important feature of such regular social drinkers was observed during fieldwork, that those who sometimes drink alone usually drink more often in group which leads to problem drinking. Some individuals were also observed at the time of drinking and it was found that when they drink alcohol alone, they do so at home and when they drink in group it may be at any location such as someone's home, at farm, at the work place etc. Table 2.7 shows the distribution of the subjects using alcohol according to the place where they usually take alcohol. It was found that 27.9 per cent subjects use alcohol at all the places such as their own home, work place, their friend's place, bar or restaurant, at the farm or cattle yard commonly known as *Tabela**, 21.5 per cent of the alcoholics said that they drink at friends' place followed by 20.6 per cent at their own home, 20.0 per cent at work place or nearby the work place, 7.5 per cent at any other convenient place and 2.5 per cent reported that they consume alcohol at bar/restaurants or *ahatas* (Table 2.7).

Table 2.7 Place where he/she usually take alcohol

Place	*No. of respondents*	*Percentage*
Home	165	20.6
Work Place	160	20.0
Friend's Place	172	21.5
Bar/Restaurant	20	2.5
All above	223	27.9
Any other place	60	7.5
Total	800	100.0

While discussing with the family members of alcoholics, it was found that a large number of daily drinkers prefer to use alcohol at their home but when it starts as group activity outside the home it

* *Tabela* is a place where cattle are kept in villages. This is a common place for men to spend their time and also where they enjoy alcohol parties.

becomes unmanageable for many of them. Some families told about it and at many places the researcher also observed that many chronic alcoholics indulge in harmful use* and drink alcohol continuously for many days and do not take even food. This is followed by a group drinking in which the alcoholic starts drinking alcohol at any of the above said places.

Company in Which Alcohol Used

In fact, the place where the alcohol is used and the company of the user are very much related to each other. The analysis of the data presented in Table 2.8 indicates that the highest percentage (70.9%) of the alcohol drinkers, drink in the company of their friends, (44.1%), co-workers (6.6%), relatives (3.9%) or with all of them (13%).

There are 24.4 per cent alcoholics who reported that they do not use alcohol in any company and always take it alone. Some of the respondents were not able to explain about the nature of company of the alcoholic members of their family, therefore, the information of 4.7 per cent alcohol users could not be recorded as they said that they do not know in which company they use alcohol (Figure 2.2).

Table 2.8 Company in which alcohol used

Company	*No. of respondents*	*Percentage*
Alone	195	24.4
With friends/acquaintance	353	44.1
With relatives	031	03.9
With co-workers	053	06.6
With family members	004	00.5
With all above	104	13.0
Any other	022	02.8
Don't know	038	04.7
Total	800	100.0

Drinking customs present an intermediate level of analysis between cultures and individual patterns of drinking. A culture

* 'Harmful use' to indicate a pattern of psychoactive substance use that is causing damage to health (ICD 10, WHO).

Figure 2.2 Company in which alcohol used

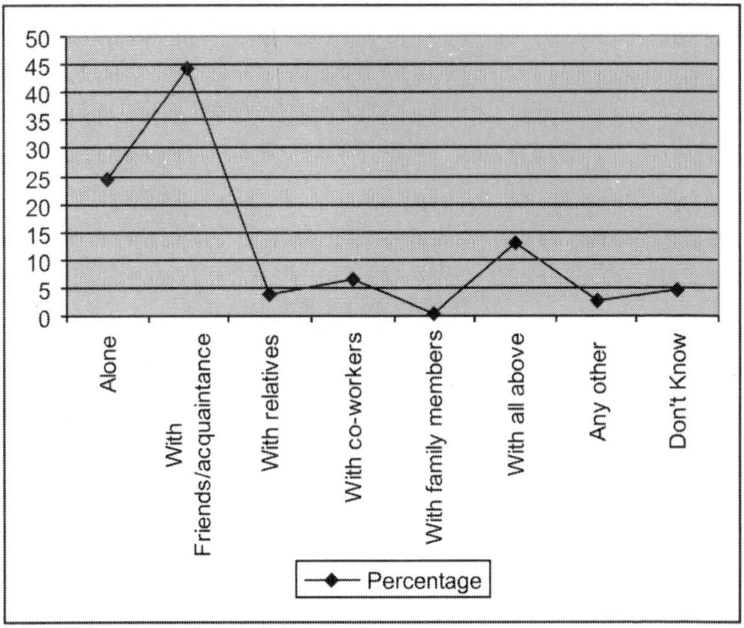

can be described as being composed of an assortment of customs, some of them centred on drinking, some potentially including it, and others specifically excluding it. Over time, the mixture of customs may change and some customs or types of occasions may become more frequent (Room et al., 2002). This was observed while interacting with the respondents and with some alcoholics. In India, there are some customs in some societies where the use of alcohol had been the part of their celebrations such as marriage, birth of male child, on the purchase of property and even at the death of the elderly member of the family. These celebrations are not considered complete till the alcohol is not served. In some of the villages, it was explained by the villagers that in panchayats sometimes before or sometimes after the meeting and proceedings of panchayat serving of alcohol is a custom. Some religious celebrations among the Hindus are also associated with the special type of intoxication such as offering of alcohol to the deities and *bhang* (cannabis) to *Shiva* on the festivals of *Shivratri* and *Holi*.

This is followed by distribution of these intoxicants among the followers in the form of a gift of the deity (*Prasad*). Such type of practices encourage group drinking which later on results to the continuous use of alcohol by some of the people. A good number of respondents explained that it is because of such customs, the person becomes a regular drinker. In some cases such practices were also held responsible for the relapse of the problem.

Type/Brand of Alcohol Used

Efforts were made to find out the type or brand of alcohol used or preferred by the alcoholics. It was observed that the use of alcohol at one side is a status symbol and on the other side it is a compulsion of the person who uses it regularly. The quality and brands of alcohol available in the market varies on the basis of its quality, price and mode of preparation. The data in Table 2.9 reveals that about 38 per cent alcohol users use *desi daru*, the locally brewed alcohol, which is illegally distillated, 18.9 per cent use country liquor, 12 per cent use Indian Made Foreign Liquor (IMFL). Good number 23.4 per cent alcoholics said that they use all types of alcohol, whichever is available (Figure 2.3).

Figure 2.3 Type/brand of alcohol used as reported by the family

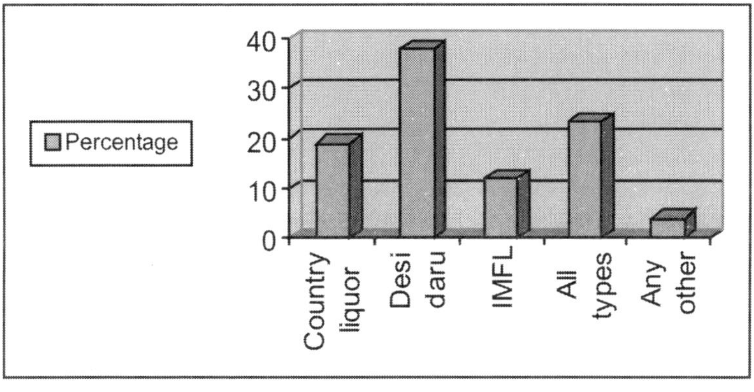

The use of alcohol and the choice of type/brand of alcohol depend on many factors such as the cost of the brand, the liking of the brand, availability in that area, the alcohol sale policy of the local government and the excise rules of the state government. The data presented in the above table shows that about 38 per cent people use *desi daru* i.e. the locally brewed alcohol, which is illegally distillated. Inspite of ban on local brewing, there is a practice of illicit distillation of alcohol in almost all villages. Some people do it for their own consumption, while many do it for sale and it is very popular in the rural areas because it is easily available at a relatively cheaper price. The research team personally visited these places in some villages with a confidence and faith expressed to them. It was observed that in many cases this activity was done with the knowledge of local police and a handsome share of the profit is given to them for this favour.

Table 2.9 Type/brand of alcohol used as reported by the family

Type/brand of alcohol	*No. of respondents*	*Percentage*
Country liquor	151	18.9
Desi daru	303	37.9
IMFL	096	12.0
All above	187	23.4
Any other	033	04.1
Don't know	125	15.6

Note: Total number of respondents is above 800 because many alcoholics were using more than one type/brand of alcohol.

Another brand popular among the alcohol users is country liquor. The alcohol content of the country liquor varied from 30 per cent to 40 per cent, while in the home made liquor, it depends upon the type of material used, the degree of fermentation in which the degree of alcohol content can go up to 60 per cent. The choice of the brand and type also depends on the easy availability. In many villages there were authorized liquor shops, in such villages people preferred country liquor, and in the villages where no such shops were available, people consumed homemade liquor. The villagers also report about professional disputes between the licensed liquor shop owners and the illegal liquor distillation centres. The licensed shop owners try to check the sale and distribution of homemade liquor, while on the other hand they set up some unauthorized/authorized small sale centres (*Khurja*) in the villages where licensed shops are not available. These small centres ensure a regular supply of liquor to the consumers. Many times the complaints were made but no effective steps were taken by the administration in this regard.

Time of Use of Alcohol

The respondents were also asked about the time of alcohol usage. It was found that a majority (57%) of the users use alcohol in the evening, which is followed by the 29.9 per cent users at any time. There were some users who use alcohol in afternoon (2.4%) and 1.3 per cent use it in morning also. Some respondents (9.4%) said that the person use alcohol in the late night usually after coming back from their business (Table 2.10).

Table 2.10 Time of drinking alcohol

Time	*No. of respondents*	*Percentage*
Morning	010	01.3
Afternoon	019	02.4
Evening	456	57.0
Late night	075	09.4
Any time	239	29.9
Total	800	100.0

When they were asked why they use alcohol in the morning the response was that it becomes difficult for them to start their routine work if they don't use alcohol. It was observed that the timings of use of alcohol was very much according to the level and duration of use. Those who use alcohol for a quiet long time were found using it any time during the day or night. While a large majority accepted that they do use it in the evening otherwise they cannot live a normal life and can't take rest at night.

Children in the Families Where Alcohol is Used

When there is a regular use of alcohol in the family a natural question arises that how it affects the children. Child is a keen observer of the minute actions, behaviour and day-to-day happenings in the family so, the chances are there that whenever he finds the opportunity he tries to imitate. Therefore, a question that does the children in family also use alcohol was asked to the respondents. Table 2.11 shows that 28 per cent respondents accepted that the children in their families use alcohol. As many as 64.2 per cent families said no, while 7.8 per cent families had not responded to this question. Many of the female members, especially, mothers and grandmothers requested the researcher to do something and save their children from this problem. They narrated their agony that they already had been suffering from, which is associated with the use of alcohol by the elder members of the family and the children who had also started using alcohol.

Table 2.11 Children in family use alcohol

Response	*No. of respondents*	*Percentage*
Yes	224	28.0
No	514	64.2
No response	062	07.8
Total	800	100.0

In nutshell, the analysis of the data shows that an overwhelming majority (92.6%) of the respondents are the Hindus. More than 43 per cent respondents belong to general castes (including high castes such as *Brahmin, Ror*, Jat*, Rajput, Khatri, Baniya*) and about 34 per cent belong to backward castes and other backward castes, while about 23 per cent belong to scheduled castes. A good number (48.6%) of the respondents are still living in joint families specially in rural areas while 47.8 per cent are living in nuclear families. A small number of 3.3 per cent of respondents are also found living in extended families. The size of the families in about 31 per cent is five members and in 29.5 per cent with four members. In rural areas, some are large sized families of nine members (1.4%), of 10 members (0.8%), and one family with 11 members are also found. Small sized families with three members (8.1%) and with two members (1.5%) are also found suffering with the problem of alcoholism. A large majority of the respondents (90.4%) have their own houses while, only 5.5 per cent are living in rented accommodation and 4.1 per cent have the government or company houses. The type of accommodation indicates that about two third of the respondents are living in *pucca* houses and less than one third are having *kacha* and *pucca* mixed houses. Rests of the respondents are living in *kacha* houses even in *jhopadis*/huts.

Occupation of the respondents' family reveals that about 34 per cent families are agriculturists and majority living in villages,

* These castes are included in Backward Castes by the Government of Haryana in 2013. A court case is also pending in Supreme Court of India against the decision of the State Government.

about 32 per cent are labourers, 22.5 per cent in jobs either government or private and 12 per cent families are doing their own business. The monthly income of the families indicates that 16 per cent families are having income between ₹ 1,000 to ₹ 2,000, about 40 per cent families have income from ₹ 2,001 to ₹ 4,000 and 44 per cent families have income more than ₹ 4,001 per month. About 50 per cent of the families were found living together while about 39 per cent have disturbed family relations and 4.6 per cent are separated, 1.5 per cent are divorced and in the case of 1.6 per cent families, the wives of the alcoholics are living with their parents.

A large part of the income is spent on alcohol (57.12% spend above ₹ 1,000 per month, 28.37% spend from ₹ 501 to ₹ 1,000 per month and 14.5% spend up to ₹ 501 per month) and rest of the income is used for other family needs such as about 64 per cent families could afford to spend up to ₹ 100 to ₹ 500 on food items and 75 per cent families on milk etc. of their income. Only 11 per cent families spend above ₹ 1,000 on food items and mere 2.5 per cent families spend ₹ 1,000 on milk. The other important family requirements such as clothing, education of children, health receive very small amount of the family income, only 2 per cent of the families spent above ₹ 1,000 on clothing and 1.1 per cent spend on health, while 72 per cent families can afford only up to ₹ 500 per month for clothing and 71 per cent for health. Education of the children is also another effected head where only 4.7 per cent families spend ₹ 1,000 and above on education of their children and 66 per cent families spend only from ₹ 100 to ₹ 500 a month. Other heads of expenditure such as house rent/repair, electricity/water bills, and entertainment also receive a very small amount of the family income.

The socio-economic characteristics of the persons using alcohol (alcoholics) reveal that in the sample 99.7 per cent are male and only 0.3 per cent females. Most of the alcoholics are married (97.87%). About 19 per cent are illiterate and among the literates 24 per cent are matriculate, 19 per cent are educated up to middle level and 13 per cent up to primary only. Some are also found with higher education, i.e. 9 per cent are graduates and 2.6 per cent postgraduates. A small number (1.1%) is having some technical diploma. In large majority (71.6%) of the families, only one member uses alcohol while 19.2 per cent families have two persons using alcohol and in 9.2 per cent families three or more persons use alcohol. The duration of regular use of alcohol indicated that 67.5 per cent alcoholics are using regularly for more than four years. Only 8.3 per cent are using alcohol for last two years. A little above of the half (54%) use alcohol daily, 23.5 per cent use it many times a week and 7.1 per cent use it once a week, 15.4 per cent alcoholics found using alcohol for several times a day. The increase in the use of alcohol during last one year indicates that a large majority (87.6%) has increased the consumption of alcohol while 12.4 per cent said no to this. The reasons found for initiating the alcohol, were that about 39 per cent alcoholics started using it under the peer group pressure and 11.10 per cent used it as a fun. Some other reasons, curiosity 4.50 per cent, to relieve depression 4.60 per cent, family problems 4.20 per cent, to imitate parents and other family members 2.60 per cent and to relieve pain 4.10 per cent were also found. About 4 per cent alcoholics said that they started using it unknowingly and about 3 per cent were tricked into taking the alcohol.

The place of using alcohol was mostly not restricted to one place, 28 per cent say that they use it at all the places where available or suitable. About 21 per cent said that they usually use it at their home and 21.4 per cent said that they use it at friends' house/place. There are 20 per cent of the alcoholics who were found using it at or near their workplace while 7.5 per cent use it at any other places such as street corner, agriculture farm, cattle shed etc., where as only 2.5 per cent use it at bar/restaurant. About 44 per cent alcoholics use alcohol in the company of friends, about 10 per cent use it with relatives and co-workers while, 13 per cent accepted that the alcoholic use it in the company of all – friends, relatives, co-workers, family members and 4.7 per cent do not know the company of the users. So far as the type or brand of alcohol is concerned about 38 per cent use *desi daru* (home made liquor) and about 19 per cent use country liquor, 12 per cent said that they use IMFL, commonly known as English brand and 15.6 per cent respondents do not know the brand or type of alcohol used by the alcoholic and 23.4 per cent said that the alcoholic can use any of the types or brands subjects to availability.

The time of alcohol use for majority, i.e. 57 per cent was told as evening while about 30 per cent use it at any time and about 10 per cent use it at late nights. The information about the use of alcohol by children in families reveal that 28 per cent families had this problem, 64 per cent say no to it while, about 8 per cent gave no response for this question.

3

Alcohol Use in Family

Some Facts

The family is universally recognized as a basic unit of society. In spite of many changes in society that have altered their roles and functions, families continue to provide the natural framework for the emotional and material support essential to the growth and well-being of their members. Family is a living, evolving institution, which is affected by socio-economic factors as well as by the changes that shape the social environment in which it functions. How families function in different situations? What are the problems the families face in the social, cultural and economic changes in society? How the members of family behave and perform their roles in the changing situations? These are some questions as well as indicators of the working of a family. The use and abuse of alcohol is one situation, which has been the traditional practice in many families. Alcohol use as a traditional custom, part of celebrations, a religious sanction, social status, and for recreational purposes has been a practice since long. But now with the changes in values and with the effect of alien culture it has changed its traditional form.

The use and abuse of alcohol has become a problem and the national and international statistics clearly explains the loss from national level to family and individual level. Excessive drinking by one or more family members results in several negative consequences for others in the family. Continuous drinking can impair the role performance of the drinker and his/her functioning as a parent, as a spouse, as a brother and as a contributor to the household responsibilities is severely effected. The rise in number of separation, desertion, divorce, broken homes, domestic violence and marital disharmony resulting from alcohol use specially problem drinking has posed a serious threat to the normal family life. Therefore, this chapter focuses on that how the family life is affected by the problematic alcohol use.

Marital and Domestic Life

Marital relations are the basis for domestic life. How marital relations are maintained is a very important question. It is a mutual give and take relationship, which is not that simple in reality. A small incidence with anyone or any situation can hurt the person and the relations can be disturbed. The use of alcohol, especially when it disturbs the role performance of the earning members results to many negative consequences. 'Alcohol problems in the family – an exploratory study in Haryana, India' (2007) offered important insights that how the use and abuse of alcohol affect the marital and domestic life in a family. To know this some questions were asked to the affected family members such as: Do the family know that when the person using alcohol has become alcoholic? Table 3.1 shows that 59.7 per cent families realized for more than last three years that the person using alcohol has become an alcoholic. About 14 per cent respondents could know it for last one year, while 12.5 per cent accepted that they know it very well for about last three years that the person in their family has become an alcoholic and 10 per cent subjects said for last two years they noticed their family member as an alcoholic. It was observed that the majority of the spouses were initially not responding to this question specially those, whose husbands were using alcohol for less than two years.

The strong family ties, the traditional customs and the status of women were some of the hindrances in the way to answer this question. But after clarification and explanation the family members were confronted with the situation, they cooperated and started exploring the events through which they told about the duration of alcohol abuse.

In the case of alcoholics who were using alcohol for more than three years it was not difficult for the wives to respond because they were so much tortured by the problems of their alcoholic husbands that they started explaining just with a first hit to the point. In the case of mothers whose sons were not married it was slightly difficult to get the response but other family members such as sister-in-law (*Bhabhi*), father, brother helped the researcher by narrating some symptoms such as physical dependence, spending how much time in the use of alcohol, increase in expenses resulting to financial burden, disturbances and troubles at work place, street brawls, frequency and quantity of alcohol use etc.

Table 3.1 Time, the family realized that the person has become an alcoholic

Response	*No. of respondents*	*Percentage*
For last one year	111	13.9
For last two years	80	10.0
For last three years	100	12.5
For more than last three years	478	59.7
No response	31	03.9
Total	800	100.0

Marital Relations

The spouses of the alcoholics were asked about their marital relations after becoming aware about the alcoholism of their husbands. Table 3.2 explains that 34.5 per cent respondents experienced changes in the behaviour of their husbands after regular and excessive use of alcohol. As many as 17.3 per cent respondents accepted that there were changes in love and care, and 16.5 per cent said that changes in interaction were noticed. About 9 per cent respondents reported for the change in faith, while 13 per cent accepted that there were serious problems regarding acceptance of their responsibilities. Only 4.8 per cent reported that they have not noticed any change in the relations, which may be because many respondents were not ready to accept the problem due to many reasons such as strong family ties, reputation of family and low status of women. About 3 per cent had refused to reply to the question (Figure 3.1).

While interacting with the respondents the researcher observed that the alcohol use in families has seriously disturbed the intra-family relationship. The alcoholics/problem drinkers in majority of the families were found either do not have any

Figure 3.1 Marital relations after knowing that the spouse has become an alcoholic

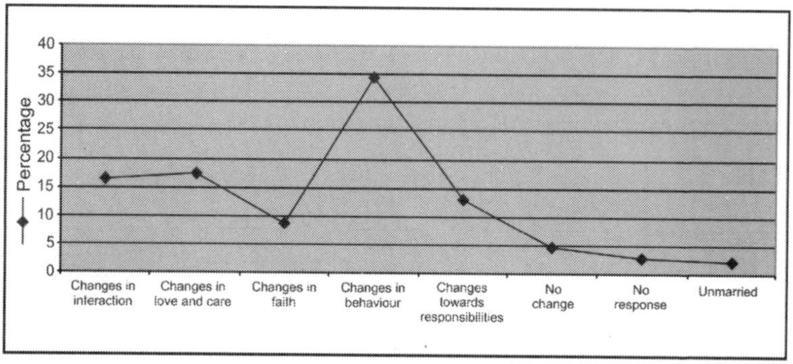

responsibility of the family affairs or they avoid their families. Many families told that alcoholics/problem drinkers were absent from their homes for months together.

Table 3.2 Marital relations after knowing that the spouse has become an alcoholic

Response	*No. of respondents*	*Percentage*
Changes in interaction	132	16.5
Changes in love and care	138	17.3
Changes in faith	70	08.8
Changes in behaviour	276	34.5
Changes towards responsibilities	104	13.0
No change	39	04.8
No response	23	02.9
Unmarried	18	02.2
Total	800	100.0

Drinking Before Coming Home

The families were asked, 'Do the person come home after drinking alcohol?' This question was asked to know how many families were suffering from the out of home drinking of alcohol. The spouses/other family members told (Table 3.3) that 38.3 per cent alcohol using family members come home daily after drinking alcohol, 30.2 per cent usually come home under the influence of alcohol and 26.1 per cent seldom do like this. Only 2.3 per cent respondents said that their alcohol using family members never come after using alcohol. About 3.1 per cent respondents did not give any response to this question. They want to avoid it because they expressed their frustration resulting from the continuous problems they were facing.

Table 3.3 Do the person come home after drinking alcohol?

Response	*No. of respondents*	*Percentage*
Never	18	02.3
Seldom	209	26.1
Usually	242	30.2
Daily	306	38.3
No response	25	03.1
Total	800	100.0

One respondent*, wife of an alcoholic explained her unending miseries, which she was suffering for last 12 years, in a village of district Kaithal clearly said, 'हमने तो इसके बारे में बात ही करनी छोड दी, क्योंकि फायदा भी नहीं है, उसे मानना तो है ही नहीं'. (Now we have stopped talking about him, because there is no use and he is not going to change). In many families it was observed that maximum time of the alcohol drinker was spent outside home in the activities related to drinking alcohol such as procuring alcohol, meeting friends, talking about alcohol, making for drinking arrangements, attending drinking sessions and enjoying after drinking the intoxicated position of the alcoholics/problem drinkers, etc. Some of the respondents and their family members said that many times the drinker was brought home in the unconscious or semi-conscious situation, when some outsider informed that the person was lying somewhere (Figure 3.2).

Fighting with Spouse

Violence against women is one of the important consequences of heavy drinking. An attempt was made to study whether the alcohol using person fight with his spouse? The data explains that 50.8 per cent respondents agreed that their husbands seldom fight with them

* Name of the respondent was not given because the spouse requested not to mention her name.

Figure 3.2 Alcoholics lying on the main road in evening after binge drinking of alcohol

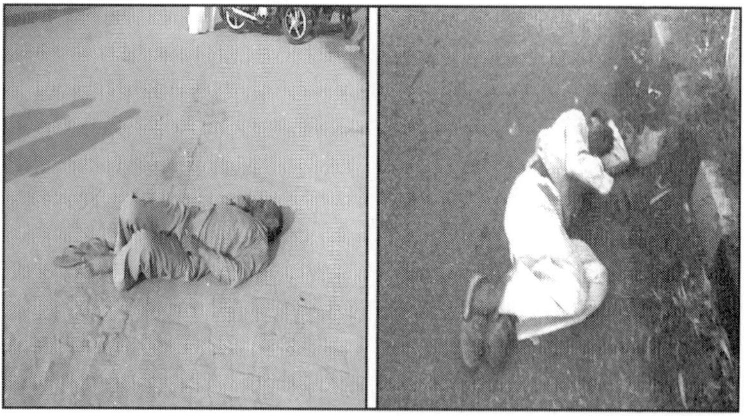

after drinking, 26.4 per cent said that it was a usual affair in their family and nearly 14 per cent wives (respondents) said that it is the everyday affair in the family. About 1.3 per cent respondents avoided this question and 5.6 per cent said that their drinking spouses never fight with them.

Table 3.4 Does the spouse fight with you after taking alcohol?

Response	*No. of respondents*	*Percentage*
Never	45	05.6
Seldom	406	50.8
Usually	211	26.4
Everyday	109	13.6
No response	11	01.3
Unmarried	18	02.3
Total	800	100.0

During interaction many ladies explained their woes and miseries to the researcher and narrated many incidences of violence. One such lady explained that she was mercilessly beaten up by her husband because she refused to give money to him. She had a bandage on her left arm, injured during the violence. She was repeatedly saying that this was not the story of one day, it happens everyday and we are now used to it (अब तो हम इसके आदि हो गये हैं) Such type of incidences are not the incidences of only Haryana or

India. Some research studies conducted in abroad also reported the incidences of violence against women by their drunkard husbands. A study conducted by Robin Room et al. (2002) and reported by WHO revealed that in Mexico a household survey of women of medium-low and low socio-economic status in the capital city showed that the male partners physically abused 14 per cent of women. The risk of violence was five times higher when the male partner was drunk everyday, as compared to a partner with no alcohol problems (Natera et al., 1996). This clearly explains the worldwide situation of the sufferings of women due to alcohol use.

Misbehaviour in the Presence of Outsiders

How the alcohol using person behaves with his/her spouse in the presence of outsiders is another area, which is the indicator of the intra-family relations of the family suffering with alcohol problems. An attempt was made to study the feelings of the wives of the alcohol using persons of how their husbands behave with their wives before others (Figure 3.3). It was found that 45 per cent respondents seldom misbehaved before others, 15 per cent usually misbehaved and 12.1 per cent were not spared to misbehave whenever the person found opportunity. a 24.4 per cent said that their spouse never misbehaved before others, and 1.2 per cent avoided responding this question (two families in which wives were the alcoholics are also included in this because the husbands avoided to respond) (Table 3.5).

Table 3.5 Spouse misbehave in the presence of outsiders

Response	*No. of respondents*	*Percentage*
Never	195	24.4
Seldom	360	45.0
Usually	120	15.0
Whenever finds opportunity	97	12.1
No response	10	01.2
Unmarried	18	02.3
Total	800	100.0

While analysing further it was found that the cases of misbehaviour were more in the families with heavy and regular drinking partners. When asked about incidence and occasions, the spouse/wife and other family members told that the alcoholic

Figure 3.3 Spouse misbehave in the presence of outsiders

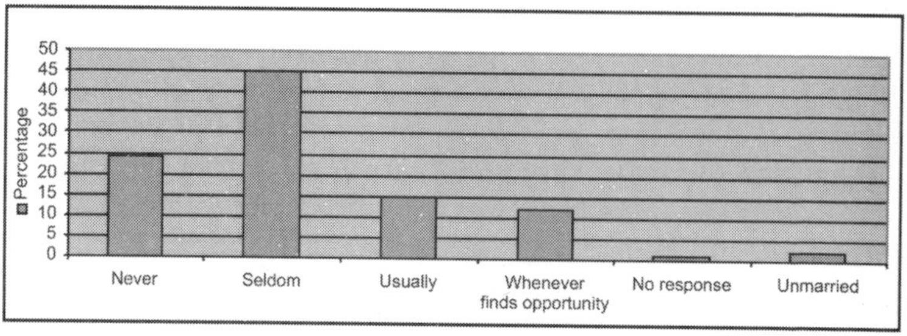

person misbehaves when he arranges the alcohol party at home and it becomes a daily affair. There were incidents of street brawls and in such situations it becomes unavoidable to leave the alcoholic outside in the street. In such situations when he was advised or forced to go inside the house he starts misbehaving with spouse particularly and with others also in general. The traditional antagonism between the sexes, which is a feature of social life, increases with drinking. Wife beating is a common feature in such situations. In almost every situation husband attacks the wife with blows directed towards the face. The researcher (author) noticed that the wives to such men were having facial scars and injuries, the

Figure 3.4 After drinking alcohol, wife beating is a common problem in India and some Asian countries

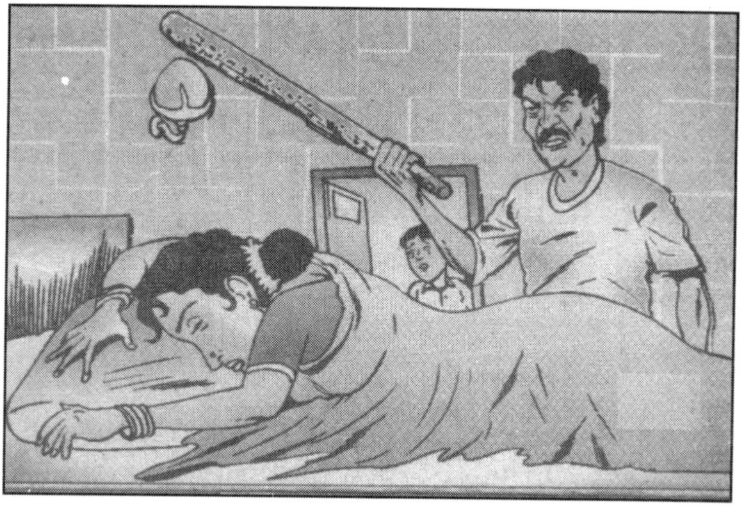

evidence of such violent incidences. It was observed and also explained by other family members that the attacks were focused on wife only (Figure 3.4) and other women particularly elder women of the family when intervene were not attacked directly, however they may get injuries in the fight. In some cases severe injuries such as breaking head with stick and breaking the arm of wife were also explained and witnessed by the researcher or his research team.

Misbehaviour in the Presence of Children

The child may experience various forms of problems in the families with alcohol use. It depends upon the age of the child that how much the child got affected with different types of problems. One such problem, which may damage the psychological and social growth of the child, is the misbehaviour with the mother in front of her children. Many families reported such incidents. The data in Table 3.6 reveals that 23.6 per cent respondents were misbehaved everyday by their alcoholic spouses in front of their children, 22.8 per cent were usually misbehaved and 34.2 were seldom. About 16.0 per cent respondents said that they never faced such situation and 1.1 per cent gave no response.

Table 3.6 Spouse misbehaves or fights in front of children

Response	*No. of respondents*	*Percentage*
Never	128	16.0
Seldom	274	34.2
Usually	182	22.8
Everyday	189	23.6
No response	09	01.1
Unmarried	18	02.3
Total	800	100.0

During discussion the respondents told that the incidents of misbehaviour start with a normal discussion but the alcoholic person take it to the point of fight many a times resulting in violence, and the focus in maximum cases was the wife. It was also found that even if the point of discussion may be the normal working in the family but the person using alcohol, after taking alcohol start focusing it to the spouse and if the children are grown up they start intervening in favour of their mother. If the children are under five years they suffer various psychological problems. The data reveals that 80.6 per cent families suffer from the misbehaviour from seldom to everyday with the spouse in front of their children. Hence, one can conclude that how much harmful it is to the physical, psychological as well as social growth of the children in the families with the problem of alcohol use.

Threats to Spouse

In the families where alcohol use has been a routine affair the atmosphere of family was found full of tense situations in many ways. It was shared by many families that initially when the use of alcohol was within the limits the family was not much disturbed but since the use of alcohol is the regular affair the problems started increasing and the situation has reached to the extent that now alcohol-using person started threatening his/her spouse or other family members. The data in Table 3.7 shows that a majority 66.1 per cent of the alcohol using persons gives one or other type of threat to their spouse or other family members. A more detailed analysis explains that 25.5 per cent threat their wives to send them to their parents, 18.6 per cent threatens of leaving the home and 13.6 per cent of living separately, 5.1 per cent threat of taking divorce and 3.3 per cent give a threat to commit suicide.

Table 3.7 Threats to the spouse and other family members

Threats	*No. of respondents*	*Percentage*
Leaving the home	149	18.6
Divorce	41	05.1
Living separately	109	13.6
To send the wife to her parents	204	25.5
To commit suicide	26	03.3
No threat	225	28.1
No response	46	05.8
Total	800	100.0

Disturbing the Family by Breaking Household Things

An attempt was made to study how many families were disturbed by the unwanted incidents of breaking household things. It was found that 30.3 per cent families accepted that they suffered seldom with such incidences, 17 per cent subjects suffered usually and in about 23 per cent families it was a routine everyday affair, while about 27 per cent said that they never faced such problem. Only 2.5 per cent respondents did not answer this question (Table 3.8).

Table 3.8 Drinking alcohol and breaking household things

Response	*No. of respondents*	*Percentage*
Never	219	27.3
Seldom	242	30.3
Usually	136	17.0
Everyday	183	22.9
No response	20	02.5
Total	800	100.0

Family Members Ever Beat the Alcohol Using Person for his Misdeeds

The researcher observed that the family members were very serious while answering the question about loss of family household things. Many of them narrated the incidents of violence, which were provoked due to everyday or usual incidents of loss to the household property. Some elderly members of the family such as mothers of alcoholic or grandparents of alcoholic bitterly explained the incidents of breaking valuable things such as TV, stereo, audio system and utensils, etc. They showed the brass and steel utensils with dents to the researcher. The family members explained that such incidents usually followed by beating up the alcoholic person and it stops only when either the person go for sleep or in coma because of excessive drinking or forcibly locked in the room. Table 3.9 shows that in 71 per cent families the alcohol using persons

Table 3.9 Do the family members beat the alcoholic for his misdeeds

Response	*No. of respondents*	*Percentage*
Never	213	26.6
Seldom	252	31.5
Usually	175	21.9
Everyday	141	17.6
No response	19	02.4
Total	800	100.0

were beaten from seldom to everyday for their misdeeds like breaking household things, 26.6 per cent said that they had never faced such incidence and about 2 per cent had not given any response to the question.

Alcohol intoxication may lead to a range of violence starting from hot verbal exchanges to physical assaults resulting to injuries. It was observed and also explained by the family members that usually the incidents started from the disturbances in normal family relations with spouse, children or parents, when the questions were raised on regular drinking the person using alcohol reacted, because he starts facing threat to his freedom to use alcohol, which has changed from a casual use to physical or psychological dependence or both. In such circumstances family brawl is inevitable in which the person intoxicated under the influence of alcohol may attack the family members. Therefore, it was enquired that do the alcohol abusing persons also attack the family members. Table 3.10 explains that 47 per cent families said that such incidences occurred seldom, about 14 per cent said yes it happens usually in their family, about 11 per cent said it happened everyday and 26 per cent said never happened.

Table 3.10 Person under the influence of alcohol attack other family members

Response	*No. of respondents*	*Percentage*
Never	208	26.0
Seldom	376	47.0
Usually	111	13.9
Everyday	85	10.6
No response	20	02.5
Total	800	100.0

The detailed analysis of all the above situations leads us to conclude that habitual drinkers always create troubles in the family. Wife of the drinker is the main sufferer and always a focus of attack. Other family members also suffer risks of all type ranging from misbehaviour to physical attack or injuries. Domestic violence is predominantly found which seriously affect the whole family including children.

Child Abuse and Neglect

How badly a child is affected by the parental alcohol drinking problems is an important question to be examined. Children of problem drinking parents are always at risk of problems and may experience various forms of neglect and abuse. In the families where drinking is a common feature the children suffer from many types of fears such as; when their father will come home? Will he come normal or drunk? He may not get involved in any accident? What will happen to their mother – will he beat her like last day or he will sleep quietly? Threat the family with verbal or physical aggression, etc. The children of the alcoholics/problem drinking parents may suffer a very disturbed life. The time when they need love, affection and care of the parents for their healthy growth and development of balanced personality they have to go through the abuse and neglect.

Schooling of the Children

The first question in this section was asked about the schooling of the child. Does your child/children go to school? Table 3.11 shows that a majority 71 per cent of the children in problem drinking families go to school, at the same time a very significant number about 15 per cent families do not send their children to school and about 10 per cent avoided to answer this question.

Table 3.11 Information about the children going to school

Go to school	*No. of respondents*	*Percentage*
Yes	568	71.0
No	117	14.6
No response	81	10.1
Not applicable	34	04.3
Total	800	100.0

In the case of about 4 per cent families the question was not applicable because 18 alcoholics were unmarried and rest were not having children. While it was further discussed in the families and it was observed that even the number of children in the families going to school is good but the type of school and the concern for education of children were the last priority or not at all in any priority. A large majority of the school going children was going to government schools where the school fee is very less or almost free. Their results were poor, attendance was very less, and they do not have books, copies or material required for school. When the researcher contacted to some school teachers it was told that the students of the families with problem drinking/alcoholism have a lot of problems ranging from continuous absence from school to the behavioural and adjustment problems.

Do the Parents go to School to Check their Children?

Table 3.12 explains that only 14.3 per cent of the parents go to school to check the performance of their children, 31.5 per cent said that they go sometimes but usually they do not get time for this and 38.3 per cent parents accepted that they never go to school of their children. A good number of parents (11.6%) denied giving any answer to this question.

Table 3.12 Do the parents go to school to check their children?

Response	*No. of respondents*	*Percentage*
Yes	114	14.3
Sometimes	252	31.5
No	307	38.3
No response	93	11.6
Not applicable	34	04.3
Total	800	100.0

In a more detailed exploration of this situation it was found that a large majority of alcoholics/problem drinking parents never bother about the education of their children. Among the respondents who visit schools for their children were either the mothers of the children or the other kin in the family such as younger uncle (*Chacha*), elder uncle (*Tau*) or in some cases grandparents (*Dada-Dadi*). It was observed that in these families education of the children was the last priority or not in any priority which was evident from the situation of the children, who do not have proper books, bags, stationary and school dress the most important and minimum requirements for any school going child. In many cases it was found that the family members or even the parents of the child do not know the class in which their child was studying.

School Performance of the Child

When it was found that the parents in the families with alcoholism/problem drinking were not able to take care of the education of their children, an attempt was made to study the performance of such children in school. The research team studied it by conducting meetings with teachers in schools, tutors (wherever applicable), going through the report cards or other records, attendance register, checking the subject note books (copies) of the children and discussions with the parents. Table 3.13 explains that in 40.4 per cent families the school performance of the children was poor, in 21.5 per cent families it was average and about 9 per cent families said that their children were doing good in their studies. As many as 4.3 per cent respondent families did not have children or if they had children, they were below school going age. Out of 4.3 per cent, 2.3 per cent alcoholics were unmarried and rest of them does not have children. About 10 per cent families refused to answer this question (Figure 3.5). The researcher and his team made good efforts through questioning, counter-questioning and cross-questioning with the help of their family friends/well wishers but they totally refused to talk in this regard. It can be concluded that the education of the children in the families with problematic use of alcohol is very severely affected.

Figure 3.5 Performance of children of alcohol affected families in their studies/school

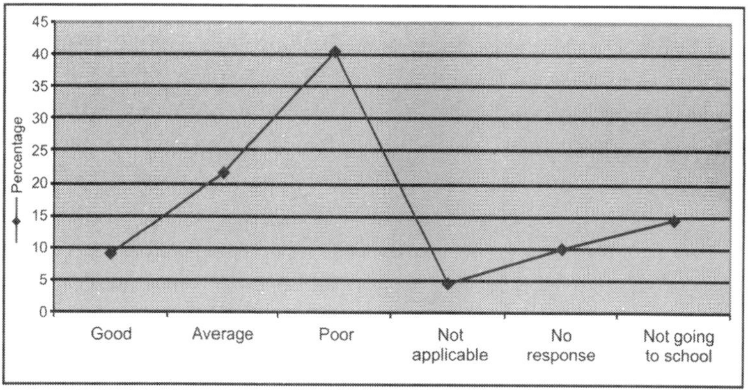

Table 3.13 Performance of children of alcohol affected families in their studies/school

Response	*No. of respondents*	*Percentage*
Good	73	09.1
Average	172	21.5
Poor	323	40.4
Not applicable	34	04.3
No response	81	10.1
Not going to school	117	14.6
Total	800	100.0

During interaction with the family members and with grown up children it was found that effect of the problems due to alcohol use in family varies as the child grows up. During discussion with some school going children it was found that they have to lose their time because of problems of alcohol use in family such as mediating in disputes in family, spending time with mother/aunty/sister-in-law for waiting or searching for the alcoholic, etc. Table 3.14 explains that 55 per cent families (N=568) accepted that their children had to lose time because of alcohol use in family. About 32 per cent said that they suffered sometimes because of it, while only 5.8 per cent said that there was no such loss in their family. Even many of them accepted that some times it becomes very difficult for them to come out from such situation. As it was generally accepted that the alcoholism/problem drinking disturb the family affairs, specially the care of children, therefore, the efforts were made to find out that do the children in the families with alcohol use start losing interest in their studies and school. It was found that 38 per cent families accepted that their children have lost their interest in school and it is because of alcohol use in their family, 31 per cent say no to this but a large number of them were unable to answer properly which means they had some hesitation in accepting the realities. About 12 per cent respondents have not given any response to this question.

Table 3.14 Loss of time because of alcohol use in family

Response	*No. of respondents*	*Percentage*
Yes	312	54.9
Sometimes	181	31.9
No	33	05.8
No response	42	07.4
Total	568*	100.0

(*Those who are not going to school are excluded from total)

One can conclude from the findings that the children in the families with alcohol use suffer a lot in their studies. It was the time when they need utmost care and attention, because of the characteristics, needs and problems of specific age span of childhood. The beginning of late childhood is marked by child's entrance in school, i.e. at six years, which is recognized entrance age in first grade in India. For young children, this is a major change in their life. While adjustment to new situation and expectations of schooling and education most children feel it as a state of disturbance, they are emotionally disturbed and as a result it becomes difficult for them to adjust with the changes. Parents, educators and psychologists give different names to this age group such as troublesome age, play age, gangue age, etc. (Hurlock, 1991). In such situation the child needs proper care, attention, love and affection from parents. But in the case of alcoholics/problem drinking parents it was found missing. Hence the children face lot of problems in their education and later life situations. The important characteristics of childhood such as immaturity, imitation or copying, plasticity or flexibility and sensitivity play a significant role in the care of children, which is severely effected due to parents' alcohol problems in the family (Table 3.15).

Table 3.15 Do the children lose interest in schools/studies?

Response	*No. of respondents*	*Percentage*
Yes	304	38.0
No	248	31.0
No response	97	12.1
Not applicable	34	04.3
Not going to school	117	14.6
Total	800	100.0

The alcohol problems in the family take a serious turn when the person using alcohol start involving children directly or indirectly with alcohol related activities. While interacting with the families it was observed that the alcohol using parents/ uncles/brother and sometimes close relatives frequently use children as a help when they use alcohol. In the families with alcohol problems the children are used actively resulting to very serious effects on their psycho-social development. A significant number (65.4 per cent families) said that the services of children were taken by the person using alcohol for alcohol related needs, while 25.5 per cent said no and 4.8 per cent had not given any response (Table 3.16).

Table 3.16 Are the services of children taken for alcohol related needs?

Response	*No. of Respondents*	*Percentage*
Yes	229	28.6
Sometimes	295	36.8
No	204	25.5
No response	38	04.8
Not applicable	34	04.3
Total	800	100.0

In a more detailed discussion and observation it was found that while taking services of children the alcoholic person do not care for the age of the child and never hesitate in using children of tender age. Therefore, the children involved in such practices may lead to using alcohol from their childhood. However, this was not accepted by anyone in the family. During informal discussion it was revealed that while extending services to alcohol users children also start using alcohol and also many times they become victim of alcohol related violence.

Care and Neglect of Children

How badly a child is affected by parents alcohol problems depend on many factors such as the age of child, status of family, level of drinking, educational level of the family etc. But it is true that child may experience various forms of neglect and experience various types of socio-psychological threats. An attempt was made to study that what the family feel about proper care of the children in the family with problematic alcohol use. Table 3.17 explains that 58.3 per cent respondents say that children in their families were not properly cared for and neglected because of alcohol use by one or more members in the family. As many as 28.8 per cent respondents feel that alcohol problems do not effect in the care of the child and in their families due care and attention is given to the children. But a good majority of them expressed their apprehension that the continuous use of alcohol may affect their children. The adverse effects of problem drinking parents were observed while interaction such as the children in these families were found neglected, suffering with physical and psychological problems, malnutrition, problem in education etc.

Table 3.17 Are the children not properly cared and neglected?

Response	*No. of respondents*	*Percentage*
Yes	467	58.3
No	230	28.8
No response	69	08.6
Not applicable	34	04.3
Total	800	100.0

A feeling of mistrust was observed on the faces of children and during discussions with them they were found shuttling with the thoughts such as, what will happen when father will come after drinking? Will he beat their mother? Will he come home or not? Will he come safe? Will we get food in the night or next day; etc.? Such types of psychological threats to the child are the hazards in the development of a healthy personality. Here the importance of Ericson's concept of the importance to 'trust' for the development of a healthy personality of child proves the adverse effects of a problem-drinking parent on the development of 'trust' in the child. A large number of such children were found suffering with the lack of 'trust in themselves', and 'trust in adults' who care for them in family.

Sufferings of Children

In the families suffering with alcoholism/problem drinking the child may experience various forms of neglect, abuse, aggression and violence from family members. An attempt has been made to study of the type of sufferings a child face in such families from father, mother and other family members. When the family suffers because of alcoholism/problem drinking the child who needs love, care, affection and warmth is neglected, rebuked, threatened and shouted at may be because of the frustration of the family members. The family members sometimes consciously or subconsciously sometimes unconsciously treat children in an unwanted and undesirable manner. Such children suffer from verbal aggression to severe violence by their father, mother and other family members (Table 3.18). It was found that children face verbal aggression in 29.1 per cent families from their father, in 37.5 per cent families from mother and, in 25.1 per cent families from other family members such as elder uncle (*Tau*), younger uncle (*Chacha*), elder aunty (*Tai*), younger aunty (*Chachi*) and in joint families from grandfather and/or grandmother. Moderate violence such as slapping or pushing aside the child was also observed and it was found that in 39.1 per cent families it was father; in 08.5 per cent families it was mother and in 5.5 per cent other family members.

Table 3.18 Sufferings of children in the family with alcohol use

Types of sufferings	*From father*	*From mother*	*From other members*
Verbal aggression	233 (29.1)	300 (37.5)	201 (25.1)
Moderate violence	313 (39.1)	68 (8.5)	44 (5.5)
Severe violence	62 (7.8)	26 (3.3)	29 (3.6)
No violence	106 (13.2)	319 (39.8)	435 (54.4)
Not response	52 (6.5)	53 (6.6)	57 (7.1)
Not applicable	34 (4.3)	34 (4.3)	34 (4.3)
Total	800 (100.0)	800 (100.0)	800 (100.0)

Note: Figures in parentheses are percentages.

The cases of severe violence such as mercilessly beating the child, resulting to physical injuries were also observed (Figure 3.7). The case of severe violence in family was 7.8 per cent by father, by mother it was 3.3 per cent and 3.6 per cent by other family members. About 20 per cent families have not given any response to this question (Figure 3.6).

Alcohol problems vary in nature, severity and persistence. How badly a child is affected by the parental alcohol use is likely to

Figure 3.6 Sufferings of children in the family with alcohol use

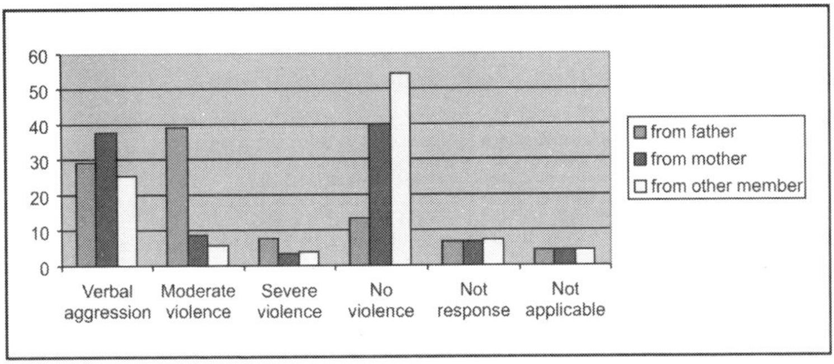

depend among other factors, on the age of the child. The child under five years of age may be more vulnerable to violence and diminished physical care because he has no other alternate, while the elder child may avoid physical torture by escaping from the situation, but more vulnerable to psychological damage. It doesn't mean that the younger child in such families does not suffer psychological damage, but it was his compulsion to stay with abusive parents, while the elder child may search some other alternates to avoid the situation. It was observed while interacting with the children in such families. 'मेरा पिता रोज पीकर आता है, मेरे को और मेरी मां को मारता है। कल रात उसने मुझे मारा और खाट से नीचे फैंक दिया। मेरी टांग पर चोट लग गई।' (My father daily comes after drinking alcohol and beats my mother and me. Yesterday night he beat me and threw me from the cot, I got my leg injured.) These were the excerpts of a five-year male child who suffered physical violence. Fear, mixed with anger was very clear on the face of the child, who further said that he and his mother could not take food yesterday night and they do not have money to get treatment for the injury he got yesterday night. They simply wrapped it with a piece of cloth, from which the blood was pouring. In such situation the child irrespective of age suffer both physical as well as psychological damage.

Hatred for the Drinking Parents

When drinking alcohol becomes a routine in the family and it had been a continuous source of family problems, what the children feel about their parents and other family members and how they

Figure 3.7 Cruelty on children after drinking alcohol is a common news in newspapers in India

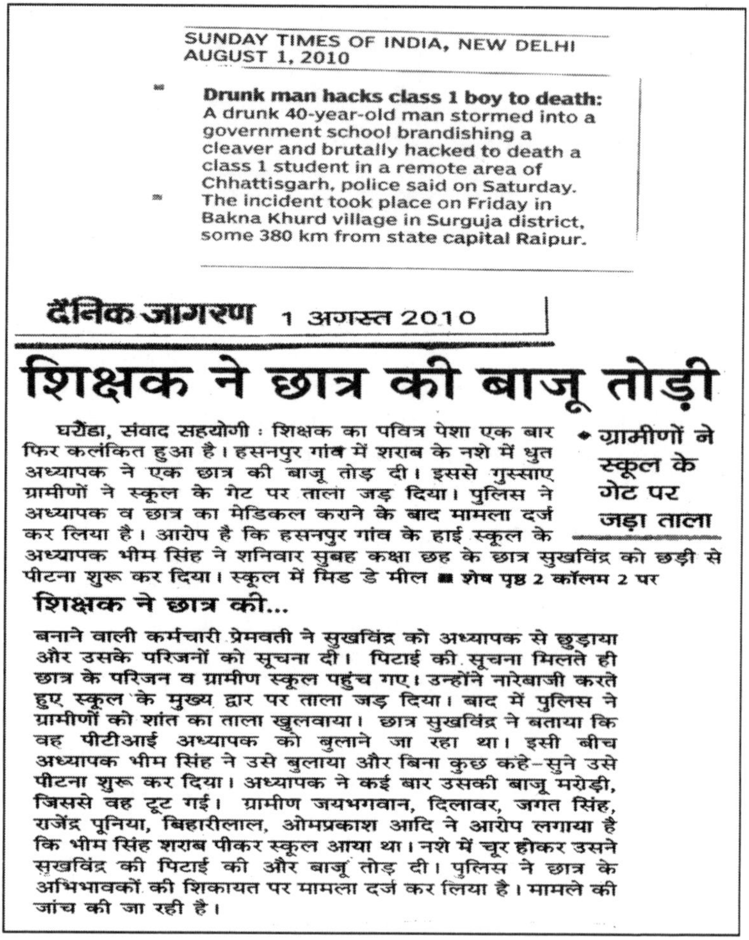

SUNDAY TIMES OF INDIA, NEW DELHI
AUGUST 1, 2010

Drunk man hacks class 1 boy to death: A drunk 40-year-old man stormed into a government school brandishing a cleaver and brutally hacked to death a class 1 student in a remote area of Chhattisgarh, police said on Saturday. The incident took place on Friday in Bakna Khurd village in Surguja district, some 380 km from state capital Raipur.

दैनिक जागरण 1 अगस्त 2010

शिक्षक ने छात्र की बाजू तोड़ी

• ग्रामीणों ने स्कूल के गेट पर जड़ा ताला

घरौंडा, संवाद सहयोगी : शिक्षक का पवित्र पेशा एक बार फिर कलंकित हुआ है। हसनपुर गांव में शराब के नशे में धुत अध्यापक ने एक छात्र की बाजू तोड़ दी। इससे गुस्साए ग्रामीणों ने स्कूल के गेट पर ताला जड़ दिया। पुलिस ने अध्यापक व छात्र का मेडिकल कराने के बाद मामला दर्ज कर लिया है। आरोप है कि हसनपुर गांव के हाई स्कूल के अध्यापक भीम सिंह ने शनिवार सुबह कक्षा छह के छात्र सुखविंद्र को छड़ी से पीटना शुरू कर दिया। स्कूल में मिड डे मील ■ शेष पृष्ठ 2 कॉलम 2 पर

शिक्षक ने छात्र की...

बनाने वाली कर्मचारी प्रेमवती ने सुखविंद्र को अध्यापक से छुड़ाया और उसके परिजनों को सूचना दी। पिटाई की सूचना मिलते ही छात्र के परिजन व ग्रामीण स्कूल पहुंच गए। उन्होंने नारेबाजी करते हुए स्कूल के मुख्य द्वार पर ताला जड़ दिया। बाद में पुलिस ने ग्रामीणों को शांत का ताला खुलवाया। छात्र सुखविंद्र ने बताया कि वह पीटीआई अध्यापक को बुलाने जा रहा था। इसी बीच अध्यापक भीम सिंह ने उसे बुलाया और बिना कुछ कहे-सुने उसे पीटना शुरू कर दिया। अध्यापक ने कई बार उसकी बाजू मरोड़ी, जिससे वह टूट गई। ग्रामीण जयभगवान, दिलावर, जगत सिंह, राजेंद्र पूनिया, बिहारीलाल, ओमप्रकाश आदि ने आरोप लगाया है कि भीम सिंह शराब पीकर स्कूल आया था। नशे में चूर होकर उसने सुखविंद्र की पिटाई की और बाजू तोड़ दी। पुलिस ने छात्र के अभिभावकों की शिकायत पर मामला दर्ज कर लिया है। मामले की जांच की जा रही है।

behave? The research team while discussion with them observed many reactions. A question was asked, 'do children express their hatred for the drinking family members?' Table 3.19 explains that a large majority of respondents (66.6%) accepted that their children express their hatred for the drinking family members including parents, while 19.5 per cent said no to this question. About 9.6 per cent respondents had not given any response.

Table 3.19 Children express their hatred for drinking parents and other family members

Response	*No. of respondents*	*Percentage*
Yes	533	66.6
No	156	19.5
No response	77	09.6
Not applicable	34	04.3
Total	800	100.0

Emotional Problems of Children

In the families with alcohol problems a child may experience various forms of neglect and feel abandoned by both parents. It may lead to many emotional sufferings on the part of the child who have to come across such situations very frequently. The fear of family brawl, beating the mother or self, what will happen to the drunkard father if not present at home are some situations which disturb the child and he may suffer from many emotional problems. An attempt was made to study the emotional problems of the children in families with problematic alcohol use.

Table 3.20 Children suffering from emotional problems

Nature of problems	*No. of respondents*	*Percentage*
Psychosomatic problems	10	01.2
Negative attitude to their parents	162	20.3
Negative attitude to themselves	40	05.0
Self-blame	73	09.1
Depression	158	19.8
Feeling guilty	297	37.1
Any other	15	01.9
No response	11	01.3
Not applicable	34	04.3
Total	800	100.0

The data indicate that highest percentage 37.1 per cent respondent families said that children suffer from feeling guilty for alcohol use in their families, while 19.8 per cent suffer from depression and 20.3 per cent from negative attitude towards their parents. About 9 per cent suffer from self-blame for the problem of alcoholism in their family, while, 5 per cent have the negative attitude

Figure 3.8 Children suffering from emotional problems

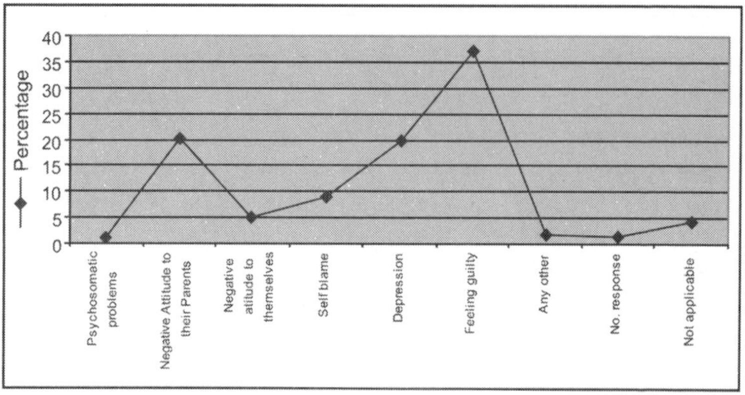

toward themselves. 1.2 per cent respondent families accepted that the children suffer from psychosomatic problems such as fever, convulsions, fits, skin problems, excessive sweating, stomach problems, etc. and 1.9 per cent suffer from other problems like every one in the family is full of anger, no body likes him, the whole family is full of bitterness and pain and there is no one in the family who can offer love, support, warmth and care to him (Figure 3.8).

From the above description the findings can conclude that a child who need emotional support at the time of his physical and psychological growth suffer emotional setbacks because of alcohol use in family, which may lead to various types of moral, developmental and social problems in the family, community and society.

How Many Times the Children were Beaten

Physical violence against children by alcohol using parents was a common feature in such families as explained by the people and also observed by the research team. Family members especially children suffer a lot due to the physical violence inflicted upon them without any fault. It was observed that in some families as the evening comes closer the children start feeling fear of the situation after the return of alcoholic father. Some children from such families were found discussing the last days/nights incidence, which was very painful. Therefore, an attempt was made to study the frequency of child beating incidents in such families.

Table 3.21 How many times children were beaten

Number	*No. of respondents*	*Percentage*
Two times	256	32.0
Three times	158	19.7
Four times	92	11.5
Almost daily	103	12.8
Never	115	14.4
No response	42	05.3
Not applicable	34	04.3
Total	800	100.0

Table 3.21 reveals that in 32 per cent families the children were beaten two times in one month and in 19.7 per cent three times, in 11.5 per cent families four times and in about 13 per cent families it happened almost daily, while 14.4 per cent families said that it never happened and 5.3 per cent had not given any response.

Whether alcohol problems are associated with violence against children or not, is an important issue in itself, which needs to be studied separately. However, the data given in Table 3.21 and during the in-depth face-to-face interviews with the family members it was revealed that violence against children and incidences of child abuse was present in such families. Children in such families bear with it because of their inability, but the grown-up children express their feelings through different reactions. While interviewing the respondent family members, the neighbour and other people in community told that in such families children were also involved in some illegal activities to fulfill their personal as well as family needs. An attempt was made to study the situation in this regard and how the suffering families take it up.

Table 3.22 Children started taking up illegal activities

Response	*No. of respondents*	*Percentage*
Yes	146	18.3
No	463	57.8
No response	157	19.6
Not applicable	34	04.3
Total	800	100.0

The data shows that 18.3 per cent families with alcohol problems accepted that their children are involved in illegal activities. Though a significant number of 57.8 per cent respondents said 'no' to this question, but they expressed their fear in one or the other way. About 20 per cent respondents had not given any response to this question (Table 3.22).

With more in-depth questioning and a mutual trust with the family it was revealed that in many cases the grown-up children were involved in criminal cases which were pending in courts. The main illegal activities were illicit brewing and sale of liquor and theft. Therefore, it can be concluded that alcoholism/problem drinking in family at one hand, disturbs the whole family and it transmits the problem in many ways to the next generation on the other hand. Many elder members in such families express their serious concern in this regard. One old lady, mother of a chronic alcoholic expressed her sufferings by saying 'इस शराब ने म्हारा तो सब कुछ उजाड़ दिया, मनै अपने बेटे का पत्थर तो छाती पै रख लिया था, पर इस पोते का क्या करूं?' (Alcohol has ruined us completely, I tolerated the problem of my son, but what should I do with the grandson). She told that her grandson was not only using alcohol but also started illicit distillation of liquor and involved in other illegal activities.

Alcoholism/problem drinking change the roles played by family members in relation to one another and the outside world. As a family member develops drinking problem, the traditional division of labour in family may breakdown. The problem drinker may cease to perform his or her functions as a breadwinner or in relation to the support and supervision of children, household chores, or other social responsibilities and recreational activities. These functions are therefore, either not performed or performed by another person, often the spouse and after some time when the children grow up they start sharing it. However, a particular pattern that has been observed is that a child, particularly the eldest child, may be forced to adopt adult roles and responsibilities. In such efforts when the child acting as a surrogate father suffer with one or the other problems and face challenges in society may divert to the same problem of alcohol use, which was observed in many families.

Sexual abuse of Child in the Families with Alcohol Problems

With many other problems in the families with alcohol problems the sexual abuse of child may be one of the serious problems. One important question in this regard arises is that, who may be the perpetrator? In the country like India where female drinking is not common or latent such incidences of child sexual abuse may occur as a result of lack of care and attention to the children in family. An attempt was made to study this difficult part of the problem with utmost care and attention. The respondents were taken in full confidence before asking this question. Because most of the respondents were the ladies therefore, girls with the help of senior members specially old ladies in the family were used to trace this problem. The answers received through this exercise may not be treated fully correct but may be helpful in knowing the nature of problem and concern of people suffering with this. Table 3.23 shows that 5.7 per cent families accepted the incidence of sexual abuse of child in family, out of which 2.5 per cent abused through exposure his/her genitals to the child, 2.8 per cent said that child suffered through 'touch', i.e. other person touching the genital organs of child or make child to touch his or her genitals, or rubbing genitals on the body of child, and 0.4 per cent respondents in such families accepted that their children suffered with penetration.

Table 3.23 Incidence of sexual abuse of children

Nature of sexual abuse	*No. of respondents*	*Percentage*
Exposure	20	02.5
Touch	23	02.8
Penetration	03	00.4
No incidence	632	71.0
No response	88	11.0
Not applicable	34	04.3
Total	800	100.0

Before asking this question very close relationship and mutual trust was established and a set of multiple questions was used to assess childhood sexual abuse. Measures of childhood sexual abuse included experiences that occurred prior to 18 years of age. A list of childhood sexual abuse incidents defined by Finkelhor (1979), and was supplemented by items from Sgroi (1982). Definition for sexual abuse was as follows:

> Victimisation experiences prior to age of 18 and that occurred against the victim's will or under conditions that would not allow the victim to consent with full knowledge.

The sexual abuse experiences as per list and definition included:

- Initiative or suggestion to do something sexual;
- Other person showing his/her genitals to the child, or compels the child to show his/her genitals to other person;
- Kissing or hugging in a sexual way;
- Fondling other person in a sexual way;
- Other person touching the genitals of child either with his/her hands or mouth;
- Other person compels the child to touch his/her genitals with the hand or mouth;
- Person rubbing his/her genitals to the body of child without penetration;
- Intercourse;
- Other person putting finger into the vagina or anus of child.

Perpetrators included any relative, family friend or anyone who forced sexual activity against the victim's will, lack of parental protection, due to father's alcohol problems, may contribute to other males known to the family perpetrating sexual abuse against daughters.

In a further more detailed face-to-face interaction it was found that there are two possible mechanisms by which father alcohol problems may be related to other adult males perpetrating sexual abuse of child especially daughters. First, daughter's growing-up in homes with an alcoholic father may not receive the typical emotional support, nurturance, and sustenance from their fathers. As a result, these girls may be more vulnerable to the manipulations of adult males outside the nuclear family who provide that support and nurturance, but at the cost of sexually abusing the girl. Second, daughters in homes with an alcoholic father may be more likely to be placed temporarily with relatives as the parents attempt to cope with the problems of alcohol dependence. These girls may then be more likely to be abused at the homes of such relatives. More detailed research is needed on this aspect of the problem to clarify many other related issues and hidden realities of the families suffering because of alcohol use.

Financial Problems

A micro study conducted in one district of Sri Lanka showed that there is a close co-relation between alcohol and tobacco use and continued poverty. The study explained that the beneficiary families during one year had spent on alcohol and tobacco more than the total loans granted to them during a period of six years (Gunasekera, 2000). The drinking alcohol of one or more family members may impair the performance of family on all fronts and most important area, which severely suffers, is the financial position of the family. The drinking of the earning members not only impair the functioning of such members and restricts the financial resources, but also exhaust the existing resources and burden the entire family. Regular drinking costs money and can totally deplete the resources of family, and put heavy pressure on other family members. They suffer in many ways. The depletion of financial resources and continuous use of alcohol results to financial mismanagement, particularly increasing debt and non-repayment of debt. It creates an enormous amount of stress-on family. An attempt was made to study the financial and economic problems in the families with alcohol problems.

The continuous use of alcohol in family disturbs the financial position of family or not was the first question in this section. Therefore, the family members were asked whether they were facing financial problems/crises due to use of alcohol. It was observed that a large number of families suffer financial problems due to continuous alcohol use in their families.

Table 3.24 Family facing financial problems/crises due to alcohol use

Response	*No. of respondents*	*Percentage*
Yes	652	81.5
No	137	17.1
No response	11	01.4
Total	800	100.0

The information received (Table 3.24) depicts that 81.5 per cent families were facing financial problems due to alcohol use in family. Only 17.1 per cent members said that they did not face any financial difficulty due to alcohol use. But many of them when counter questioned accepted that some areas of their personal and family life suffered, and they had to make adjustments. They themselves agreed that the use of alcohol by the family members has not reached to the extent to affect their financial needs but if it continues very soon the situation will become out of control. Among these respondents a good majority was of the families where the alcoholics were not the earning members but the dependent member of the family and family members were making adjustments to his needs. One younger brother in a respondent family said, 'क्या करें भाई साहब बड़े हैं घर में, हम तो समझा, बुझा कर थक गये पर नहीं मानते। अब घर की सारी जिम्मेवारी तो हमने संम्भाल ली । इन्हें तो बस पीने से मतलब है। चार साल से मैनें काम सम्भाल लिया नहीं तो इनके भरोसे सब चौपट हो गया था।' (What we can do? He (alcoholic) is the elder member in family, but now we got tired because he do not understand. Now, I have taken over the whole responsibility of the family, he has the only business of drinking alcohol. I am looking after the family business for last four years, otherwise he would have destroyed everything). Like this many families shared their experiences where the total family business, family property, family occupation, earning sources of family were destroyed by the alcoholic members, and other family members had to take the charge to save the family business or occupation.

In a further discussion the family members in many families disclosed that their personal as well as important family needs were not fulfilled because either the large part of family income is drained off in the use of alcohol or the earning family members has lost his earning capacity. The next question put to the respondents was about the satisfaction of family needs.

While enquiring the sufferings of the families with alcohol use, Table 3.25 shows that 10.6 per cent families were effected to the extent that even the food requirements of the family members were not fulfilled and a large part of family income is used in alcohol by the alcohol using family members. After food, the requirement of clothing about which 17.7 per cent respondents said that this need was not being fulfilled and the family have to suffer a lot. Many female members in such families said that they had to suffer to the extent that they depend upon others for clothing themselves and their

Table 3.25 Information about the family needs not fulfilled due to alcohol use

Needs	*No. of respondents*	*Percentage*
Food and food products	85	10.6
Clothes and related needs	142	17.7
Educational needs	216	27.0
Health needs	447	55.9
Social and religious needs	406	50.7
Other needs	173	21.6
No response	08	01.0

children. It was also observed by the researcher and his team that children and women members in such families were either half clad or wearing poorly torn clothes. There are 27 per cent families suffering with insufficient educational needs of their children, so the children had to leave their studies in between or performing very poor in their studies. Health needs of family also suffer severely in these families as 55.9 per cent families accepted it (Figure 3.9). Health being the last priority among all needs was found as the main casualty in such families. In many such families children and women were found without any care in their illness. If the problem increases they go to the local quacks. During fieldwork it was observed that,

Figure 3.9 Information about the family needs not fulfilled due to alcohol use

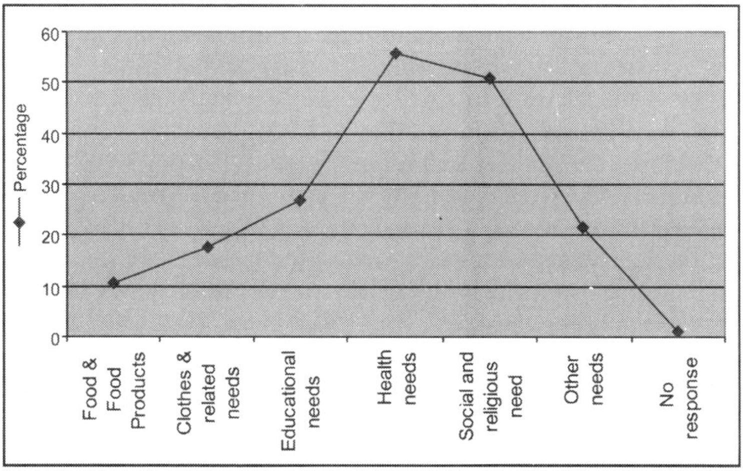

due to lack of care to health needs, the children become vulnerable to many health risks such as because of improper or partial immunization they suffer from all the diseases, which can be treated by complete course of immunization. This course was either not taken or left in-between because of the problems caused by alcoholism/problem drinking. A detailed description will be given on the health problems in family in separate chapter.

A very important need of the family members is the social and religious need. In the country like India where social relations play a very dominant role in personal, family, community and even occupational life such needs should be properly taken care. Table 3.25 shows that 50.7 per cent families with alcohol problems accepted that their social and religious needs were either not satisfied or partially satisfied. When further questioned about the types of social and religious needs the respondents explained with sorrow that maintaining relationships with close relations, friends, neighbours become impossible. The celebration of festivals, religious functions such as *Devi Jagran, Ramayan Path, Bhajan Kirtan, Sunder Kand Path*, *Akhand Path* of Guru Granth Sahib and visit to various religious places were not possible. The proper celebration of some festivals was also not possible in these families for many years.

In Indian families the social relations are maintained by honouring the married daughters by giving gifts to them and their family members whenever they visit the parental family. Among the kinship usages the usages of 'Amitate' gives special role to the father's sister, she is given more respect than the mother in family. So in such a social system, when the daughter of a mother and the sister of the drunkard brother leave the parental family unattended it is very painful to the mother and also socially unapproved. Therefore, the social relationships in such families were totally disturbed which results to harm the status and reputation of such familv/families in society because this kinship system is important for the maintenance of social structure and these relationships work as a pivot around which the social structure revolves. An old lady very painfully explained her agony 'मेरी छोरी आवै अर न्यू ये चली जावै। इस ऊत का अपणा ई नी पूरा पाटदा, मेरी छोरी न के देवैगा। सारा दिन पीण पै लाग्या रह। मनै तो आस ई छोड़दी' (My daughter comes and goes bare hand. This idiot fellow (her drunkard son) could not fulfill his own needs, what he can give to my daughter (sister of the alcoholic). He remains drunkard whole day, so I have left all hope.)

The agony of children for not fulfilling the need of celebration of religious functions such as *Diwali, Janmashtami, Gurupurab, Holi* etc. was also noticed. In some families it was explained that the religious ceremony was totally disturbed with the fear of what will happen when the drunkard person will come or where the person is at the time of worship during celebration. It was found that a psychological fear always dominate in the mind of spouse, mother, sister or elderly members of the family. Therefore, the religious and social celebrations become secondary to them. It results to poor socialization of the children in such families and may be one of the reasons for deviant behaviour of children.

A good member of respondents 21.6 per cent said that apart of these needs some other needs such as love, care and affection were also not fulfilled in the families with alcohol problems. The drunkard spouse, father/brother always think and work for his own needs and never think about the needs of his or her spouse, children, parents or other members in the family. So it can be fairly consulted that at one side it results to the disturbing family relations and at other side it leads to poor socialization of children. One elderly women explained with anguish 'त्योहार बार अर जीने मनाने की छोड़ इस नै तो महारा मरने मैं भी पी कै खेल मचा दिया। हम तो किते के बि ना छोडे' (What to say of celebrating festivals, birth etc. he (the drunkard son) had disturbed the function of last rites on the death of a relative). Alcoholic son of this elderly lady drink alcohol in the death function in relations and created problems.

Family Assets

How the use of alcohol affects the financial position of family is important part of the study. It was observed that a large majority of non-drinkers felt that drinking alcohol affects economic life of the family. It was also found that 81.5 per cent of the sample accepted (Table 3.24) that they face financial crises due to the use of alcohol by one or more family members. An important part of family's economic position is the family assets. At one side the assets of family are the indicators of family status, they are the security for the family in emergency at another side. What are the assets of a family with alcohol problems and how the consumption of alcohol affects the family assets was examined in this study. Table 3.26 indicates that 37 per cent families had agricultural land and 13.5 per cent had plots/shops as the important family assets. The study reveals that 27.8 per cent had jewellery and 18.6 per cent bank balances. As many as 81.2 per cent respondent families had their own houses and 13.5 per cent had vehicle (motor vehicles two wheeler and four wheelers). The study showed that 53.3 per cent families had livestock, as an important asset (majority of which were rural families). All the 800 families interviewed in the sample accepted that they had their personal savings of money, which they keep for their personal use (Figure 3.10).

Figure 3.10 Family assets of the alcohol affected families

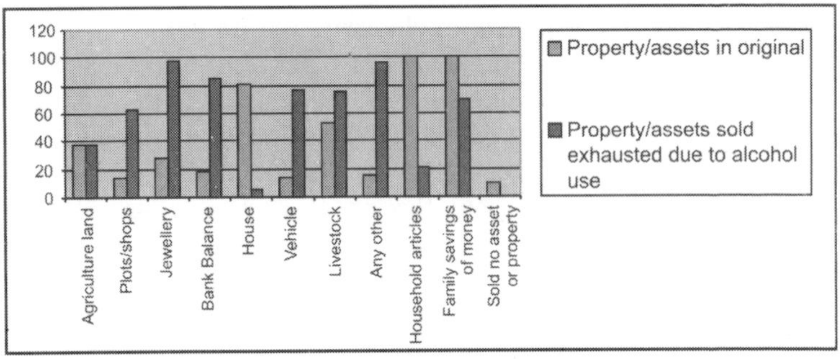

Table 3.26 Information about the family assets

Assets	*Property/ assets in original*		*Property/assets sold/exhausted due to alcohol*	
	Number of respondents	*Per cent*	*Number of respondents*	*Per cent*
Agriculture land	296	37.0	111	37.5
Plots/shops	108	13.5	68	62.9
Jewellery	223	27.8	218	97.7
Bank Balance	149	18.6	127	85.2
House	650	81.2	37	5.6
Vehicle	108	13.5	83	76.8
Livestock	427	53.3	321	75.1
Any other	122	15.2	117	95.9
Household articles	800	100.0	164	20.5
Family savings of money	800	100.0	560	70.0
Sold no asset or property	77	09.6	–	–

It is believed that alcoholic beverages are inexpensive in India (Riley and Marshall, 1999), but expenditure on alcohol by alcoholic still requires a substantial portion of family income. It is more significant when about 40 per cent of the population lives below poverty line, that how the expenditure on alcohol adversely affects the family economy. Besides the money spent on alcohol, a heavy drinker also suffers other adverse effects such as fewer wages, increased medical expenditure for illness and accidents, expenses on litigation because of drink-related offences and decreased eligibility for loans. A direct effect of all this disturbed economic situation of family comes to the family assets. Therefore, an attempt was made to study that how the use of alcohol in family disturbed the family economy and assets. Table 3.26 shows that out of 296 families that hold agricultural land as important family asset that was also the source of family income 37.5 per cent had sold it. It is a very significant number, which indicate toward the consequences of alcohol use and the seriousness of the problem. Out of 108 respondent families about 62.9 per cent had lost their plots or shops, which they purchased for their family as an important asset and it was because of heavy alcohol use in the family by the head of the family. There are 97.7 per cent respondent families out of the 223 families had sold their jewellery and 85.2 per cent (N=149) had lost their bank balance. Out of 650 respondent families 5.6 per cent had sold their houses because of financial crises in the family due to chronic alcohol use by one or more family members. 75.1 per cent (N=427) had to sell their livestock and 70 per cent (N=800) had lost their family savings and 76.8 per cent (N=108) also sold the vehicle of the family (Table 3.26).

In a detailed discussion, the family members narrated their lengthy and sensitive stories regarding the financial problems of the family and the loss of their assets due to the chronic and heavy use of alcohol.

In a village in district Kaithal an old lady explained her agony that she had three sons and all the three, use alcohol. They had sold their agriculture land, jewellery of the family and at last the house in which they reside. But when the brothers of this old lady came to know about it they purchased the house. For the sake of the prestige of family they executed the deal in my name (old lady)*. 'भाई मेरे बेटों ने तो मैं बर्बाद कर दी पर आप मेरे और मेरे गाम का नाम मत छापियो - बदनामी दूर-दूर तक जागी। मैं क्या करूं इस बुढापे मैं मनै काम करना पडै इन पौते-पोती के वास्ते'. (Brother, my sons had ruined me and my family but you please do

* She requested not to mention her name and the name of her village.

not publish my name and the name of my village because bad name goes far away. Now in this old age I had to work for the care of my grand children.) It was observed that all family was run by the woman members who go to fields to work so that they can earn to satisfy the family needs.

In another village a lady told that they had good agriculture land, tractor and other implements, but her alcoholic husband had sold almost all the agriculture land and tractor, now only one and half acre of land is left. 'मेरे धोरै बहुत जमीन थी, ट्रैक्टर था, अर सारा सांदा भी था। इब तो सारी जमीन, ट्रैक्टर अर सांदा सबकुछ बेच दिया बस डेढ एकड धारती बची है।' (I had plenty of agriculture land, tractor, all other implements for agriculture and farming. Now almost all the land, tractor and implements are sold by this man [her alcoholic husband] left only one and a half acre of land). It was observed that the family was going through severe financial crises, the children left their schools and play in streets, ladies go for daily labour and it was all because of heavy alcohol use in the family.

Loan and Indebtedness of the Family

The continuous use of alcohol in the family disturbs the economy and household budget of family. It affects the earning sources in terms of poor work performance and depletion of financial resources, which leads to liquidation of family assets. To satisfy the family needs many families go for taking loans from various sources, e.g. moneylenders, commission agents in grain markets, personal friends, relatives, banks, cooperative societies etc. An attempt was made to know that how many families with alcohol problems had taken loans from various sources and how many of them were suffering from the problem of indebtedness.

Table 3.27 Information about loan and indebtedness

	Response	*No. of respondent*	*Percentage*
I	Taken loan	414	51.7
	Not taken any loan	223	27.9
	No response	163	20.4
	Total	800	100.0
II	Problem of indebtedness	331	79.9
	No indebtedness	72	17.4
	No response	11	02.7
	Total	414	100.0

Table 3.27 reveals that 51.7 per cent of the respondent families agreed they had taken loans. 27.9 per cent said that they had not taken any loan and 20.4 per cent families had given no response to this question. But in informal discussions and the information given by the neighbours, friends, shopkeepers in the local areas it was found that almost all of them had taken loans may be of smaller amounts and were suffering from poor repaying capacities. It was not a confirmed source of information so all such cases were covered under no response. If this number (20.4%) is also considered in the case of 'taken any loan' the total percentage may engorge to 72.1 per cent, which is a very significant number. In the further enquiry to know about their loan repaying capacity it was found that a significant majority of the families with alcohol problems were suffering with the problem of indebtedness. The part-II of the Table 3.27 indicate that about 80 per cent (N=414) of the families who had taken loan from one or the other source were suffering from the problem of indebtedness. In the discussion with family members it was found that the loans were taken to satisfy the important family needs such as marriage of daughter, health problems or for some other needs but because of poor repaying capacity the loans were not returned and the family suffered serious financial crises. In Faridabad district, in a village, a lady, wife of an alcoholic who committed suicide narrated her problem bitterly weeping – 'हम तो शराब ने बर्बाद कर दिये, उसने (इसके पति ने) तो पी के खुदकुषी कर ली, आधी से ज्यादा जमीन भी बेच दी, बची जमीन पे कर्जा ले लिया, सारा परिवार कर्जे में डूब गया, हम क्या करें'. (We are ruined because of alcohol, my husband committed suicide because of alcohol, he sold more than half of the land and he had taken loan on the remaining land, now my whole family is suffering from the indebtedness – what we should do ...). This was the one case which I referred here, during data collection the research team and the author during his practice with alcoholic cases of about two decades found many such families suffering with severe financial problems because of alcohol use. A separate detailed investigation on the problem of indebtedness can reveal much more about this aspect of alcohol use.

In nutshell, the chapter discussed that how the family life is affected by the alcohol use in family. It was found that the use of alcohol in family has seriously disturbed the family relations and the worst effected relationship was the marital relations. Changes in the behaviour, changes in love and care, changes in interaction and changes in mutual faith due to use of alcohol were explained by a large number of respondents and the same was also observed by the researcher and his team. The alcohol drinkers in majority of the respondent families do not undertake any responsibility for their families rather burden the families with psychological, social and financial problems. More the use of alcohol increases, more the irresponsible behaviour towards family was reported, coming home after drinking alcohol was found very common as 38.3 per cent respondents said that the alcohol using family members daily come late to their home after drinking alcohol, 30.2 per cent normally do this and 26.1 per cent seldom do like this. Fighting with spouse was a common feature in such families, about 14 per cent families face this problem everyday while 26.4 per cent accepted as a usual affair and they had accepted it as unavoidable event. About 51 per cent respondents said that their husbands seldom fight with them. Therefore, it was observed that fighting with wives increased with the increase in frequency and quantity of alcohol use.

About 72 per cent respondents said that their alcoholic spouses misbehaved with them before the outsiders at different occasions and 80.6 per cent reported that they were misbehaved in front of their children. This all leads to family violence in which wife beating was a common feature and many a times small children were also the victim of violent drunkard behaviour. The families with regular alcohol use face various types of threats from the alcohol using persons out of which to send the wife to her parents was reported by 25.5 per cent and living separately was reported by about 14 per cent, 18.6 per cent threatened of leaving the home, about 5 per cent threatened to give divorce and 3.3 per cent threatened to commit suicide. Breaking household things after drinking was another common feature in such families, which was, reported by about 90 per cent families from occasionally to everyday.

A continuous disturbance to the family life by the alcohol-using member causes a counter reaction to the situation and it was reported that after a particular level of tolerance the alcohol-using member was also threatened for his misdeeds. About 8 per cent families said it was a daily incident when family members beat up the alcoholic person, while about 22 per cent families said it happened normally and 31.5 per cent accepted it occurring seldom. About 71 per cent families said alcohol-using person also retaliates to it, which resulted to severe violence many times.

There also appears to be an association between problem drinking, child abuse and child neglect in the family. The children of problem drinking parents were found at risk and experience various forms of neglect such as about 15 per cent families do not send their children to school. Among those who send their children to school, 40.4 per cent respondent families accept that the performance of children was poor and about 22 per cent said it is average but continuously going below. About 55 per cent families accepted that children suffered heavy loss of time because of alcohol use in their family and as a result of this about 38 per cent respondent families said that their children had lost interest in studies and had started performing poor while in the beginning they were good in their studies. A large majority of families (65%) with moderate to heavy drinking problems said that directly or indirectly the alcohol using persons took the services of children for alcohol related tasks and needs. The alcohol using person/s do not care about the age or other needs of the children while using them for their alcohol related needs. It seriously affects the growth and development of these children and also increases the chances of using alcohol by them. A majority of the respondent families (58.3%) feel that their children were continuously neglected because of alcohol use in the family, and 8.6 per cent gave no response regarding this. Because of continuous use of alcohol the children in the family suffer from various types of neglect, aggression and violence, the study found that children face verbal aggression in nearly 30 per cent families is from father, in 37.5 per cent families from mother and in nearly 25 per cent families from other family members. In 39 per cent families the children suffer moderate violence from father, in 8.5 per cent families from mother and in 5.5 per cent families from other family members. While in 7.8 per cent families children suffer from severe violence from father, in 3.3 per cent families from mother and in 3.6 per cent families from other family members.

A large majority (66.6%) of respondent families said that their children had developed a feeling of hatred for drinking parents or other drinking members. The children in such families were found suffering from various types of emotional problems, in 10 per cent families the children were suffering from psychosomatic problems, in 20.3 per cent families from negative attitude for their parents, and in 5 per cent families from negative attitude towards themselves. About 9 per cent suffer from self-blame and about 20 per cent from depression, 37.1 per cent families said that their children suffer from guilt feeling. Physical violence (beating the children) by the alcohol using parents was a common feature, and it was found that in 32 per cent such families the children were beaten up at least two times in one month, in 19.7 per cent three times, in 11.5 per cent four times and in about 13 per cent families almost daily. In the evening or at the time of coming home of the drunkard family member, the fear of the children was visible on their faces. The children in such families found involved in illegal activities, 18.3 per cent families accepted this fact and many more expressed their fear and concern in this regard. Sexual abuse of children in alcohol using families was also found, 5.7 per cent families said that such incidences happened in families in which the children suffered from exposure to penetration. The drunkard people as well as the close friends of family or relatives were also found involved in the sexual abuse of the children in heavy drinking/problem drinking families.

A large majority of families (21.5%) suffer from financial problems due to alcohol use of one or more family members. The families suffer to the extent that the basic family needs and essential personal requirements of the family members were not fulfilled because a large share of family income is drained of in the use of alcohol. The financial problems also increased because of the loss of earning capacity of the alcoholic member of the family and loss of work habit, loss of job, inability to work because of physical or mental damage due to continuous use of alcohol were found as main reasons. Family assets were also used to satisfy the needs when the regular source of income were either lost or not found sufficient. About 37 per cent families had agricultural land as an important family assert, 13.5 per cent had plots/shops, about 28 per cent had jewellery and 18.6 per cent had bank balance, 81.2 per cent families had their own houses, 13.5 per cent had vehicles and 53.3 per cent had livestock as an important family asset. These family assets were used as a main source by the alcohol using family members to fulfill their alcohol related needs and it was found that 37.5 per cent had sold their agricultural land, 62.9 per cent sold plots/shops, which were the important assets of these families. Jewellery was also another main target for such families. 97.7 per cent had to sell their jewellery because of alcohol use in family and 85.2 per cent had lost their bank balances. In some of the respondent families (5.6%), their house had been sold because of financial problems of the family. About 52 per cent respondent families had taken loans from different sources out of which about 80 per cent were found suffering from the problem of indebtedness.

Thus on the whole it can be said that the use of alcohol which gradually develops as heavy or problem drinking is responsible for several disturbances and problems for other family members. The women and children are the main sufferers. Children were not able to continue their schooling, wife and child battering were found common in such families, which leads to very serious physical, mental and social problems in the families. Women family members were found suffering from various threats and they had to play the role of breadwinners and forced into work. Increased responsibilities, work and poor financial condition affect the health of women and children in such families. Insufficient financial resources leads to selling the family assets like agriculture land, jewellery, plots, bank balance and even the own house. These factors contribute toward the greater poverty often to the point of destitution.

4

Alcohol Use and Health Problems in Family

World wide consumption of alcohol in 2005 was 6.13 litres of pure alcohol consumed per person aged of 15 years or older. Global Status Report on Alcohol and Health Analysis 2001–05 showed countries in the WHO Americans, European, Eastern Mediterranean and Western Pacific regions had relatively stable consumption level during that time but marked increases were seen in Africa and South East Asia during the five year period.The recent WHO report on the Global Burden of Disease (GBD) projects in stark terms the heavy toll of death and disability due to drinking. The study put alcohol's global health impact on a par with unsafe sex and above tobacco in terms of its contribution to the total number of years of life lost to death and disability as recorded in Disability Adjusted Life Years (DALYs) (Murray and Lopez, 1996) (Figure 4.1). In addition to chronic diseases that may affect drinkers after many years of heavy use, alcohol contributes to traumatic outcomes that kill or disable at a relatively young age, resulting in the loss of many years of life to death or disability.

The use and abuse of alcohol is related to a wide range of physical, mental and social harm to the person who use it and also to the others around him or her. Most health professionals now agree that practically no organ in the body is immune from alcohol related harm (Bower, 1992). The scientific studies regarding alcohol related health and social problems are very limited in India, but there are sufficient indications available in the literature and

Figure 4.1 DALYs lost attributable to 10 leading risk factors for the age group 15–59 years in the world (2004)

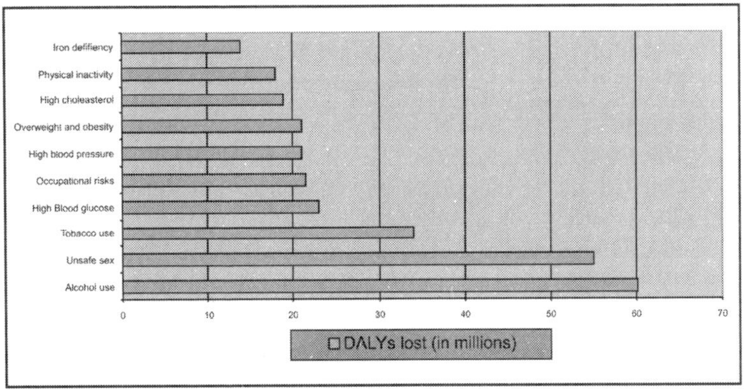

Source: The Globe, Issue 1, 2011.

records in many health institutions across the country that the harm is substantial. Few scientific studies in India deal with the health problems caused because of alcohol use. Sharma and Murthy (1988) in a study of four-to-five years follow up study of patients diagnosed as alcohol dependent found that 11.3 per cent of those who could be traced had died. In another study, Desai and Ray (1989) documented a mortality of 5.5 per cent during an 18-month follow up among hospital patients with alcohol dependence of number of other health problems such as alcoholic liver cirrhosis, cancer, accidents and injuries, alcoholic psychosis, alcoholic gastritis, alcoholic polyneuropathy, ethanol toxicity and methanol toxicity have been identified.

Research over the past two decades has found that the level of alcohol problems is related both to the overall amount of drinking in the country (per capita alcohol consumption) and to the particular patterns of drinking (Global Status Report on Alcohol, WHO, 1999 and 2004). A review of Indian studies during the period from 1933 to 1975 reveals that among biopsy-proven cirrhosis cases, between 0.0 per cent and 66 per cent (cumulative mean = 16%) had the history of alcohol use and alcoholism (Bhagwat and Islam, 1980). Another study among patients who presented with cirrhosis found only a minority of them to have had excessive alcohol intake (Rajwanshi et al., 1985). However, for all of these studies, since drinking history often is not elicited or reliably recorded, these proportions may be underestimates. Studies of heavy drinkers have revealed a much higher prevalence of liver and other diseases.

Harmful use of alcohol is defined as excessive use to the point that it causes damage to health and often includes adverse social consequences. Many countries recognize the serious public health problems caused by the harmful use of alcohol and have taken steps to prevent the health and social burdens and treat those in need of care. But clearly much more needs to be done to reduce the loss of life and suffering associated with harmful alcohol use (Alwan, 2011).

The report also recognizes that there is a broad range of people adversely affected by the drinking of others. It presents Australian data to show that around 1 per cent of the population was hospitalized due to another person's drinking in the course of a year, and about the same proportion suffered a domestic assault related to alcohol, according to police records. But much larger numbers report being negatively impacted by somebody else's drinking in the workplace, household or public place, and by a family member, friend, stranger or someone not well known to the victim. More than two thirds of the survey respondents were adversely affected by drinking of a stranger negatively impacted a total of 10.5 million people.

The report presents evidence that, measured in terms of Disability Adjusted Life Years (DALYs), alcohol is the leading global risk factor for 15–59 year olds. Harmful use of alcohol has many implications on public health. Nearly 4 per cent of all deaths are related to alcohol. Most alcohol-related deaths are caused by problems resulting from injuries, cancer, cardiovascular diseases and liver cirrhosis. Globally, 6.2 per cent of all male deaths are related to alcohol, compared to 1.1 per cent of female deaths. One in five men in the Russian Federation and neighbouring countries die due to alcohol-related causes. Globally, 3,20,000 young people aged 15–29 years die annually, from alcohol-related causes, resulting in 9 per cent of all deaths in that age group (ibid.).

The WHO complains that too few countries use effective policy options to prevent death, disease and injury from alcohol use. From 1999, when WHO first began to report on alcohol policies, at least 34 countries have adopted some type of formal policies to reduce harmful use of alcohol. Restrictions on alcohol marketing and on drink-driving have increased, but there are no clear trends on most preventive measures. Many countries have weak alcohol policies and prevention programmes. Alcohol consumption patterns indicate that 35 per cent of adult men and 5 per cent of women consume alcohol (70 million alcohol users, 12 million of whom are alcohol dependent). More than 50 per cent of regular users fall into the category of hazardous drinking. Alcohol use is high in poor communities, contributing to increasing expenditure on alcohol and increasing resources spent on managing alcohol related problems. The average age of starting alcohol use has reduced from 28 years during the 1980s to 17 years in 2007 (Gururaj, 2011).

Therefore, keeping in view the above position an effort has been made to study the health problems in the families with alcohol use in Haryana, India. The first question put to the respondents was about the health of the person who uses alcohol. The information given in Table 4.1 explained that 75.6 per cent families said that the health of the alcohol users was not satisfactory and only 19.1 per cent accepted it as satisfactory, while 5.3 per cent respondents refused to answer the question.

Table 4.1 Health of the person using alcohol in family

Response	*No. of respondents*	*Per cent*
Satisfactory	153	19.1
Not Satisfactory	605	75.6
No Response	42	5.3
Total	800	100.0

Physical Health Problems

Alcohol causes damage to health in two ways, firstly, long-term use of alcohol results to cumulative harm and secondly, accidents and violence, caused by a simple bout of drinking. The harm done by long-term drinking is far reaching, especially in damage to health. Drinking on average more than three units of alcohol per day for men and two units for women increases the likelihood of health problems (Rutherford, 1997). Among regular drinkers (those who drink more than one unit per day) one in three adult males and one in five females drink at or over the above level. Alcohol is absorbed from the stomach and the small intestine, and gets distributed to every organ, tissue, and cell in the body through blood circulation. The liver at a rapid pace absorbs most of the alcohol circulating in the blood. The continuous alcohol use adversely affects multiple organs of the body. Physical health complications due to alcohol use can range from acute damage to the stomach, to severe chronic liver damage, sterility and loss of intellectual functions. Some complications are acute such as liver damage like developing a fatty liver, cirrhosis, brain damage, stomach pains, blood pressure, cancers of orpharynx, larynx, liver, stomach, oesophagus, rectum, breast, disorders of the immune system (ibid.). While studying the alcohol problems in family various types of health problems also came into picture. The damage to health of the person using alcohol was very common and a variety of problems were explained. Therefore, the health problems both physical and psychiatric of the person who use alcohol and its effect on others are covered in this chapter.

The harm done by drinking is not only to the drinker, the spouse, children and other family members often suffer because of it. Table 4.2 shows that the alcohol users suffer from many types of physical problems. A good number of users, i.e. in 24.6 per cent families were found suffering from changes in their physical appearance such as change in skin colour (dark and dry) and scratches on face etc. Such changes were quite visible among the chronic alcoholics.

Table 4.2 Information about the physical health problems of alcohol using persons in family

Nature of physical problems	*No. of respondents*	*Per cent*
Changes in physical appearance	197	24.6
Loss of weight	333	41.6
Gastritis and acid peptic disease	045	5.6
Alcoholic liver disease	163	20.4
Cirrhosis	09	1.1
Malabsorption syndrome	112	14.0
Pancreatitis (Stomach pain)	220	27.5
Cardiovascular complication	30	3.8
Loss of appetite	132	10.5
Loss of sight	46	5.8
No problem	153	19.1

Note: The total number exceeds 800 as many respondents gave more than one response.

Figure 4.2 Physical health problem of alcohol using persons in family

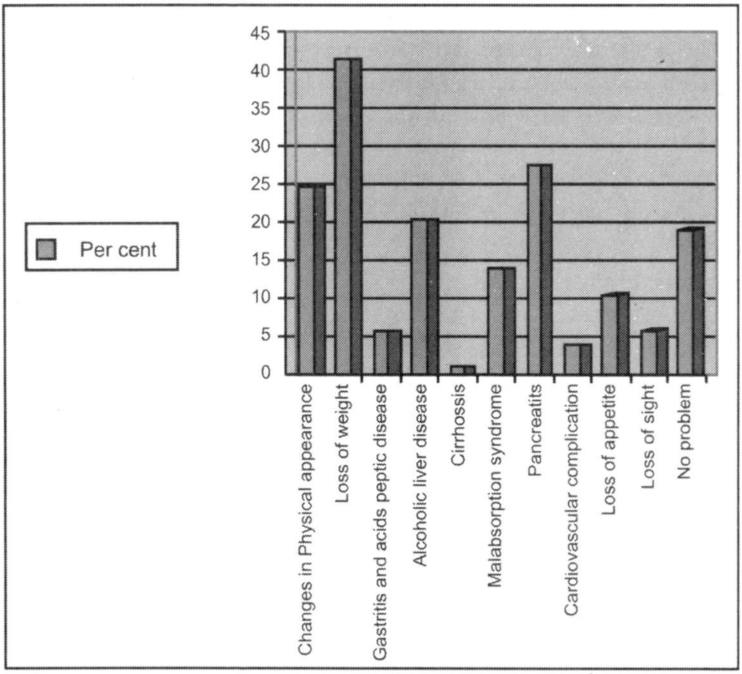

In 41.6 per cent families, alcoholics were found suffering from the problem of loss in their body weight and in 15.6 per cent were having gastritis and peptic disease, in 20.4 per cent families were suffering from alcoholic liver diseases and in 1.1 per cent families the alcohol using persons were suffering from cirrhosis medical reports of the suffering alcoholics. While discussing about the health problems of the alcohol using persons the respondents revealed that in 14 per cent families the alcoholics face the problems of malabsorption syndrome (digestive problems) and in 27.5 per cent from stomach pains for which the doctors diagnosed as pancreatitis. 03.8 per cent families said that their alcohol using members were having cardiovascular complications while 10.5 per cent complained for loss of appetite and 5.8 per cent were suffering from eye sight and vision problems (Figure 4.2).

During interview the respondents were not able to disclose the nature of ailment but they explained it in terms of symptoms and with common names used in their community as per their knowledge and experience. The research team consulted the doctors (wherever possible), records at drug de-addiction centres and examined the prescriptions of the treatment. In some cases the alcohol using person was also consulted wherever possible and inferences were drawn about the diseases.

Hospitalization for Treatment

The health problems of the alcoholics/problem drinkers in family create many types of other problems for the family members. At one side their physical condition gradually start deteriorating, on the other side the continuous use of alcohol makes it more critical. Many times it becomes unmanageable for the family. In such conditions hospitalization is very essential but the family members who become habitual of such incidences because of daily routine of alcoholic/problem drinker either avoid it or in many cases do not know the importance and need of hospitalizing the patient. Moreover, heavy drinkers always try to avoid going to doctors, probably because of shame or not want to be lectured. Therefore, delay in referral for proper treatment including hospitalization and other professional help results to many serious problems for the family.

Table 4.3 Hospitalized during last six months*

Response	*No. of respondents*	*Per cent*
One time	258	32.3
Two times	161	20.1
More than two times	64	08.0
Never	307	38.4
No response	10	01.2
Total	800	100.0

Note: * The study was conducted in the year 2004–2007.

Table 4.3 reveals that 32.3 per cent families had to get the persons using alcohol hospitalized at least one time for treatment for one or the other health problems, 20.1 per cent had to be hospitalized for two times and 8 per cent were to be hospitalized for more than two times during last six months. It means about 60 per cent families with the problem of alcohol use got their alcohol using family members admitted in the hospital for treatment and 38.4 per cent have not felt any such need and 1.2 per cent refused to reply. While enquiring further about the type of hospital where they had to get the person admitted, the duration of hospitalization and the nature of treatment and cooperation from the patient varying responses were reported. In majority of the cases the hospitalization was done in private clinics/nursing homes. In some cases the hospitalization was in the government hospitals and drug de-addiction centres but the nature of services and care provided were not satisfactory. The family members narrated lot of stories about the carelessness and negligence of hospital staff and the workers of de-addiction centres. The non-cooperation of alcoholic/problem drinkers were also reported by the family members such as they do not take medicines, do not cooperate with the staff, misbehave with the staff/doctor, throw away the medicines and run away from the hospital and sometimes become violent also. This is a hard reality which the family have to face and feel handicap. It is true that early identification of problem drinking and proper care and attempt by the trained and qualified staff can pay good results but neither the drunker nor the family can work at appropriate time to break the cycle, which results to serious health problems for drinker and other problems for family.

Mental Health Problems

Alcohol use can also lead to or exacerbate many types of mental health problems. The range of problems associated with drinking is very wide from affective disorders such as depression and anxiety to alcoholic psychosis and suicide. The International Consortium in Psychiatric Epidemiology (ICPE) using WHO's Composite International Diagnostic Instrument (CIDI) for psychiatric disorders in six countries found that those with alcohol dependence also had high rate of depression (18%) and of anxiety disorders (35%). In a study conducted by Merikangas et al. (1998) found that in Mexico, those with alcohol dependence were 2.4 times as likely as others to have a mood disorder, and 2.7 times as likely to have an anxiety disorder. In a survey of heads of household in the middle belt region of Nigeria, Obot (1993) reports significantly higher rates of indicators of psychological problems among drinkers than non-drinkers. Therefore, various mental health/psychiatric problems of the alcohol users in the family are studied and analysed.

Table 4.4 Information about the mental health problems of alcohol users in family

Nature of problem	*No. of respondents*	*Per cent*
Sleeping difficulties	289	36.1
Dementia	31	3.9
Loss of memory	213	26.6
Epilepsy	38	4.8
Alcohol induced jealousy	115	14.4
Alcohol induced mood disorders	77	9.6
Suicide	126	15.8
No problem	153	19.1
No response	116	14.5

Note: The total number exceeds 800 because many respondents gave more than one responses.

Table 4.4 reveals that 36.1 per cent respondents said that the alcohol users suffer from sleeping difficulties. According to their statement the person using alcohol cannot sleep till he/she takes alcohol in the evening, many of them get up in between and create

Figure 4.3 Mental health problems of alcohol users in family

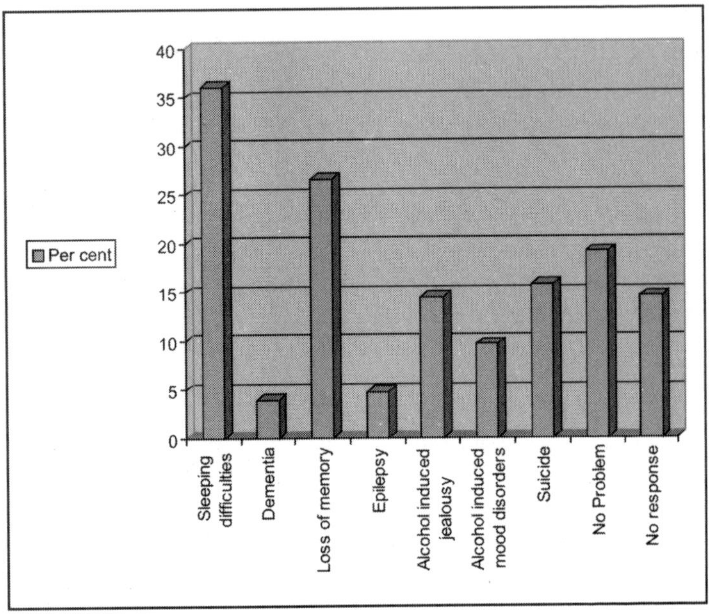

problems. Irregular sleeping timings, getting up early in the morning, disturbed sleep and problem of insomnia were very common as per the medical records of alcohol using members with other symptoms explained by their family members. About 4 per cent respondents complained about dementia, 26.6 per cent loss of memory and 4.8 per cent accepted that their alcohol using family members suffer from epilepsy (Figure 4.3).

Some other problems were also explained like 14.4 per cent recorded the problems of alcohol-induced jealousy, 9.6 per cent alcohol induced mood disorders such as depression and bipolar disorders, 15.8 per cent families said that their alcohol using family members attempted to commit suicide and 14.5 per cent refused to reply for this question. Thus, one can conclude from the above data that mental health problems are common among the alcohol dependents and family confronts it by its own. Every family has a sad story to narrate and every alcohol dependent has his personal justification for using alcohol as a coping mechanism.

In addition to the effects of alcohol on the drinker, there is considerable evidence of the effect of alcohol consumption on the health of people other than the drinker in areas such as spouse and child abuse, violence after use of alcohol and road and traffic accidents. The public health impact of alcohol on others is of great importance in both developed and developing countries.

Range and magnitude of alcohol's harm to others in Australia in 2008

Deaths due to another's drinking	367
Hospitalizations due to another's drinking	13,699
Substantiated child protection cases involving a caregiver's drinking	19,443
Alcohol-related domestic assault in police records	24,581
Alcohol-attributable assaults in police records	69,433

Source: The Globe, Issue 1, 2011.

As association between drinking and some forms of victimization, including robbery, rape and aggressive behaviour is consistently reported in literature (Edwards et al., 1994). Particularly in developing countries, alcohol consumption may lead to significant effects on the health of the drinker's family, through financial difficulties arising when a large part of the family's income is spent on aggravated by poor living conditions and malnutrition (Saxena, 1999).

Children in Family Suffering from Malnutrition

The alcohol use in family disturbs the entire family in many different ways. The financial difficulties due to the large part of income used in alcohol leads to disturb the entire family budget and the first axe falls on the food and on the share of children. Table 4.5 shows that in 32 per cent families, children were suffering from malnutrition. 3.5 per cent avoided this question, but it was observed that a significant number out of these were having the symptoms of malnutrition.

Table 4.5 Children in family suffering from malnutrition

Response	*No. of respondents*	*Per cent*
Yes	256	32.0
No	516	64.5
No Response	28	03.5
Total	800	100.0

In many families there was no regular source of income and whatsoever was earned the large share was drained of in the use of alcohol. The family does not have sufficient sources to arrange for two square meals. In many families women members go for work and try to procure the resources. In many cases discussions with local doctors, PHC doctors, ANMs, Anganwadi Supervisors and workers revealed that such problems in the alcohol using families are much more serious than it looks. In the case of the children found suffering from malnutrition in such families the symptoms of malnutrition among them were clearly visible and confirmed from doctor's report or prescription from where the families take

Table 4.6 Information about the symptoms of malnutrition among children in the families with alcohol use

Symptoms	*No. of respondents*	*Per cent*
Under Weight	94	36.8
Anaemic	50	19.5
Dry-skin	53	20.7
Pale eyes	59	23.0
Total	256*	100.0

Note: * The number of children suffering from malnutrition is 256.

treatment, in the case of small children anganwadi workers were contacted and records available there were consulted. The common symptoms found are given in Table 4.6 which shows that 36.8 per cent children in the families with the problem of alcohol use were suffering from under weight and 19.5 per cent were found anaemic. The symptoms like dry-skin were reported in 20.7 per cent cases and 23 per cent found with pale eyes.

Health of Spouse

As per the characteristics of Indian patriarchal system the male member is the head of family in any condition. The role of the women family members is restricted to household work such as cooking food, washing clothes, taking care of children and old members of family etc. Even if the women members in the family take responsibility of family matters in odd situations but only male member has the social sanction. Women who take care of the entire family, what about her health? It was a very important question. During discussion with the women family members it was observed that a large majority of them was not much concerned about their health and health problems. The health status of the wives of alcoholics/problem drinkers disclosed many important facts and issues about the health of women family members specially wives.

Table 4.7 Health status of the spouse (wives) of alcoholics/problem drinkers

Health status	*No. of respondents*	*Per cent*
Normal	314	39.2
Poor health	427	53.4
Sick	32	4.0
Suffering from chronic disease	12	1.5
No Response	13	1.6
Husbands*	02	0.3
Total	800	100.0

Note: * In two families the alcoholics were women.

Table 4.7 reveals that about 61 per cent spouse were not having normal health conditions and were suffering from one or the other health problem. 53.4 per cent reported that they had poor health, 4 per cent were found sick and taking very casual treatment,

Figure 4.4 Health status of the spouse (wives) of alcoholics/problem drinkers

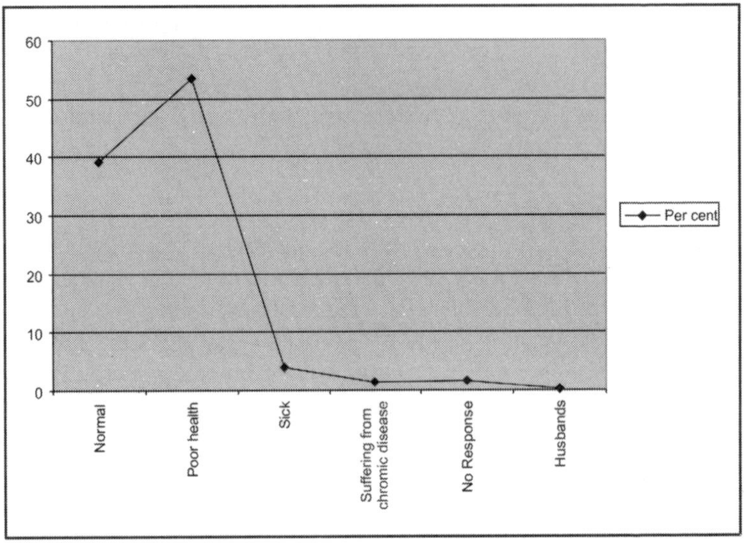

1.5 per cent suffering from one or the other chronic disease such as T.B., epilepsy, 1.6 per cent had not given any response (Figure 4.4). While discussing regarding health problems of women it was found that because of the problem drinking by one or more family members the health becomes the last priority and even not at all in any priority in some cases. They only go for treatment when the things become unmanageable. In large majority they take treatment from the local doctors (quacks) who do not have any authorized qualification. In some cases the women told that they go to government PHC or dispensary. But when the doctor was consulted and records were scanned, it was found that the treatment taken was very casual. PHC doctor also confirmed that these patients were not serious for their health and for treatment. In some cases when it was asked that why you were so casual about your health problems, a very spontaneous response was 'किस तरां बीमारी ने देखां रे भाई, इस शराबी न तो सब कुछ खो दिया । हमनै तो अपणी सोधी नही रहीं इसके करतब देख-देख कै। (This alcoholic man has disturbed everything, how I can go for my treatment in such situation. I have lost all sense for my self because of his (alcoholic) deeds).

In the families with alcoholic/problem drinkers the majority of women were suffering from one or the other health problem and very careless about their health. In some cases the relapse of disease like TB was also reported, such as a lady explained that: 'पहलां दवाई खाई तो ठीक होगी थी मैं पर इब एक महीने से फेर बिमार होगी, सांस ठीक नी आंदा, दवाई लेन जाने की हिम्मत ही ना होई, रोज का खाड़ा कर कै राखे यो जुल्मी।' (I got relief when I took medicine but now for about last one month again I have the problem in respiration and cough. I could not go to doctor for medicine because this man (alcoholic) creates one or the other problem daily). This was the case of a TB patient (wife of an alcoholic) for which she took treatment and got relief. She left the treatment in between because of the alcohol problems of her husband and now again started suffering from same disease probably more serious than earlier for which she had not gone for treatment. Her health was very poor, her house was in shambles, children were also not cared at all.

Alcoholics/Problem Drinker's Concern about the Health Problems of Family

How for the alcohol using person is concerned about the health problems of family? The family members specially the wives of the alcoholics/problem drinkers had many types of health problems as discussed earlier, therefore, in such situation who is there to take care and how the family take care of health needs of the family specially when the head of the family is an alcoholic.

Table 4.8 Alcoholics/problem drinker's concern about the health problems of family

Response	*No. of respondents*	*Per cent*
Yes	391	48.9
No	337	42.1
No response	72	9.0
Total	800	100.0

Who takes care about health problems of family, the family members responded that about 49 per cent alcohol users take care while 42 per cent do not take care for the health needs of family. As many as 9 per cent families did not reply to this question because of their own reservations. When a close relationship was established and the family members started sharing very personal matters it was revealed by the spouses that when their husbands are normal (very rarely) or drink up to normal levels they are very caring but when they themselves need care, which goes for weeks or even for months, so the health problems of spouses or family members becomes secondary.

Efforts to Stop the Use of Alcohol

The onset of use of alcohol is due to many reasons such as curiosity, peer pressure, to ward of anxiety. The person may become alcoholic because of other precipitating factors such as property disputes with family, financial problems, carelessness or unhealthy behaviour of children, family disputes and/or other personal problems. Do the alcoholics at any point of time want to stop the use of alcohol or continue with it. It was observed that after continuous use of alcohol a time comes when the alcoholic himself feels that he/she should now leave it but the physical and/or psychological dependence do not allow for it.

Table 4.9 Information about the alcoholic who tried to stop the use of alcohol

Response	*No. of respondents*	*Per cent*
Yes	551	68.9
No	246	30.8
No response	03	0.3
Total	800	100.0

The data shows in Table 4.9 that 68.9 per cent families said that the alcoholics want to stop the use of alcohol and also tried at one or the other time, 30.8 per cent said that the alcoholics never tried to leave alcohol. A further enquiry on why the person want to leave alcohol and what were the means to stop the use was very interesting and useful information was shared by the family members. It was found that many of them become the victims of quacks and professionals who advertise about helping such people and exploit the feelings of patients (alcoholics) and their family members. During interaction with family members it was noticed that among the majority of the families there was total ignorance about the effects of alcohol and the ways of treatment for alcohol related problems. They have tried their own ways and when asked that whether they had gone to the drug de-addiction centre, the simple reply was 'no'. In some cases/patients who said 'yes' a total dissatisfaction was explained with regard to the working and service delivery system of the centres. The type of treatment the families take to get rid of the problem of alcohol use is presented in the Table 4.10 which shows that the 15 per cent families out of 800 approached Ojjhas/Sadhus/Sufi/Maulvi to find out the solutions regarding the alcohol use of their alcoholic family member, 15.9 per cent contacted qualified medical practitioners at their private clinics, 11 per cent took treatment from government hospitals or PHC, 4.4 per cent contacted quacks and 13.1 per cent tried at drug de-addiction/counseling centres. 30.7 per cent had never tried for any treatment because the alcoholic person either not created any problem for the family or the family was not concerned about his/her alcohol use. About 10 per cent of the respondents refused to reply to this question (Figure 4.5).

Table 4.10 Type of treatment taken to give up alcohol

Type of Treatment	*No. of respondents*	*Per cent*
Quacks	35	4.4
Ojjha/Sadhu/Sufi/Maulvi	120	15.0
Govt. hospital/PHC	88	11.0
Private clinic (qualified doctor)	127	15.9
Drug de-addiction/counseling centre	105	13.1
No treatment	246	30.7
No response	79	9.9
Total	800	100.0

In more detailed observation of the alcoholics and the families, the family members shared many information and experiences. A very important experience shared by the families was that initially majority of them were not much concerned about this problem and they had never thought that alcohol use could be such a big problem for them. Some of the family members (women) explained their personal efforts such as taking row (मन्नत मानना, व्रत रखना) so that the

Figure 4.5 Type of treatment taken to give up alcohol

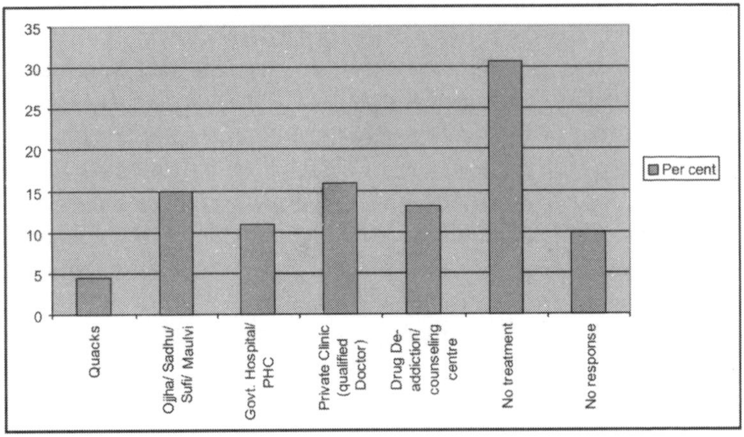

person could be helped by the superior powers and leave using alcohol. Some families shared their experiences of being cheated by *Religious Faith Healers* or private doctors/quacks advertising for the treatment of alcoholics. A common and interesting experience shared by a majority of the respondent family members was that giving of medicine to the alcoholic by mixing it in food or any beverage like milk, curd, buttermilk etc. This medicine was easily available to them at the shops of quacks/private clinics or even at chemist shops, known as 'Pudia' (पुड़िया). The women family members take active interest in it because it is very easy for them to use and the alcoholic person could not know about it, because of which he couldn't use alcohol. In some cases the alcoholics had to be admitted in the hospital because of serious complications due to such practice.

Therefore, one can conclude that so far as the source of treatment for health problems, type of treatment and its continuation is concerned, it is not satisfactory. The majority of the families started treatment of their own in the family itself on the basis of their experiences and local wisdom, then shift to *Religious Faith Healers* (Ojhas, Sadhu, Maulvi etc.). When the situation becomes more complicated then they go to private practitioners, who were often quacks. The suffering family members specially women try their best to help the alcoholics but the steps taken for this were non-scientific, based on their beliefs and moreover a total non-cooperation from the alcohol using person.

Resources in Family for Treatment at the Time of Illness

Income inequalities and the increased cost of medical care are some important factors, which affect the health concerns of individuals. When it comes to the families of alcoholics/addicts where a large part of income is being drained off in the use of alcohol, health of family members nowhere comes in any priority. It was observed at the time of interview and informal discussions that the family members were extremely casual for health problems and treatment because they have to struggle for the fulfillment of other important needs of the family. This can be inferred from the words of an old lady in a village of Faridabad district in Haryana who said, ''घर के खाने को देखें या बीमारी को देखें, नौकरी से तो निकाल दिया, जमीन रही नहीं, सब कुछ शराब पी गयी तो दवाई-बूटी कहां से लायें' (what should we see, food for family or illness? He (alcoholic) is fired from job, he has sold his agricultural land, everything is finished by alcohol so how we can arrange for treatment and medicines).

After going through a continuous interaction on various aspects of the sufferings an important aspect emerged that how many such families have sufficient resources for the proper treatment in case any member of the family fell sick. The information reveals that 48 per cent families with the problem of alcohol use clearly said that they do not have any resources for the treatment. Another 11.6 per cent refused to answer this question, expressing their own reservations regarding resources. They questioned about the steps taken by the government regarding sale and supply of alcohol, which is the root cause of all these problems, a serious question about alcohol policy in the country. A good number of respondents reacted regarding the steps taken by the government for the treatment of alcoholics and help given to the families in their crisis. They also accused government for encouraging sale of alcohol to increase the state revenue. While 40.4 per cent respondents said that they have sufficient resources for treatment at the time of illness, but they had also expressed their dissatisfaction about the health provisions and services given by the government (Table 4.11).

Table 4.11 Does the family have sufficient resources for the treatment of sick person in family?

Response	*No. of Respondents*	*Per cent*
Yes	323	40.4
No	384	48.0
No Response	93	11.6
Total	800	100.0

So far as the family resources are concerned it was observed that some of the families do have sufficient resources for the treatment of alcoholic and other family members at the time of need. But, what is more important that how these resources could be properly utilized specially for the treatment of alcoholics. They want proper treatment but no proper treatment facility is available for such problems. The drug counseling and de-addiction centres wherever working are not able to establish their credibility within the community. This leads to develop a sense of mistrust and dissatisfaction among the suffering families. They lose faith in the system and it affects the health of other family members. Those who do not have sufficient resources suffer in the want of proper treatment facility, which is nowhere available, and a majority of them become the victims of quacks and traditional faith healers. These further adds to the poor health status of entire family that's why the health status of spouse (wives) was also found poor and the children were suffering from the problem of malnutrition and other diseases.

There is a common belief that small intake of alcohol is psychologically, socially and even physically beneficial. Some studies have shown that occasional and moderate drinking helps a person alleviate the tension and pressure of their harsh life situations. The aged who use alcoholic beverages moderately also enjoy improved sleep, high tuned moral and general well-being. Moreover, light drinkers have lower death rate than complete abstainers (Neff and Husaini, 1985). It is also believed that moderate drinkers are much less likely than teetotallers to suffer from heart disease. But the fact that a little bit is good does not mean that a lot would be better. Many casual and moderate drinkers become heavy drinkers and lead to harmful drinking because of many reasons and the chances of which are very much present in our system and basic human weakness of pleasure seeking, it is heavy drinkers who are likely to harm their own health and the health of entire family in various ways.

It was found that in majority of the families the use of alcohol was initiated moderately but gradually it shifted to heavy and harmful drinking which severely effected the health of the drinker. Earlier it was used for improved sleep, alleviation of tension and decrease of pressure now it acted otherwise for other family members who started suffering from many types of health problems (specially wives and children) and increased tension and pressure for their smooth and healthy family life.

To summarize, the use of alcohol is responsible for many types of health problems for drinkers and the majority (75.6%) do not have satisfactory health. The most common damage done to the body by heavy drinking involves the liver (20.4%), loss of weight (41.6%), stomach pain (27.5%), changes in physical appearance (24.6%). A most common response found at the time of interaction was that the respondents were not able to disclose the nature of ailment but they only explain in terms of symptoms such as stomach pain etc. It was also revealed that 32.3 per cent persons using alcohol were hospitalized once during last six months, 20.1 per cent two times, 8 per cent more than two times and 38.4 per cent were not hospitalized.

A large number of alcohol users were found suffering from one or the other mental health problem such as 36.1 per cent found suffering from sleeping difficulties, 26.6 per cent were suffering from loss of memory, 15.8 per cent tried to commit suicide, 14.4 per cent were suffering from alcohol induced jealousy, 9.6 per cent were suffering from alcohol induced mood disorders, 4.8 per cent from epilepsy, and 3.9 per cent from dementia. About 19 per cent respondents said that there was no mental health problem with the person using alcohol in their family, but in this case a majority was found confusing within themselves while answering this question, therefore, one cannot conclude this number as confirmed non-sufferers. 14.5 per cent refused to reply this question because of many personal reasons explained by them. Children in these families were also found suffering from many problems including malnutrition, in 32 per cent families the children suffered from malnutrition for which 36.8 per cent found suffering with under-weight, 19.5 per cent were suffering with anaemia, 20.7 per cent had dry-skin, and 23 per cent had the symptoms of pale eyes.

Wives of the alcohol using persons are the main suffers and they have to bear the whole burden. It is because of this, their health is the most neglected area of family life. It was found that 53.4 per cent spouse (wives) were having poor health, 4 per cent found sick, 1.5 per cent were suffering from chronic disease. About 39 per cent said that their health was normal and 1.6 per cent gave no answer to this question. About 49 per cent alcoholics said that they feel concerned about the health problems of their family members while 42.1 per cent said that they have no such concern, 9 per cent refused to answer this question. About 69 per cent respondents said that the alcohol using persons tried to stop the use of alcohol and 38.8 per cent said that they never tried to stop the use. It was found that 15 per cent families contacted *Traditional Faith Healers* (Ojjhas/Sadhus/Sufi/Maulvi) for the treatment of alcoholics, 15.9 per cent approached qualified medical practitioners, 11 per cent took treatment from government hospitals or PHCs, 4.4 per cent contacted quacks and 13.1 per cent tried at drug de-addiction/counseling centres. 30.7 per cent never tried for any treatment. The families suffer from the scarcity of resources even for the treatment for the ill persons as it was found that 48 per cent families do not have sufficient resources for getting treatment for the sick family members while 40.4 per cent said 'yes to' this question and 11.6 per cent refused to respond.

5

Social Implications of Alcohol Use in Family

In addition to causing health problems to the alcohol users and to other family members discussed in the previous chapter, continuous use of alcohol may bring various types of social complications to the family. Social life of the family has two aspects (i) activities within the family and (ii) family's relationships to the outside world. It was observed that the continuous and excessive use of alcohol disturbs the family from both sides, within as well as outside relations, because the normal family life required to be acquainted with the social relations is disturbed in many ways. Family activities particularly social and recreational activities within the family are likely to be restricted because of the drinkers unpredictable behaviour, or inability to participate or the family members feel themselves reluctant to participate out of the fear of the behaviour of the drinker.

It is generally recognized and said that alcohol use not only affects a person's economic life, his/her personal health (also observed in the pervious chapters) but also the social life of the user and his/her family. In order to examine the relationship of drinking behaviour and social life, detailed discussions were held with the families effected with the problem and the questions focused on the important aspects of interfamily and intra-family relations such as social status, feelings of neighbours, associations with relatives, reactions of family friends, participation in social and religious functions, social and religious ceremonies, problems created by alcoholics, encounters with police, effect on recreational activities, street brawls etc.

Alcohol Use and Social Status of Family

While studying the effects of alcohol use on the social status of the family, it was found that an overwhelming majority of the drinkers' family feel that drinking leads to degradation of family's social status, as much as 92.5 per cent respondents said 'yes' alcohol use in family affects the social status and reputation of family. It was also observed that the reaction of many family members including wives of the users were very hostile about the problematic behaviour of their alcoholic spouse. Many of them said that they can live without husband but not with the alcoholic one. It is clear from the words of Roshni Devi* 'जब भी मेरा पति घर पर पी कर आता है तो वह इतना शोर मचाता है, मार-पीट करता है कि पड़ोसी भी जाग जाते हैं। हमारी तो जिंदगी नरक कर दी है इसने। यदि मेरे को बिना पति के जीवन काटना हो तो मैं तैयार हूं पर शराबी पति और इस जैसा तो बड़ा मुश्किल है' (whenever my husband comes to home after drinking alcohol, he always makes so much noise, and beats that disturbs neighbours. He has made our life hell. If I have to spend life without husband, I am ready but not with an alcoholic husband). Only 2.6 per cent respondents said 'no' to this question. When it was discussed and analysed that about saying 'no' for such type of enquiry, it was found that either the respondent was not interested to share this information or the respondent was so much concerned that she was not ready to compromise on the reputation of family. The answers such as 'यो तो अपणा मामला है, सुलझ ल्यांगे इज्जत बेजती की क्या बात है ...' (This is our own matter, we will solve it. There is nothing like respect and disrespect ...).

Some important observations also came into picture when a detailed discussion was held with the wives and other family members of alcoholics. The family tradition in drinking, the permissive attitude of the father, lack of education, various myths and misconceptions about the beneficial effects of alcohol are some important factors which obstruct them to link it with the social status and reputation of family reason for 'no' to the question or refusal to reply. A very important observation was that at one side use of alcohol is a symbol of social status in society, for example in

* Name changed, from a village in Kaithal District.

all socio-economic sections of society serving alcohol to guests, visit bars, serving alcohol in social functions/ceremonies like marriages, parties etc. is considered as a status symbol, whereas another aspect of alcohol abuse is that effected families feel that it leads to degradation of social status. But the reality is that the entry point in the name of social status is one of the root causes of problematic use in many cases.

Neighbours of Alcohol Effected Families

Neighbours are the most important part of a person's social life. In traditional Indian culture the place of neighbour is compared with brothers and it is said that neighbours play an important role in the families of each other. A common proverb in Haryana is भाई दूर पड़ौसी नेड़े (Brothers are far but neighbours are more close and near) signifies the importance to the neighbours who acquires a role like a family member. Therefore, it is very essential to have a good relationship with neighbours, which is a mutual concern and based on both side's feelings for each other. In case of the families in which alcohol is used a question arises, can a mutual relationship be possible with alcoholic's family? This question was asked, explored and analysed that what your neighbours feel about your family (alcoholic's family)? The results show that a 44.8 per cent respondent said that their neighbours were sympathetic for them and feel concerned about the problems of the family. There are 15.5 per cent who said that their neighbours feel disturbed and label the family as a stigma on the locality. These families shared their experiences and also showed their helplessness and guilt because of the problems of heavy alcohol use by their family member. Another response to the question was how many feel unconcerned, 28.5 per cent respondents said that their neighbours were not at all concerned with them and have no relationship with them. Around 9.8 per cent respondents said that their neighbours want to get rid of our family. As many as 1.4 per cent respondent refused to reply this question, but their gesture was not very appropriate on this issue which is the indicator of a negative feeling and sufferings (Table 5.1).

A further observation and analysis of this response found that the majority of the families with alcohol problems do not have good neighbourhood relationships. There were cases of fights, disputes and police reports against each other. When contacts with some of the neighbours of alcohol affected families were made, they shared their agony and explained the problems they suffer with. The most common problem explained by them was ill effects on their children, disturbance to peaceful life etc. In one of the Mohalla of Palwal city in Faridabad district when a neighbour came to know about my visit to the alcoholic's family (his neighbour) he, himself contacted the research team and insisted to help him by convincing the alcohol affected family to change their place of residence. He explained that how they spent their nights and were always fearful of any unexpected incidence because of the alcohol drinking in their neighbourhood.

Table 5.1 What your neighbours feel about your family

Response	*No. of respondents*	*Percentage*
Sympathetic	359	44.8
Stigma on locality	124	15.5
Feel unconcerned	228	28.5
Want to get rid of	78	09.8
No response	11	01.4
Total	800	100.0

What the Relatives Feel and How they Behave

Alcohol drinking especially excessive drinking by one or more family members results in several negative consequences for others including the relatives. In Indian social system where network of kinship relations determine the family interaction, and play very important role in important family matters like, settlement of marriages, consultations for sale and purchase of property, family disputes, division of property, education of female members etc., some relations are given so much importance that the decision taken by the relative is last and final and the effected family members had no option other than to obey it, among these kinship relations the important relationship is 'Amitate'* relations in which the sister of father and her in-laws are given a very special status. The decisions taken by them are given due importance.

* Amitate: when a special role is given to the father's sister. The father's sister gets more respect than the mother.

It was observed that relatives of the drinkers' family were also affected and have to play a role in many ways. Specially the relatives from the wife side of the alcoholic were seriously concerned. Other relatives such as drinker's sister and brother-in-law (sister's husband), daughter and her in-laws etc. were also found playing important roles in many ways such as financial help, educating, counseling, pressurizing the drinker, helping children in education, helping in agriculture/farming/business etc. in different capacities. Therefore, the feelings of the relatives of the alcoholics towards the family affected by alcohol use were observed and analysed. The feelings and reactions of the relatives shows that response of the relatives varies from an active help to that their relatives feel sympathy towards the condition of the family and also tried to help, but now when there is no solution from the drinker's side they started withdrawing them. On the other side 14.8 per cent families said that now the relations are ceased. Nearly 32.7 per cent families accepted that their relatives help at the time of need, while 16.4 per cent families said that now the relatives have no concern with them (Table 5.2).

Table 5.2 Feelings of relatives about the alcohol affected families

Response	*No. of respondents*	*Percentage*
Sympathetic	258	32.2
Relations ceased	118	14.8
Help at the time of need	262	32.7
No concern	131	16.4
No response	31	03.9
Total	800	100.0

A detailed and informal discussion with the family members was held and it was found that in the initial stage when alcohol use was casual and for the sake of entertainment and hospitality to the relatives, the relatives were equally enjoying. But when gradually the situation started worsening, for some time, some relatives helped, co-operated and extended their helping hand sympathetically. As the level of drinking started increasing and the alcoholic person involved in excessive drinking the relatives started withdrawing themselves. It was also observed that only some relatives expressed their concern for these families. Otherwise the people who enjoyed drinking alcohol with the alcoholic person, now completely withdrew themselves. In many cases financial limitations were also found responsible for the ceased relations with close relatives.

Friends of the Alcohol Affected Families and their Feelings

The reactions and feelings of the family friends were also examined by the present study. The family friends who were the main persons and significantly influence the family decisions have an important say in the event of crisis in a family. Usually next to the important family members, the family friends were consulted in almost all-important family matters and in many cases it is reciprocal. But when alcohol entered in the family and the male members in alcohol-affected family gradually become incapable of performing family roles the position of family friends becomes very crucial. To know the feelings and reactions of family friends in such situation a question was asked, 'How do the family friends react at this stage of your family'?

Table 5.3 Feelings of family friends about the alcohol affected families

Response	*No. of respondents*	*Percentage*
Co-operative for proper solutions	298	37.2
Started alienation	156	19.5
No concern	203	25.4
Total dissociation	135	16.9
No response	08	1.0
Total	800	100.0

Table 5.3 explains that 37.2 per cent families accepted that the family friends were co-operative in various difficult situations and for finding proper solutions of the problems. A very good percentage of families (19.5%) said that now their family friends have started alienating. About 25.4 per cent respondents said that now the friends of their hay days have no concern with them, even after sending messages and requests to come and see, they never respond. Some respondents became emotional and started discussing that how all these friends used to come and participate in almost all the affairs of their family, they remembered some events of mutual help, but now everything is disturbed and it was only because of alcohol. A total dissociation was reported by 16.9 per cent families and 1 per cent refused to answer this question (Figure 5.1).

Figure 5.1 Feelings of family friends about the alcohol affected families

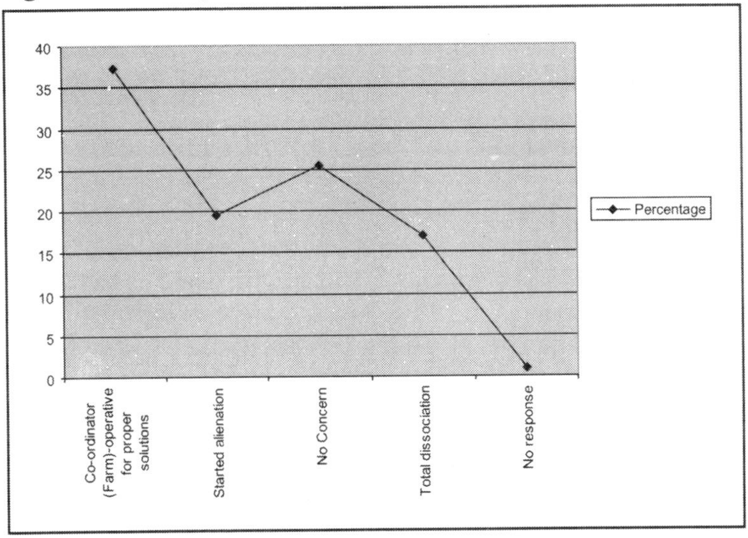

Therefore, it can be concluded that a large majority (61.8%) of the family friends had ceased their relations, when the family suffered in many ways because of regular and excessive use of alcohol by the problem drinker/drinkers in the family. When the matter was discussed in details many versions were explained by the suffering families such as, in majority cases these friends initiated the use of alcohol in the suffering family. They all used to enjoy parties, late night drink celebrations (even in very small and insignificant events), it was a common routine of these friends, sometimes at home and sometimes outside home, may be at another friend's home. But now when one of their friends has lost everything because of, regular and excessive use of alcohol, these friends started disappearing gradually.

Celebration of Social and Religious Festivals and Family Rituals

Family gatherings on some social and religious festivals or family functions may be subject to disruption because of the problems of alcoholics/problem drinkers. It was observed and also supported by the data that in many families either such occasions were avoided or if celebrated the family members suffered because of the problems created by the alcoholic person in the family itself. Moreover, in India, some festivals are linked with the use of intoxicants such as *Shivaratri* (distribution of *bhang* as *prashad* of Lord Shiva) and *Holi* linked with use of alcohol and *pakoras of bhang* (snacks prepared of cannabis). A good number of gods in Hindu mythology are even today offered alcohol/wine usually described as an offering to the deity.

The ancient Indian literature has many references of use of alcohol usually described as *somras* on various occasions of festivities and sacred rites. Aryans used to drink this liquid on all festivals and religious celebrations. *Rigveda* has more than hundred hymns to describe various uses of *somras*, for example, it described *somras* as *amrita* and all the gods drank Soma:

अपाम सोमममृता अभूम
अगन्म ज्योतिरविदाम देवान् ।
किं नूनमस्मान्कृणवदरातिः
किमु धूर्तिरमृतं मर्त्यस्य ।। (Rigveda viii, 48.3)

'We have drunk Soma; we have become immortal; we have gone to the light; we have found the gods. What can hostility now do to us and what the malice of mortal man. O immortal one?' In other words, it can be said that the exhilerating power of *'Soma'* led to its being regarded as a device drink bestowing immortal life. Hence, it is called *amrita*, draught of immortality. All the gods drank *Soma*: they drank it to gain immortality, it confers immortality not only on gods, but also on men.

Such examples in the religious literatures were supported by the venerated *rishimunis* (hindu saints) who use various drugs such as *somras, bhang* (cannabis) for concentration, or perhaps to strengthen their capacity to keep their mind away from worldly things. This conveys a powerful message to a common man about the utility of such intoxicating substances. Therefore, it is now recognized that a large number of 'alcoholics' drink in a manner heavily influenced by drinking customs and the general rate of consumption in the socio-cultural environment (Ahlstrom-Laasko, 1975).

The initial use of alcohol in the name of religious celebrations or social customs may gradually become the problem of heavy drinking. Alcohol used in the name of cultural practices slowly and gradually become a problem drinking and neither the alcoholic nor the family over, thought that it will result to the family disturbances to the extent that the heavy drinking started disturbing important religious celebrations and family festivals. When, it was explored that how the problem drinking in such families affects the family festivals or social ceremonies, the respondents shared many important information. Table 5.4 explains that what happens during celebrations in the families suffering from alcohol drinking.

Table 5.4 What happens at the time of festivals or any social function in family

Response	*No. of respondents*	*Percentage*
All celebrate joyfully	109	13.6
Fear of some mishappening	478	59.8
Members other than alcoholic celebrate	121	15.1
Not able to participate in celebrations	78	9.8
No response	14	1.7
Total	800	100.0

The data shows that a large majority 59.8 per cent of the respondents suffers from the fear that there must be some mishappening in the function. The absence of drinker was also reported in some families as 15.1 per cent said that members other than alcoholics celebrate, while 13.6 per cent respondents said that we all celebrate and enjoy because consuming alcohol is an important part on these functions and if the problem arises the drinkers manage it of their own, it has been a common affair for them. Some respondents (9.8%) said that they were not able to participate in the celebrations and 1.7 per cent refused to reply this question. In a detailed discussion the respondents and other family members revealed many interesting and important information. A big majority said that when the matter for celebration of any such occasion or function comes before the family an inherent fear of some mishappening start coming in their mind and they suffer with it till the celebration is over. In some villages the cases of fights, brawls, use of arms, firing, police case and even death of some one were also shared. A lady* in one of the villages in district Faridabad

* Name is kept confidential.

Figure 5.2 What happens at the time of festivals or any social function in family?

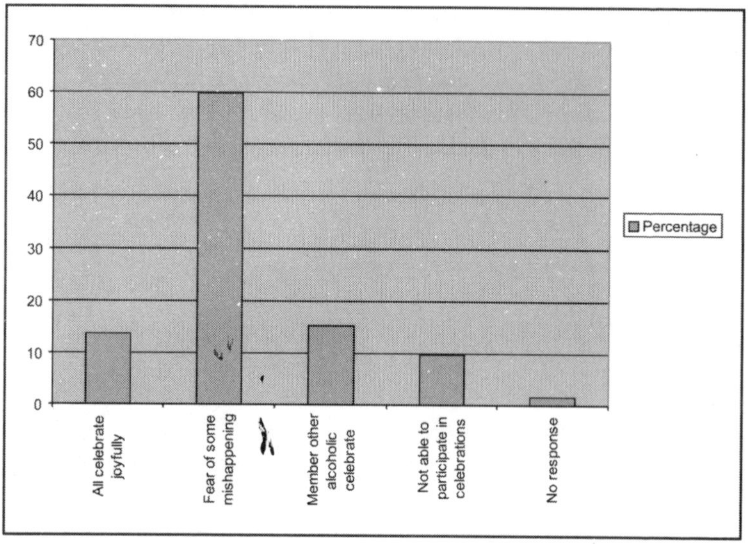

explained her agony that how the marriage ceremony of her daughter was disturbed by her drunkard husband. The situation became so critical that the marriage ceremony could only be performed when some important community people intervened and the drunkard father was taken to some other place. Another incidence was explained by an employees family in Karnal city where a child (with his mother) explained the story that how his birthday cake was thrown away by his drunkard father and his mother was beaten before his friends who came to celebrate his birthday 'मेरे बर्थडे केक को डैडी ने फेंक दिया और मेरी मम्मी को बहुत मारा।' Thus, the data reveals that the families suffer a lot because of problem drinking and the important functions such as marriages, birthdays, family gatherings, celebration of festivals were celebrated with a psychological fear of some mishappening. Some of the families has started avoiding such functions and only perform important ceremonies so that the problems can be avoided. One of the lady said 'हम तो बस सब्र कर लेते हैं। काम चलाऊ सा प्रोग्राम बना के सब कुछ निपटा देते हैं क्योंकि इसने (शराबी पति) कुछ छोड़ा ही नही; और यदि कुछ करें तो कब उत्पात कर दे यह नहीं पता।' (We keep patience, perform only basic needed ceremonies and finish the programme as early as possible because we never know that when he (alcoholic) will create problem). The social celebrations and participation in these celebrations is a mutual and reciprocal affair. For the families, it is essential to participate in social functions. But in such families where the problem drinking can lead to disruption of such functions, participation in other's functions also becomes a problem. Therefore, it was also explored that how the families with alcohol problems cope up with such situations. A question in this context was asked, 'Do you or your family members participate in the social functions/ceremonies of your relatives'? Table 5.5 explains that how the families cope up with the situation.

Table 5.5 Do you or your family participate in social functions/ceremonies of relatives?

Response	*No. of respondents*	*Percentage*
Yes, under compulsion	383	47.9
Send some representative	213	26.6
Only symbolic	150	18.8
Not able to participate	50	6.2
No response	04	0.5
Total	800	100.0

It is evident from the table that about 48 per cent respondents participate in such functions but under compulsion. Some of them explained that they have experiences of going together in functions and had to face the problems created by the alcoholic after consuming alcohol for which they have no words to explain. 26.6 per cent respondents said they send some other family member as the family members representative in the function and avoid sending the problem drinker, while 18.8 per cent said that they have to participate because of social compulsions, otherwise they always suffer with fear of something untoward, which can give bad name to them, and 6.2 per cent showed their inability to participate in any function because of the reasons clear, that alcohol is the main problem but they were unable to explain (Figure 5.3).

Figure 5.3 Do you or your family participate in social functions/ceremonies of relatives?

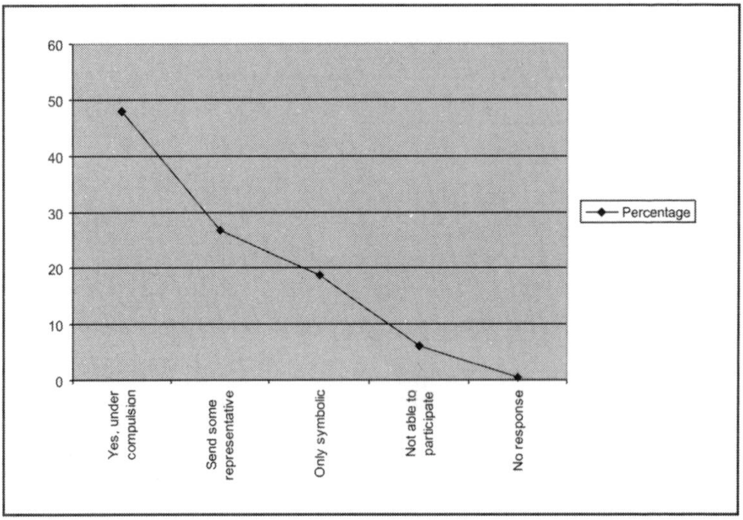

Behaviour of Problem Drinkers/Alcoholics in Social Functions/Family Celebrations and Social Ceremonies

An attempt has been made to see that how the problem drinkers behave in social functions/celebrations and social ceremonies. The family members especially the spouse of the alcoholics/problem drinkers remains under severe psychological strain because of two main reasons, (i) whether they should participate in social functions/celebrations or not? (ii) what will happen if they participate? So far as the first reason is concerned the participation in such family functions is a social compulsion for them and, which is reciprocal in nature. In India social customs and rituals are considered as an important part of celebrations into which whole family, relatives and friends join the function. If the family misses the function because of alcoholic's behaviour the entire family suffer isolation. Then the next question, that what will happen if they participate? The family members always have apprehension of something wrong on the part of the alcoholic/problem drinking and suffer from the fear of problems, which may be created by the alcoholic/problem drinker. The entire burden of keeping social relations intact remains with the spouse of the alcoholic (mainly wife) who suffer with multi devotional problems and unable to explain to anybody. The situation is only limited up to lip sympathy.

Table 5.6 Alcoholic/problem drinker created problems in social functions/ceremonies

Response	*No. of respondents*	*Per cent*
Never	135	16.9
Seldom	415	51.8
Usually	114	14.3
All the time	133	16.6
No response	03	00.4
Total	800	100.0

Table 5.6 indicates that the overwhelming majority of the respondents, 82.7 per cent, said that the alcohol drinkers of their family created problems in one or the other way in such functions. In a further analysis about the frequency of incidences 51.8 per cent seldom created problems , 14.3 per cent usually and 16.6 per cent always, while 16.9 per cent said that their family member drink alcohol but he never created any problem.

Thus, one can conclude from the analysis that the alcohol use in families specially heavy drinking creates problems in social functions and celebrations which affect the social life, status and reputation of the family and the main sufferers are the female members specially wife and children.

Alcohol Abuse and Visiting Police Station/Jail by the Family

Excessive drinking produces a variety of closely interrelated social problems in Indian society. Confronting with law and going to police station or imprisonment are still considered as stigmatic in Indian society. Violence within and outside the home is frequent in many Indian communities and a substantial proportion of it is believed to be alcohol-related (Saxena, 1999). Street brawls and group violence often happen after drinking and approach to law enforcement agencies specially police are the most common ways to deal with. Therefore, it becomes necessary to study how frequently the families with alcohol problems have to go to police station or jail.

Table 5.7 Do the alcoholic or family members have to go to police station/jail because of alcohol use

Response	*No. of respondents*	*Percentage*
Never	381	47.6
Seldom	221	27.6
Usually	80	10.0
As a routine	63	7.9
No response	55	06.9
Total	800	100.0

Table 5.7 gives the information that do the families suffering with alcohol use have to go to police/jail. The question asked was a very personal question and the family members were reluctant to respond. The efforts were made through counter-questioning and cross-checking to find out the proper response. The data indicates that 47.6 per cent respondents said that they had never faced any such problem because of alcohol using family member. But this information may not be fully true because the family does not want to share such information for family prestige and social stigma. There are 27.6 per cent families who reported that they seldom had to go to police station or jail because of alcohol using person and 10 per cent said that it had been a usual affair. For 7.9 per cent families it was a routine and 6.9 per cent respondents refused to reply this question.

Accidents and Injuries

Many aspects of alcohol relate problems were found during discussions at the time of fieldwork. Accidents and injuries are one of the important parts of alcohol related problems the families face. The literature on alcohol's role in injuries is conventionally split into three divisions, (i) unintentional injuries or accidents, (ii) intentional act, (iii) self-directed violence (Room et al., 2002). Injuries or sometimes casualties because of intentional or unintentional reasons to the drunker or others add to the problems of the already suffering families. In many cases it was difficult to differentiate the intentional acts or unintentional or intentional injuries because it was difficult to draw a boundary between these. For instance, although automobile crash one conventionally assumed to be unintentional, a particular crash may have been intentional. Provoking for fight under the influence of alcohol resulting to violence and injuries to the involved may be an intentional act. During discussions with the alcohol affected families many such cases were found.

Alcohol is held responsible for a large number of accidents and injuries in India, which include road accidents, farm machinery accidents, e.g. threshers, tractor, and other agricultural equipment, pedestrian injuries, and household accidents. The studies reveal that alcohol plays a role in whole range of injuries, ranging from falls, mishandling of tools and equipment, road traffic injuries, violence and assaults. Unfortunately, in most of the developing countries no proper record is available to scientifically analyse the role of alcohol in accidents and injuries. But the available records and literature reveal that such figures are high (ibid.). For example, in the cape Metropolitan Area of South Africa it is estimated that, among patients attending public hospitals, alcohol plays a contributory role in between 38 per cent and 49 per cent of cases involving trauma. Road traffic injuries are by far the most common cause of alcohol-related death in many developing countries. The National Road Research Institute in India summarized that a third of all drivers on intercity roads were under the influence of alcohol, and a quarter of all major traffic crashes are alcohol related. The Agriculture Research Institute estimated that half of all farm machinery accidents that led to loss of limbs or life were related to alcohol, with or without the presence of other drug. Increased traffic congestion on roads, poor vehicle and road maintenance and the presence of unlicensed and unskilled drivers on the roads are contributory factors, but alcohol consumption certainly adds another potent influence to India's high accident rates (WHO, 1999).

Therefore, keeping in mind the above situation about the role of alcohol an effort was made to know how many alcohol drinkers were involved in accidents in the families with alcohol problems.

Table 5.8 Alcohol drinkers involved in accident because of drinking

Response	*No. of respondents*	*Percentage*
Yes	422	52.7
No	318	39.8
Don't know	36	4.5
No response	24	3.0
Total	800	100.0

Table 5.8 shows that 52.7 per cent of the respondents families accepted that alcohol drinkers in their family were involved in one or the other accident, which resulted to many serious problems in the family, about 40 per cent said no to this question and 4.5 per cent said that they do not know anything about it. 3 per cent have not given any response to this question. In a further analysis it was revealed by the family members that in many families it had become a routine that the drinkers were found involved with one or the other type of accident or injury. In one such family in a village in Karnal district (Haryana) the drinker was on bed with plaster on his left leg. While talking with him he himself told that he got this injury when he was badly drunk and fell down in his farm. A spouse (wife) in one other family very bitterly explained her grief and sorrows she had to suffer due to her husband's physical injuries and accidents because of heavy drinking.

It can be concluded from the data as well as observation that the accidents and injuries because of alcohol use are of many types and affect the families very seriously in many ways.

Alcohol Use and Violence

Violence inside and outside the home is frequent in India and a substantial proportion of it is believed to be alcohol-related (Saxena, 2002). Domestic violence such as wife beating, child abuse, and breaking household material under the influence of alcohol is common. Another aspect of the violence is the outside home violence which is in the form of street brawls and group violence which also happen after drinking. Therefore, an attempt was also made to study this part of alcohol problems.

Table 5.9 Alcohol drinkers involved in street brawls after use of alcohol

Response	*No. of respondents*	*Percentage*
Never	189	23.6
Seldom	455	56.9
Usually	94	11.8
Daily	56	7.0
No response	06	0.7
Total	800	100.0

Table 5.9 explains that 23.6 per cent respondents said the alcohol drinkers in their family never involved in any street brawls or any fight, while about 57 per cent of the alcohol using families said such incidences happen seldom and 11.8 per cent said the alcoholics in family are usually involved in street brawls. 7 per cent respondents said that it had been a daily affair in the family and the family is suffering a lot because of it.

During fieldwork the researcher himself witnessed such incidences in some villages as well as mohallas in cities. In one such incidence in a village* in the night of winter season, in the month of December at about 9.00 p.m., an alcoholic started shouting from the roof of his house. He was heavily drunk and was shouting in a very high volume. After sometime some neighbours started rebuking him and then he came down keeping a long stick (Lathi) in his hand and started hitting on the doors of the neighbour. Some women from his (drinker's) family tried to stop him but he started pushing them aside and attacked on these women with fist blows. Some male members came there and fisticuffs started. Meantime the neighbour on whose door the drunkard was hitting came with a long stick in his hand with other male members and a severe fight took place in which many people were injured including the drunkard and some women. The whole incidence occurred up to midnight and ended with the police intervention only.

Therefore, one can conclude that the incidences of street brawls are common after drinking, which many a times leads to serious consequences for the families in which alcohol is used. Some families explained their woe that how they had to face police and court because of it, and suffered heavy financial loss.

Social Ostracism

The effects of drinking on family and the sufferings of families with alcohol problems have been discussed in detail. Greater use of alcohol results in a greater number of problems in different areas of social and personal life. It has also been established that frequency of heavy drinking or intoxication is a major predictor of alcohol-related problems (Knupher, 1984; Greenfield, 1986; Single and Wortley, 1993; Room et al., 1995). It was observed that after a considerable

* Name is not disclosed to maintain confidentiality as desired by the villages.

period of sufferings from alcohol related problems the family came across a very critical situation in their social relationships. During data collection and interaction with the family members it was noticed that after sometime the family suffers social ostracism, which further effects the family and its members in many ways.

Table 5.10 Does the family suffer from social ostracism?

Response	*No. of respondents*	*Percentage*
Yes	542	67.8
No	189	23.6
Don't know	47	5.9
No response	22	2.7
Total	800	100.0

Because of continuous and heavy use of alcohol in the family a good number of families (67.8%) accepted that they suffer social ostracism (Table 5.10). In more detailed and informal discussions with the family members many new and hidden facts came into picture. The family members explained that many times they had to come across through humiliating situations not only before the relatives, neighbours but also with those who had been the part of this game at one time but not reached to the level where we have reached. They explained it in clear words, 'हम तो अब उनके आगे भी शर्मशार हो जाते हैं जो कभी हमारे घर में हमारे आदमी के साथ बैठ कर शराब पीते थे। अब वो स्याणे हैं और हम बरबाद। सच है जिसकी गाड़ी उल्टी हो जाये उसे सब अहमक कहते हैं। हमारे साथ भी यही हो रहा है।' (We have to feel ashamed before the people who had been drinking alcohol with our person in our home. Now they became wise and we are ruined. It is true that when things go otherwise everybody label as fool, the same happened with us.)

The family explained that how the relatives, neighbours, friends, and other acquaintances had now started ignoring their family from social functions such as marriage parties, birthday parties, common festivals and even many of them do not give any information of death or illness of their family members. Children of alcoholic parents suffer humiliations at school, playgroups, in friend circle and even in the grocery shops where many of such families have their accounts. This all lead to social ostracism of the family.

It was also observed that the problem of social ostracism does not come in the early days of alcohol consumption and related behaviour but it seems to be a spontaneous response to the continuous and longer period of alcohol use and problems associated with it. Many families accepted that it was not four or five years back with us what we are facing now. It is because the alcohol use in a limited level has social sanction. Therefore, one can conclude that out of 23.6 per cent families who said no to the sufferings of social ostracism may suffer from this problem after sometime if the quantity and frequency of alcohol use increases and the problems of alcohol use and intoxicated behaviour will be more apparent.

Thus, on the basis of above discussion it can be summarized that, the family/families with alcohol problems have many social complications and the longer and greater the use of alcohol the problems become more and more complicated. The continuous use of alcohol significantly effects the social position of the family in society as 92.5 per cent families accepted it. So far as the relationship with neighbours is concerned about 45 per cent respondents said that their neighbours were sympathetic for them and feel concerned about their problems, 15.5 per cent labeled it as a stigma on locality, 28.5 per cent feel unconcerned while about 10 per cent neighbours want to get rid of them. It was found that the relations with relatives were also severely disturbed due to continuous and heavy drinking of alcohol. About 15 per cent of the respondents said that their relatives had ceased their relations with them and 16.4 per cent had no concern. The continuous and problematic use of alcohol also affected the friendly relations of family the data indicate that 19.5 per cent respondents said that their family friends had started alienating and 25.4 per cent friends had no concern with them, while about 17 per cent had total dissociation for quite long time, it means that a majority (11.8%) of family friends had ceased their relations.

Indian social life, which is very rich in festivals and social celebrations, was also found severely disturbed in the alcohol using families. It was reported that all the family members especially female members (wife, grown-up daughters and mother) of the alcoholics suffer a psychological stress at the time of celebration of festivals or social functions and ceremonies in the family. About 60 per cent respondents suffer from the fear of some mishappening;

about 10 per cent were not able to even participate in festivals due to continuous and heavy drinking of alcohol by one or in some cases more family members. About 15 per cent respondents said that the alcoholic members of the family do not participate in the festivals while others celebrate. So far as the participation in social functions/ceremonies is concerned about 48 per cent said that even the situation doesn't allow, yet they have to participate under compulsion, 26.6 per cent said that whatsoever the situation, but one have to live in society and to maintain relations they send some representative, while 18.8 per cent said that their participation remains only symbolic. Nearly 6 per cent respondent families said that the situation has become so worse that now they are not able to participate in any social function or ceremony. The previous experiences family members had suffered because of the behaviour of the alcoholic/problem drinker compel them to think many times about participating in these functions and then they take decision keeping in view the prestige of their own family as well as the host family. About 52 per cent respondent families accepted that the alcohol using members of their families seldom created problems in social functions, and 14.3 per cent said usually the problems were created, while 16.6 per cent said that alcoholics all the time create problems in their families after drinking. Some of the respondent families were found suffering with the problems of visiting police stations/jails. About 45.5 per cent families said that they had to visit police stations and jails because of various offences of the alcohol using persons in their family. Out of this about 8 per cent families visit police station or jail as a routine.

While enquiring about involvement in accident, the respondent families reported that 52.7 per cent were involved in accidents, 39.8 said no and 4.5 per cent said they don't know about it. Therefore, it can be concluded from the data and discussions, that the accidents and injuries because of alcohol use are of various types and the families have to suffer a lot and in many ways. About 57 per cent respondents said that the alcoholics in their families seldom involved in street brawls, 11.8 per cent were usually involved and for 7 per cent it was a daily affair, which is a very serious problem for peaceful social life. Because of continuous and heavy use of alcohol and the problems related to alcohol use a situation comes when the family feels social ostracism. The study reveals that about 68 per cent families were suffering from social ostracism, a serious threat to the family and for the next generation.

Therefore, on the basis of above discussion, available data and the observation of the research team, it can be concluded that the social life of the families with alcohol use is disturbed to serious extents. Both aspects of social life, within the family and outside relations suffer seriously because of continuous and excessive use of alcohol. It has direct impact on the socialization process, the main sufferers are the children in family, who become the victim, and in many cases it was found that male children also become alcoholics or problem drinkers in adulthood/later life and female children were abused in many ways. Women suffer to an extent that they loose their self-identity and keep her involved in managing the family problems created by alcoholics/problems drinkers.

6

Treatment and Rehabilitation of Alcoholics

Social Work Intervention Through Family

Alcoholism, alcohol dependence, heavy drinking, problem drinking are various forms of alcohol abuse which is a serious social problem across the world including India. This is responsible for many problems in family as discussed in the preceding chapters. The complications of this problem, its nature, magnitude, prevalence, causes and precipitating factors present in the social systems need a concerted effort to deal with it. Moreover, the myths and misconceptions about alcohol and its effects and socio-cultural link to it makes it more complex specially in rural Indian society where illiteracy and faith in superstitions are very common. It is important to deal with this problem through a scientific process and professional approach so that its devastating effects on 'family' (basic institution of society) can be controlled effectively.

The family, is a primary and the most intimate and influential institution in which human development takes place, can play an effective role in the treatment, recovery and rehabilitation of alcoholics. Family is defined as 'a group of persons united by the ties of marriage, blood or adoption, consisting of a single household, interacting and inter-communicating with each other in their respective social roles of husband and wife, mother and father, son and daughter, brother and sister creating a common culture' (Burgess and Locke, 1945). This explains its characteristics which has significant influence on family members and can be used to sort-out many problems within its relationships. The important part is that these relationships must be used positively and constructively with a clear understanding of human behaviour and social conditions. Therefore, these important and inmate features of the 'family' can be aptly used by the social workers when they come across with such problems during their work in different communities.

This chapter provides the guidelines for basic skills and processes needed to be used by social workers as a counselor and as a family therapist. The chapter is divided in two parts; part I deals with family counseling and part II with family therapy.

Part I
Family Counseling

Family counseling is a process of helping a family to find out solutions for the problems through a professional relationship based on trust. It helps to understand and cope better with stresses and strains of family life. It is based on the premise that family is a source of care, support, encouragement, love and affection which can be powerful means to help alcoholics and the suffering families to come out of the problem. Sometimes relationships within families are under doubt and full of strain and stress to the extent that the suffering family members feel isolated and overlooked in the family.

Families with alcoholics face a number of problems including violence, separation, divorce, problems of children, disturbances in family functions and cultural celebrations, inappropriate role models and financial difficulties. Alcohol dependence does not disturb and ruin the family abruptly instead it enters slowly and silently, until it is finally detected and is perhaps then the loss is realized by the family. However, by that time it had already affected the family to serious extent. Alcohol dependence is not a condition which once treated can be completely cured but as a progressive disease and chronic problem, with a tendency to relapse, it is always likely to topple the individual back to the same situation of dependence if the individual and his/her family do not take adequate precautions.

Treating alcoholics therefore involves more than just getting the alcohol user to stop using alcohol. It also needs a professional expertise through scientific intervention with continuous counseling and other therapeutic approaches to the family and thus improving family relationships and functioning of each member of the family. At this stage if the social worker feels that the whole family is needed to be involved, family counseling is considered appropriate with the following steps:

Steps in Family Counseling

There are different steps in family counseling, which are carried out in the course of sessions with the client and his/her family (Nirmala and Murthy, 2005). In the ideal situation, the social worker as a counselor should follow the steps in the sequence given here; for instance, before counseling is started it is important to make a proper assessment of the impact of the client's alcohol use on the family and on himself/herself. The families of alcoholic do not have proper and adequate knowledge about the problem of alcohol abuse and the loss they have suffered because of this. These families often come with different myths and misconceptions about alcohol, its use and effects and expectations from the social worker. In such situation social worker as a counselor will have to be flexible and should select the appropriate intervention techniques. The intervention process should be carefully developed and divided in different sessions in consultation with the family members. Different sessions may address different issues and should be structured according to the need of the family members. Active involvement of all the family members is necessary for effective results.

Establish Positive Relationship

Addiction to alcohol is often understood as a problem stemming from the lack of voluntary control. Family members often feel angry, disappointed and frustrated because they think the person takes alcohol deliberately. The spouse and children of the alcoholic are unable to discuss the problem with anyone due to the stigma attached to such issues, and keep all their emotions suppressed. The family is disturbed to the extent that often, negative emotions towards the alcoholic are expressed, and there are lot of manifestations in the form of anger, hostility and resentment towards the person. In such situation family members have no option other than to leave the family to the fate. This all leads to disturb the intra-family relationship and lacks to establish faith in any outside individual or agency coming forward to help the family.

Relationship is the base of all help therefore, it is most important for the social worker to establish positive and purposeful relation with the affected family and the person.

Ventilation

It means helping the client to express strong feelings when he/she is hesitant to do so because of his/her uncertainty regarding the worker's response, or because he simply does not have the words to express these feelings (Upadhyay, 2003). In alcohol affected families such hindrances are very common. Ventilation helps family members in removing their suppressed emotions and feelings. This intervention provides emotional support by listening, being sympathetic and non-judgemental, and acknowledging the family members' feelings. As a result it allows rapport to be built up with the family members so that further counseling becomes effective.

Preparing

While preparing the family, the social worker should introduce himself/herself and express concern with genuineness and warmth. Try to collect general information about the family and the client like individual's name, family composition, occupation and social status etc. instead of directly starting and identifying them only as

Figure 6.1 Social worker and NGO representatives in session with the affected person

the patient's relative. Family members as well as the individual should be assured about the confidentiality of the information shared, and give response to the questions (Figure 6.1). The social worker should keenly observe the problems that the family members are facing and allow them to talk in the way they like to communicate but, suitable to the process of treatment.

The course of the interview is determined by the family members (with the help of social worker) and what he/she would like to talk about is decided. The social worker as a counselor basically works as a link to supportive listening and communicates an understanding to the family members and other relatives who show concern.

Assessment of the Problem

Assessment includes identifying strengths and resources that exist within the client, within the systems that makeup the client's environment and in the transactions within this ecosystem (Johnson and Yanca, 2011). In developing a proper understanding of person and his/her problem the worker tries to understand the feelings, thoughts and actions of the clients (alcoholic) and members of his/her family. 'Assessment is a process and product of understanding on which action is based'(Siporin, 1975). Alcoholism affects a number of areas in life such as personal life of family members, health of alcoholic, spouse, children, social life of family, financial, occupational and professional areas of family members, education of children etc. Before intervention, the social worker should have a comprehensive understanding of the impact of addiction on the family as well as on the alcoholic. Therefore, assessment is useful in collection and analysis of information and related with available facts so that the problem could be identified in its reality.

The social worker should talk to the family member(s) on the important aspects of the problem such as knowledge about alcohol use and level of dependence, the reactions of family members towards the alcoholic, changes in the roles of the family members, the effect of alcohol dependence on the alcoholic's job/profession/occupation. While discussing with the family, neighbours, relatives and friends available social support that the family members have in terms of immediate family, friends and other tertiary support groups (like the religious groups, self-help group etc.) must be carefully assessed.

The factors responsible for continuous alcohol use in terms of craving, withdrawal symptoms, negative moods, peer pressure, coping with stress, handling pain, family problems and any other should be taken care. Perceptions of family members about these issues are useful to understand, as they may be quite different from the alcoholic's own perceptions. Such differences should be carefully noted and should be addressed at appropriate time during intervention.

Psycho-social Education

It has been observed that the members of the family generally expect the alcohol dependent person to have voluntary control over alcohol use but it is not possible for the alcoholic due to his/her physical and psychological compulsions, e.g. physical as well as psychological dependence on alcohol and in some cases social factors precipitating alcohol use. They need to be educated about the individual's problem as an illness that cannot be cured by will power alone. The factors responsible for dependence of alcohol are to be identified and family members are made aware of these factors.

The social worker should discuss the effects of alcohol abuse with facts and compare alcoholism with any other physical illness and explain with the help of examples and symptoms and experiences. The family members should be helped by explaining in simple terms that just as any physical illness affects your ability to function normally, e.g. your appetite, sleep and work, alcohol dependence also affects these functions. Alcohol addiction can be treated like any physical illness. However, its treatment is not 'one time' like treating cholera and malaria. It is rather illness that needs life-long precautions and care, as in the case of diabetes. The earlier the illness (alcohol addiction) is identified and treated the easier it is to control, similar to any other chronic illness.

Discuss the pattern with which the problem started in the client, right from first-use of alcohol, and how it progressed. Inform and alert them about social factors which are present in surroundings of the suffering family and precipitate alcohol use, such as social functions, the role of friends and relatives, profit or loss in business, in agriculture and farming, tension or pressure of work/job.

Relapse Prevention

Relapse is a process which is very common among alcohol dependent persons. Normally it is understood as the act of taking a drink after a period of abstinence, following treatment. While the individual may be motivated to give up the alcohol when first seeking treatment, the will-power to stay sober is not sufficient by itself in the long run. The individual needs to be equipped with very practical strategies to handle high-risk situations. The family needs to provide support in these efforts.

Inform firmly the client and his/her family members that alcohol abuse/dependence can be a chronic and relapsing condition, and that will-power alone is not enough for staying sober. Support your statement with facts and examples which have been collected during discussion and collection of facts. Make the family aware that they need to assist the individual in identifying common relapse triggers. Educate both client and family members on how to handle these triggers. Give responsibilities to the spouse/elder brother/sister/uncle for taking care of time schedule of the alcoholic for personal care such as timings for breakfast, lunch, dinner, bathing, attending to the routine work at his/her job or other occupation. Make family aware that it must consult family doctor/social worker when needed.

Handling peer pressure

With the help of examples and facts the social worker should explain the family that peer pressure is one of the most important factor leading to relapse. Family members often feel that the best solution is for the individual to avoid contact with alcohol users or alcoholic/s, and therefore prevent the person from meeting such friends. This does not solve the problem, and may even make the person defensive and hostile towards the family because meeting friends and sharing time with them is one of the important needs of a human being. Therefore, to prevent a person from meeting friends is not always possible.

The individual thus needs to be helped to cope with peer pressure by teaching him/her skills to refuse the use of alcohol, without affecting the relationship with alcohol-using friends (Nirmala and Murthy, 2005). Such action need a thorough understanding of age group of the alcoholic, his needs, interests, ability to cope with changes and adapting capabilities social worker is required to play an active role here. Keeps a constant watch on the activities of alcoholic and peer group. As far as possible avoids attending social functions (marriage, etc.) by the alcoholic.

Handling craving

Craving is a strong and irresistible desire to consume a particular substance such as food, chocolate, any drug or alcohol. But this fact is many times confusing the family of the alcoholic. Therefore, social worker should explain the family that craving is one of the main problems of continuing addiction to alcohol, and that the individual is likely to come across many situations that trigger craving. The family can help the client by supporting and encouraging him/her to express craving to the family or to anyone in the family whom he/she has trust. Neither criticizing nor confronting or panicking, as craving can be handled in ways other than using alcohol (though it may take time). Clarifying and understanding that the process of craving is temporary and after sometime it starts reducing. The family members should be advised to provide placebo whenever needed and give him/her something to eat or drink to direct the mind and attention. The craving is often reduced when a person's hunger or thirst is quenched. The responsible family members may be given specific assignment of distracting the individual by playing a game, reading a book, going to a movie, listening to music or going out to visit some relatives, etc. While selecting relatives precaution to be taken as alcohol use is avoided.

Coping with conflicts and stress

Conflicts and stress are common in everybody's life. Alcohol dependent person is also not exception to it. Generally, alcohol dependent persons tend to use alcohol as a way of coping with their conflicts and stressful situations. They need to re-learn adaptive coping strategies to deal with such situations. Coping strategies are of two types, i.e. emotion-focused and problem-focused:

Emotion-focused coping

Encourage the family to listen attentively to the person and support wherever needed. Getting emotional support from the family members helps significantly in facing problems.

Problem-focused coping

Educate the entire family about the process of problem solving. Using a systematic approach to problem solving lets people feel that they have control over problems in their lives. As the problems are put in a different perspective and significant family members are involved in finding a solution, the alcohol user recovers and feels unburdened and lowers his/her chance of relapse as a dysfunctional way of coping.

Alcohol-free Lifestyle

In the successful attempts made by the social worker and family a situation may come that after a long time when a person who has been spending most of his/her time in getting, using or recovering from the effects of alcohol, does not know what to do with him/her, with the time and the extra money available after quitting alcohol. This can be a difficult and worrying situation for the convalescing user and his/her family. Social worker should handle this situation by:

(a) Management of time: Without alcohol, the individual will be left with a lot of time on his/her hands. If this time is not managed wisely, it can lead to boredom, which may trigger a relapse. The family can be helped by helping the individual to schedule activities, not leaving him/her alone too often and engaging the person in some mutually interesting activity.

(b) Role functions: With progressive stage of alcoholism the alcoholic often reduces or stops taking responsibility and playing his/her role within the family. Another family member undertakes his/her role. Once the alcoholic recovers, he/she may be keen to take on that responsibility or role again (for example, earning for the family, making decisions). Family members may be hesitant to restore these roles and responsibilities to the recovering user because of lack of trust, doubt, or because someone else has taken up that role. Defining (or redefining) the role of recovering alcohol user in the context of the family is very important in order to reintegrate the person within the family. Therefore, the social worker should:

- Discuss this issue very carefully and tactfully with the family

- Encourage the issue and try to understand each other's views
- The client needs to be helped to accept the lack of trust from family members due to a number of experiences of broken promises
- The family also needs to be counseled on the need to normalize the activities of the individual and encourage role and responsibility
- Both need to sit together with the social worker/counselor settle and decide on what each needs to do (such issues may not be handled in a single attempt, if needed and some new situation comes it should be handled in different sessions)
- Emphasize the family about the need for positive reinforcement of the recovering person
- Caution the family against constantly bringing up past issue/s and putting the recovering person down for all the problems that he/she had created in the past.

(c) Management of finances: Alcohol dependence is associated with many financial losses as discussed earlier. During recovery the person is often confronted with financial difficulties of which he/she was earlier unaware. Encourage the family to work with the individual towards clearing debts, budgeting current expenses and taking decisions about future investments.

Coping with Relapse

As discussed earlier relapse is a very common problem with alcohol dependents. Family members often find it difficult to accept that the process of recovery is not easy rather it is uneven. They may believe that once the alcohol dependent person is admitted for treatment, he will remain alcohol-free for life. A lapse or relapse may come as a rude shock and for which they are not prepared to deal with the situation, and feel hurt and betrayed.

The social worker must prepare the family in clear and simple terms that relapse is very common during recovery, stress the need for continuous and regular follow-up, and advise the family to bring the individual to the treatment centre at the earliest in case of relapse.

Handling crises and emergency situations

- If the alcoholic becomes very violent and is a threat to the health and safety of the family members advise them to take the help of neighbours or even the law.
- If the person is not motivated for treatment and repeatedly troubles or threatens them, teach the family members to set limits by not compromising with his/her threats, and to take the help of other resources like temporarily shifting the place of residence, or shifting the family (at least the alcoholic and spouse) to more advanced treatment centre, or consulting more experienced professionals (psychiatrist, psychiatric social worker) ... to handle such threats.
- Encourage the family to be in touch with the social worker/counselor even if the alcoholic is unprepared to change. There are critical and crucial times such as illness, withdrawal, or following threat of job loss, financial difficulties when the individual can be persuaded by the family to seek treatment. This will provide emotional support to the family and strengthen to cope.

Indications for referral to family therapy

In certain situations during simply counseling the family may not be adequate. If at this stage counseling is not proving appropriate, and desired results are not coming, referral can be made for family therapy. Indications for family therapy include:

- Frequent relapses precipitated by interpersonal problems within the family
- Family problems that tend to maintain the dependence of the individual
- Non-compliance of family members with the counseling process.

II
Family Therapy

Family therapy is a range of techniques and strategies for helping families to resolve relationship problems, attain goals and functions more harmoniously. There are many variants of family therapy and more of them work on the central premise that relationship between family members can become rigid, so that behaviours between members tends to repeat compulsively a destructive pattern. This pattern may involve blaming or scapegoating a particular member of the family or coercive behaviours such as shouting, physical abuse, isolation and withdrawal. Such patterns of behaviour are very common in the families suffering with the problem of alcohol abuse and alcoholism.

Family therapy as a distinct professional practice within western cultures can be argued to have its origin in the social work movements of the 19th century in the United Kingdom and the United States (Broderick and Schrader, 1991). But formal development of family therapy dated to the 1940s and early 1950s with the founding of the American Association of Marriage Counselors and through the work of various independent clinicians and groups in 1942.

Family network therapy is a more recent mode of intervention. Its focus is on the individual, but the widest possible range of significant family members, as well as other important people in the individual's environment, deal together with an identified problem such as alcohol/drug abuse. The family and significant others are considered to be an important source of concrete social support, aid, and stability for the individual who is having disturbed functioning. The process is one of linking an individual whose life has become unhinged into a stressful and satisfying role in his or her social network (Friedlander and Apte, 1982).

In the families affected by alcohol abuse the relationship between family members are disturbed, faith on each other is lost and the whole family is in situation of obliteration. Therefore, this part provides the guidelines for basic skills, functions and competence needed to be used by social workers to intervene as a family therapist for the treatment of alcoholics and help the families effected with the problems due to alcohol abuse/alcoholism/ problem drinking (Leticia et al., 1996). These are given in a step-by-step process on the following broad topics:

- Engagement
- Problem Identification
- Developing a Social Diagnosis
- Change Facilitation

- Termination

These are guidelines, which the social worker (as a family therapist) may use with the affected families. As his experience grows, the social worker should then become more comfortable in using these guidelines in the therapy sessions. Examples are provided in boxes to illustrate the different phases. These had been derived from experiences of supervising postgraduate social work students in fieldwork settings, dealing with cases of alcoholism, case studies in the de-addiction clinics/centres, from the individual and group conferences, and from follow-up supervisory visits. It is important to note that each family and each situation is unique. There were many other interactions related to the individual, family, occupational and other related aspects of the problem.

Techniques

Family therapy has been used effectively in the full range of human dilemmas; there is no category of relationship or psychological problem that has not been addressed with this approach, hence it can also be used with the families suffering with the problems of alcohol abuse and problem drinking.

Family therapy uses a range of counseling and other techniques including communication theory, psycho education, psychotherapy, relationship education, systemic coaching, systems theory, reality therapy, media psychology as per the need and requirement of the problem.

The number of sessions depends on the situation, but the average is 5–20 sessions. Social worker as a family therapist usually meets several members of the family at the same time. This has the advantage of making differences between the ways family members perceive mutual relations as well as interaction patterns in the session apparent both for the therapist and the family. These patterns frequently mirror habitual interaction patterns at home, even though the therapist is now incorporated into the family system. Therapy interventions usually focus on relationship patterns rather than on analysing impulses of the unconscious mind or early childhood trauma of individuals. The use of genogram may also be used to find out the patterns of relationship across generations, it may help the family members to understand in simple language the causes of disturbances in their present relationships.

Social workers as family therapists with such families needed to be more interested in the maintenance and/or solving of problems rather than in trying to identify a single cause. The families disturbed with the alcohol problems generally perceive cause-effect analysis as attempts to put blame to one or more individuals, with the effects that for many families a focus on causation is of little or no clinical utility. Understanding of issues affecting the family is important for purposes of education and to aid in communication.

The Engagement Process

The engagement process is the most important initial stage in family therapy intervention. This is the situation when the expectations of the family and the social worker as therapist are defined, the processes are clarified and the roles and responsibilities of each participant are discussed. The process includes five points:

- developing rationale for the family approach
- clarifying the person's view of the problem
- establishing positive and purposeful relationship
- conveying professional competence
- maintaining the social worker and family concordance

Developing rationale for the family approach

The family approach brings the family together and explains clearly the importance of family participation in various ways such as stopping a family member from further involvement in alcoholism; from preventing mental illness; avoiding stress and strains in family and helping alcoholics to cope up in a positive way in facilitating and encouraging them to undergo rehabilitation process. Ideally, the families themselves would request for treatment. But in Indian situations where the myths and misconceptions about use of alcohol, socio-cultural sanctions linked to alcohol accompanied by illiteracy and unawareness family therapy is not in practice. It can be a very useful approach in the treatment of alcohol related problems (Box 1).

When family therapy is required? It is a very important question particularly in Asian countries like India where this method is not known to the common people. It does not mean that in these countries family therapy do not have any importance in difficult situations, it has, but it is not used as a scientific process. A

Box 1

Basic Skills, Functions and Competence of the Social Worker as Family Therapist

1. *Engagement*
   Develop rationale for the family approach
   Establish positive and purposeful relationships
   Convey professional competence
   Maintain the social worker and family concordance
2. *Problem Identification*
   Clarify the problem presented
   Focus on the immediate process
   Identify and explore interpersonal problems
   Clarify individual problems
   Integrate the assessment
3. *Social Diagnosis*
   Carefully distillate the accumulated and filtered evidence
   Conscious assembling of material
   Encouraging relationship between the social organization of the community and the individual psychological organization
4. *Change Facilitation*
   Exercise good clinical judgement
   Break maladaptive interaction patterns
   Clarify problematic consequences
   Alter affective blocks
   Implement new adaptive patterns
   Mobilize external resources as required
5. *Termination*
   Review therapeutic process
   Accept family initiative to terminate
   Initiate termination when indicated
   Develop alternate assignments
   Conclude treatment constructively

traditional approach of informal role of family members, pressure of elders or kinship relations is commonly used to find solutions to various family problems. Some situations/symptoms where one can need family therapy as a method to solve problems are as under:

- when symptoms of an individual (e.g. stress due to family responsibilities, family conflicts, adolescent children in constant arguments with parents and siblings, staying away from home whenever family members quarrel) reflect family disturbance and one member of the family is singled out as the person with problem;
- when the family (or significant others – e.g. teachers, social worker, employers, supervisor, friends, aunts, uncles) identify an area of conflict that need family therapy;
- when the person undergoing individual treatment is unable to contain his/her own stress due to family conflict and disturbance;
- when family ignorance or high anxiety is felt to exert pressure on a person especially where the patient depends on family support;
- when the family has to participate in patient's treatment as in the case of patients with mental illness such as schizophrenia, manic depressive psychosis and alcohol/substance abuse;
- when treatment reaches a stalemate because expected changes in the family systems have not occurred: for example, non-cooperation of family members on socio-cultural aspects, patient's unending complaints about his or her marital problems, disturbed relations with grown up children, joint family disputes;
- when the patient's relationship in social situations like schools, work and work-place, marriage, relatives etc. is turbulent especially when the same problem is found within the family.

The client with problem of alcohol use is best understood in the context of the family system. Factors in the family may determine the cause; or the reverse may be true in that, these factors could lead to the therapeutic solution of the alcohol problem. At this stage, it is appropriate for the family to begin to understand dynamics of alcohol dependence particularly as this relates to the identified patient. It is important to note that the problem of one member could affect the lives of others in the family. Oftentimes, family members may feel irritable, disturbed, or develop guilt with the alcohol dependent family member. Informing and raising their awareness is therefore an important initial step to reduce tension and stress for all family members. This is one component where the educational process for the family is important as the *family as a whole unit* must understand the problems of the identified patient. As the social worker as a therapist explores the problem identified at the beginning of the session, he/she gathers all information surrounding the case, taking every factor into account, including determinants of the problem as well as therapeutic elements that can be helpful in involving the family in treatment.

Setting of goals and direction

The social worker should make it clear to the family that the goal is to promote good health for each member of the family and not only of the identified patient. Following the identification of the problem, possible solutions and ways of strengthening coping mechanisms should be discussed (Box 2).

Box 2

When the family visited the social worker, they pointed out to the son's alcohol abuse as a problem of their son. On exploring deeper, the social worker searched through the problem and saw that the problem was more complex, as explained by the family and indicated the need and appropriateness of family therapy for proper treatment.

The family was asked how they understood the client's problem. The parents and other family members said that they had tried everything possible.

Father to social worker: 'You are the expert, and we would like you to help us in dealing with this problem, Please do everything what you can for us.'

At this point, the social worker should emphasize and explain to them that they (family members) are in an ideal position. That they can work effectively with everybody, and can deal with the problem directly but they must accept the problem in its real perspective and understand their role. A feeling of positive outlook is very essential for each member of the family.

Social worker: 'My role as a guide and therapist is to facilitate that everybody in family could work through the problems with your son.' This is a complex problem in which role of each family member is very important. I can help you to understand the problem, its intricacies and how the family should deal with this. The role of each family member is important and all have to co-operate with me as and when required.

Communication techniques

The social worker may recognize the importance of each member of the family. He/she should not be frustrated with the resistance shown by some members, and should be able to overcome these barriers. To open the family sessions, the social worker as a therapist should consider the example in (Box 3). During the course of the sessions, the social worker should identify the different ways by which members express their feelings: Assess how they 'communicate' while watching TV, or while passing each other in the corridor/street or discussing a point with family friends/relatives about the problem in question. Do they bother to look at each other's eyes? Do they show appreciation for each other? Are they too embarrassed to acknowledge each others' little achievements – like achievements in business, good earning from agriculture and allied activities, praise for religious or community work initiated voluntarily, good grades in school, new haircut, well-pressed clothes, good ideas? Do family members resort to nagging to show anger, praise, and affection?

It is important that at the outset, the family is clear about the implications of family therapy. This should be clarified before family members commit themselves to the intervention.

Box 3

Social worker: I would like to spend sometime getting to know you better. I want more information from you and your family so I will ask you about situations that you find stressful in your life and how your family helps to overcome these problems. First, I would like to ask you about your understanding of your condition. Then, I would like to know about your own goals, and how your family helps you to achieve these. This will help me to decide the best way we can help your family to work together for everyone's benefit. Do you have any questions before we start?

Establish positive relationship

To enhance the engagement process, the social worker should deliberately recognize and acknowledge each of the family members. He/she should give recognition and importance to each member of the family through direct interaction. Empathy, warmth, and genuineness accompanied by easy and local communication – all tend to strengthen interpersonal involvement and to maintain positive relationship. One should be sensitive and consistent in relating to each member of the family. Any family member who shows indifference and resistance to the therapy should be given special attention from the outset.

Recognize the internal and external manifestations of distress in the family, which resulted in seeking professional help. For example, in the Indian context, a family may seek help only in times of crisis and when problems become severe. The family often keeps the problem of alcohol abuse and/or mental illness secret. Provide the family with directions and rules regarding the therapeutic process. Guilt-provoking statements do not help and should be avoided.

To help the patient and family members, real situations/incidences may be presented (when needed) through videotaping or tape recording. For this, permission should first be sought from the family.

Convey professional competence

Determine the level of cognitive development and functioning of family members, particularly of children. It is important for the family to understand the communication process that is going on with the social worker. If possible, use language, which is easily understood and accepted by the family (preferably in local dialect). When working with the family, the social worker should use expressive phrases familiar to family members, including their pet names. Be familiar with these, and use them.

Qualities of the Social Worker as a Therapist

It is not easy to be calm in the midst of warring members but the therapist social worker should try to remain calm, even at the height of emotional turmoil. Family members should be allowed to express their individual feelings. The social worker must be ready to tolerate a wide range of emotions by allowing members of the family to express themselves freely. Request the family to allow the social worker to enter their private life but at the same time assure them of confidentiality.

Allow the family to 'let go'. Do not pressure family members; instead take time with them, make them feel secure. Needless to say, the social worker must be well versed with the methods and strategies on drug/alcohol abuse prevention and rehabilitation.

Ideally, a social worker as family therapist must be an experienced professional worker. Knowledge and skills of interpersonal and family functioning are required in the successful employment of any approach to family therapy. No matter what specific methods are applied, empathy is needed for the social worker to appreciate tension and anxiety at various levels. For example, while looking at individual family members, the social worker must be able to appreciate not only conflict over desires, attitudes and goals, but also conflicts centred around narcissism, vulnerability, personality disorganization or conflicts over separation from the family and individuation from within. The social worker should regard, as a serious problem, any failure of the family to show empathy with the patient. This applies in particular to adolescents who have been at the centre of the family's upheaval who may not have had the opportunity to clarify some of his/her confusions as a teenager. The social worker should try to come to grips with and to address the specific problem of the family member.

The social worker as family therapist must be willing to look at his own role in the process of the therapy. His/her empathy should extend to all family members including those who are absent because of unreliability, hostile attitudes, unavailability, or even death. The extended family in its cultural context should be appreciated; its relationships should be considered. The construction of a genogram is often crucial in understanding the difficulties in therapy, e.g. such topics as injustice, excessive fragility, gender difference, family myths, and power. The social worker's mastery of these areas is essential to attain a balanced approach towards the family problem.

Maintain the social worker and family concordance

An agreement should be reached with the family on the estimated number of sessions, which would be needed to work on specific problems. Sessions could be held once a week, for a period of three months. The family as a whole should evaluate progress. Each session could last from one to one and half hours. After six months, the family may meet with the social worker for another three months if necessary. Following this period, the therapy could be terminated after ensuring that the family meets the criteria.

Problem Identification

The following steps are included in problem identification:

- Clarify the problem presented by the family
- Focus on the immediate process
- Identify and explore interpersonal problems
- Clarify individual problems
- Make an integrated assessment

Clarify the problem presented by the family

The social worker should listen to each member of the family and observe how each one of them presents the 'problem'. Different members of the family may have their own views about the problem. To get a balanced view it is important to assess everybody's perception. While listening social worker must observe carefully the level of participation of every member by their body posture, use of language, tone of voice, facial expression. The social worker should check information gathered with different members of the family (Box 4).

Box 4

Some lead questions might be necessary in the early sessions.

How the problem arose? (Client's perception)

How do you see the problem?

How do you get along as a family?

What do you do in the evening when everybody is in home, or when you are gathered together on evenings, nights and or weekends?

Focus on the immediate process

The social worker must be observant and cautious, and must listen intently to the problem presented by the family members. Premature conclusions must be avoided. The social worker may be inclined to reassure some members of the family immediately because the inexperienced social worker may feel anxious to help in the beginning. Be aware of this trap. Hold your emotions, energy and eagerness. Social worker should clearly understand that in the beginning, you don't know very much about the case. As you learn more about the problem, you will most likely change your assessment as the session proceeds.

It is important to recognize relevant behaviour that can help to get a full and detailed appreciation of the problem. The attention of the family members should be re-directed and focused on the most of the problem through appropriate questions. In the problem of alcohol abuse, the family may deny the existence of the problem leading them to either avoid or confuse the issue. One should select the most important points of enquiry by focusing on the problems of issues, which may be not about alcohol abuse alone (Box 5).

Box 5

Kewal is a 41-years-old adult. He was admitted to Drug-de addiction centre because of his alcohol problems. During the course of the sessions, it was disclosed that Kewal started drinking during his adolescence age with friends and relatives. His father, a farmer with good land holding also uses alcohol and was an opium addict, died because of cancer. His father being illiterate could not look after his property and agriculture, which had been looked after by his old grandfather and other kins. Kewal has two sons and a daughter. Elder son studied in a good English medium school up to 10th standard but could not do well in studies and now casually looking after farming and family tasks.

Wife of Kewal is a semi-literate lady believes in superstitions and traditional faith healers. She tried her level best to stop Kewal from drinking alcohol with the help of usual prevailing practices in rural areas such as through traditional faith healers and quacks as well as by qualified medical practitioners when the situation became out of control. Kewal stops drinking for sometime but when starts drinking again indulges in binge drinking, continuously drink day and night and even do not take food. He was diagnosed for liver damage. Kewal believe that family property and other joint family problems are responsible for his drinking alcohol, which is precipitated by the arrogant behaviour of his elder son. His wife became very irritable, and often castigated her children for petty reasons. Perhaps it was her way of coping, but she could no longer hold out. Other children, as well as the mother of Kewal saw his problem as an aggravating factor to the disturbed family.

Identify and explore interpersonal problems

The underlying relationship among the family members could be shown by letting the family express their views freely. The social worker should carefully observe non-verbal communications. Make clarification or confirmation to the family members. The social worker as therapist should clarify non-verbal communications that have been practiced by the family and understood only by them and which they use in the therapy sessions. The family members should be able to conform whether the interpretation of the social worker as to its meaning is what the family meant. Focus how the family sees the problem. At this point the social worker should be able to identify the interpersonal relationship and problems among the different family members. He/she should now see how the presenting problem is compounded by these interpersonal relationships (Box 6).

Box 6

Wife, who is frustrated, blames the family for the alcohol dependency of the husband. The family members feel vindictive and withdraw from the problem. The wife feels more frustrated and continues to blame the elder and other family members who were taking care of the property.

Resist obvious or hidden pressures when interpreting problematic beliefs. Avoid conforming to the family expectations which constrict the therapeutic process. An example of 'constriction' is feeling that such sessions lead to nothing or the session is not going anywhere. If necessary, leave the room temporarily and discuss the process with a supervisor or with the co-worker.

Beliefs on family myths should be recognized as it could have strong influence on the present situation. They need not be explicit. Recognize behaviour, which reflect implicit beliefs, that operate as disguised family rules and which suppress individual growth. Carefully watch for different types of family behaviours which conform, clarify and deny adaptive family rules.

Clarify individual problems

Recognize individual characteristics and let each individual understand himself/herself better. Remember that each individual member of the family is unique and has its own style of relating to others. The individual problems of each member of the family should be explored. Initially, asking how each family member perceives himself and his relationship with the other members of the family, could do this.

After interviewing individual family members, their permission should be asked to disclose their views to the rest of the family. The trainee social worker could comment on the problematic behaviour of the individual seen and observed by the other members of the family and could encourage the individual to reflect and analyse his/her own behaviour, and to speak out. Clarify further the relevant information send in the verbal and non-verbal communication can tell much about the individual or the situation (Box 7).

Box 7

Non-verbal communication could be imparted by means of body language. One may shrug the shoulders for 'no comment', pout the lips 'when displeased', rile eyes for 'negative response', 'sitting with legs and feet somewhat facing a person to indicate approval of that person', and so on.

Summarize the individual problems in a way that can be understood by the family. Seek clarification and feedback from the members (Box 8). The social worker can use certain strategies and techniques such as verbalizing the feelings, conveying acceptance, reassurance and encouragement etc. which can assist him/her in exercising, correct clinical judgement. Constantly look out for positive behaviour. Plan the strategies for change, appropriate timing, optimize results.

Family members are often willing to change when facing a moderate crisis. This is the time to introduce changes if the social

Box 8

The individual problem of each family should be explained. Each member of the family should be given time to answer questions such as 'Do you have a problem with his present behaviour?' or "Is his behaviour affecting you?"

Box 9

Mehar regularly bullied his younger brother while doing work in farm. His brother tolerated his all such activities including alcohol use but felt frustrated because of the problems created by him. Now his younger brother stopped talking to him because of this Mehar reacted and tortured his brother more severely. The social worker asked him during the sessions to explain such behaviour. It took a while for Mehar to respond. He remained silent. After some minutes, when other members of the family had spoken, Mehar decided to talk about the bullying incidents.

worker wants to have immediate response from the family and to have lasting results. Some people could regress to a more primitive level of functioning when under stress. The social worker must in this case provide immediate support (Box 9).

One should look out for counter transference to a particular member of the family, or to the family in general. The social worker may displace his/or her feelings towards any family member because of his own experience, and previous relationships. For example, the negative feelings of the social worker could come out during the therapy. This can be a disturbing element in the therapy if not properly acknowledged by the worker to himself. The social worker should be aware of this and use his/her professional self in order to proceed smoothly. Principle of conscious use of self and non-judgemental attitude should be used in such situation and the worker must trust the practice. Remember though that it is anti-therapeutic for the social worker to raise unrealistic expectations for family members. When a crisis is too stressful, introduce changes which could mobilize other family members to act in support of these changes.

Integrate the assessment

For the completion of the brief assessment, consider the strengths and the weaknesses of the family, and the underlying factors that may have been involved in the problem. It would be important to explore the possibility of multiple problems and to maintain a problem list rather than adhere to a single diagnosis. These problems could be classified into primary individual and primary interpersonal problems (Box 10).

Box 10

Examples of Primary Individual Problems

- Mother is severely sick
- Daughter fears possible maladjustment at her in-laws
- Son is poor in studies
- Extra-marital relations of wife

Examples of Primary Interpersonal Problems

- Father/mother relationship has been affected by an extra-marital conflict
- Father/son relationship has been affected by father's alcoholic problem
- Sister/brother relationship has been affected by sibling rivalry

Maintain clear awareness of the interpersonal relationship, the personal and the presenting problems, and discuss these with the family. Problems should be prioritized. Prepare a list of the possible hazards within the family so that these can be taken at appropriate time. Identify the most important problem and focus on it jointly with the family. The family must agree to concentrate on the priority of the problem to facilitate change. Define specific goals and obtain the agreement of the family on how to attain them. Study how available family resources could be used systematically in improving family problem solving capabilities and skills.

Social Diagnosis

Also known as psycho-social diagnosis emphasizes on understanding of biological, psychological, social and environmental factors operating and responsible for the problem. Establishing an appropriate relationship of the factors responsible for the problem of alcohal addiction and other alcohol related problems in the family is very important. Therefore, the social worker should carefully scrutinize the relevant information and try to avoid irrelevant part. In this process the material available in the form of facts, explanations, incidences, assertions, promises, commitments etc. should be carefully assembled and organized in a way to establish their relatedness to each other as well as to the problem. Social worker after a careful observation of the family members, their roles and concern should properly understand the way through which the facts and other information fit together and formulate a diagnosis (psycho-social) to help in taking further steps.

Change Facilitation

Guidelines and directions towards change facilitation include the following processes:

- Exercise good clinical judgement
- Break maladaptive patterns
- Implement new adaptive patterns
- Mobilize external resources
- Establishing congenial atmosphere to deal with hostility, aggression and violence
- Providing protection and control

Exercise good clinical judgement

At this juncture the family should have a deeper knowledge of the family life development, support systems, communication relationship system, problem solving processes, and coping. With this information, the therapist social worker relate the diagnosis which is validated together with the family; then a plan of management is developed jointly. The message could be exemplified by the following statements (Box 11).

Break maladaptive interaction patterns

Negative interaction patterns are bound to happen during the sessions. Take control if it becomes destructive to the therapeutic

Box 11

Social worker to the family: I see that now you're aware of your different strengths in your family. You are also aware that you could use these strengths in many ways. But perhaps you should now plan specifically. Of course I will be helping you along the way. Many of you may come up with different approaches to solutions. But what is important is that you all reach a consensus. All the family members accept the problem as a disease and cooperate in treatment as suggested.

sessions. Break resistance, but let the family know that some behaviour may not always be avoidable; if they feel that this approach is getting some results they should not be put off and they should persist in getting on with the session. Educate the family on the behavioural patterns of the alcohol dependent and their role in dealing with him. Demonstrate this to the family whenever they are to overcome their resistance (Box 12).

Box 12

For three meetings now Ram Chand, the identified patient always turned to his younger brother, in anger. He blamed him no end for almost every difficulty the family had been going through including his alcohol abuse. He said he was older, yet he did not help out in the family finances. That his parents who had to eke out a living from selling old newspapers and bottles, still had to support his brother, his wife and their newborn. That his parents did not seem to mind that sort of dependence because the brother seemed to be the favourite, being the eldest.

The social worker allowed these outbursts to happen because it was important for everybody to know how Ram Chand felt. The social worker then explained the basis of this anger to the rest of the family not only in terms of resentment, sibling rivalry and poverty, but also as regards the negative effects of alcohol to his mood and behaviour.

Clear and focused expression of anger could be destructive to relationship. The therapist social worker would really want to see some examples of such difficult behaviour: support and direct the expression by directing the expression of anger.

If in a particular session, one member of the family is observed to be resisting, this resistance should not be ignored, instead it should be evaluated and resolved, if needed. A special session could be scheduled with a resistant family member (Box 13).

Clarify problematic consequences

When the behaviour is perceived as accurate the family to describe the problematic behaviour and reinforce their awareness. Encourage

Box 13

Different expression of anger from family members:

- Do not think that this therapy will be effective
- Unless she (wife) listens, this whole session will come to nothing
- He knows it is wrong. Why does he have to keep on doing it?
- I just hope that this time, it works. But I do not have much hope

the family members to accept the responsibility for their problematic behaviours. Owning the problems would facilitate change to adaptive patterns of behaviour. Of course, one might say, how can they own the problem, if they do not have the adequate insight to them? The social worker in such situation should intervene and the client and others associated who are in fix. The process of clarification enables such insight to be acquired (Box 14).

Box 14

After several sessions, held at regular intervals the father realized that it was his alcoholic problem, which had driven the family and the alcoholic into their patterns of behaviour, he would modify their respective behaviour, and he would need to initiate the change first. He decided to attend a rehabilitation programme for himself; at the same time working with the family in sessions. The social worker carefully monitored this decision and the sessions keeping in view the professional approach and reactions of the client and other family members. This was appreciated as well as obstructed by the father as well as other family members time to time.

Alter affective blocks

Allow a family member to express and clarify affective experience in order to understand behaviour patterns more completely. By doing this, other family members could understand the behaviour. The social worker could now come in and interpret the possible meaning of the emotions as well the behaviour presented.

For example crying is a normal response to loss. While allowing family members to weep, the social worker should encourage them at the same time about the cause of this weeping. Openly communicating the causes, as well as the effects of weeping enables the therapist social worker to assist, the family in altering affective blocks and suppressed feelings. Encourage the family members to verbalize their feelings to enable the therapist to learn more about their personality make up, their intellectual capabilities, and thus enable them to assist their personal constructs and family beliefs. Personal constructs refers to how one sees oneself in terms of thinking, feeling, and relating to others, of which language and non verbal communication are important elements such as posture, gesture, way of talking, gait, tone and pitch of voice etc.

Awareness of their past experiences and their earlier beliefs enables them to realize that these could have influenced their present behaviour and make the members of the family aware of such irrationalities. Let the family members see how these patterns of behaviour have arisen. Summarize the various aspects of their maladaptive behaviour, and allow the family members to react to your summary. Carefully observe the reactions of all present there and also take a feedback time to time. This will help the social worker to get correct response. This is your aim at this point, as a social worker (Box 15).

Box 15

The belief of some families that elders in family know best, and that there is no need to consult other members of their families for their decisions have often brought about many problems. This is especially problematic of a decision that has to be taken, and that decision concerns a member with whom the parents and other family members must discuss the issues.

Every individual has his own knowledge and perception of the world; this makes him behave in the way he does. In the beginning social worker does not know much about that. Perhaps, not even family members may have much insight. Even if they do, their knowledge of what the other family members think or feel may not very profound, nor helpful. Encourage the family members to talk about their personal constructs and their beliefs. The individual may not remember past experiences, nor would they understand how their current perceptions and behaviour to relate to those past events. Encourage open discussion of these beliefs, values or goals which appear to interfere with problem solving and adaptive behavioural changes. It might help encounter emotions which block adaptive change. Share these with them. You may have to keep going back to this stage during the course of the sessions (Box 16).

Box 16

Social worker to the alcohol dependent: All these years you believed that your parents did not care for you; despite some indications that they might have? Did the constant struggle of your parents to make ends not mean anything to you?

Alcohol dependent: No I only knew that they had no time for me. They scold me every time. Never care for me, my friends are good who always help me.

Father: Perhaps he is right. We spent too much time in the farm. Of course, we thought that our efforts were appreciated because we work for family and we are illiterate.

Mother: He has spent his whole time with his friends who are useless, but don't you think that we also think that he could have taken care for himself. We expected him to understand that everybody had to make their contribution to the family life. But we never so much verbalize this because we thought that he will himself understand and work but he started drinking alcohol.

Implement new adaptive interaction patterns

Initiate adaptive change by restructuring relationships in the therapy process. Identify eventual changes on involvement and performance of the family members and individual's roles. Common behavioural interaction that would support the attainment of their common goals should be given importance. It would be important to recognize that each individual family member is different and that their behaviour at any given time may be different. On the other hand, a very timid family member may hesitate to take initiatives during the interview. One could then help him by more direct questions and at the same time, give him verbal support to express his/her view. Encourage family members to overcome negative behaviour in a constructive manner (Box 17).

Box 17

Father to alcohol dependent son: Okay, I see that I have relegated everything to your mother. Do you think it will help if you begin to share hand with me in our business whenever you feel like? Perhaps it could help you in realizing the situation more practically?

Son: Yes, that may help. But I really think that the most important thing is that you show genuine concern. I see how irritable you get when I do not concentrate in work.

Mother: But why don't you concentrate? It is your own work, we do not expect much from you? What else do you need?

Social Worker: So these are the most important things for him to think? (Mother did not answer, reflected on the social worker's comment.)

Older Brother: Of course I get envious of what he has. During my time I worked very hard, father many times slapped me but I never reacted. So what's wrong with him? I realize that those were very different days.

Allow the family to talk about positive experiences and stimulate the process of giving feed back to one another; this is a constructive initiative. For example, praise and acknowledge positive experiences or positive statements made by any family member. Encourage the family to show approval even of small accomplishments of other family members, and try not to disqualify that praise by saying 'I like what you did, but …'. Family members should say exactly what it was that pleased them, and he/she should tell the person concerned how he felt about it.

Family members are more likely to carry out a task when there is explicit commitment to make them do so. The therapist social worker should therefore get this commitment from them to carry out a specific task within a specified period of time. Make them understand that by stimulating interaction between family members, future positive change from individuals or the group may be easier to accomplish.

Mobilize external resources as required

During the whole course of the session, the social worker could encounter several instances where he/she would feel totally at a loss. For example when the identified patient shows verbal and physical violence or expresses his suicidal intent. The social worker should recognize these situations, as well as his inability to cope. He should in these instances not hesitate to seek immediate guidance from his supervisor. There may even be a need for the social worker to hand over the sessions completely to the supervisor.

Social networking is an important element in the therapeutic process. It is specifically important when family starts to alienate itself from others outside the family or the people start avoiding the family due to increasing problems in the family. Facilitate the contact of family members with outside sources while working on their own resources. Such outside support are particularly important during the early stages to termination or conclusion of therapy. Reassure family members that it is alright to secure outside support, if they feel they will need it. This can be in the area of education, work, spiritual matters, and another community based support system.

Termination

This section discusses the guidelines and directions for termination or conclusion of therapy as well as the timing and the reasons for termination. Termination can be initiated by either therapist or by family.

Periodic review of the therapy process

Periodic progress assessment should be done. Find out how the family members perceive the status in solving the problem. For example, clarify how maladaptive behaviour of some family members influences the problem of alcohol abuse with a family member. The improvement of family's problem-solving skills could now be determined by asking how their contributions to the process have helped. Allow each member of the family to talk and to communicate these skills to each other. At this point family members should be given to show confidence in their acquired adaptive patterns and the therapist social worker should let them see this (Box 18).

Recognize how the therapeutic goals have been attained, once that problem coping has improved and much insight into the relationships have been acquired. Some members might continue to show reluctance in termination of the therapy out of anxiety. Let the family member talk about these worries and give some examples of situations where these may or may not happen. As a therapist, social

Box 18

Social worker: I see that Ram Chand listens attentively now to his older brother's comments. You do not seem to be irritated anymore by him?

Ram Chand: Yes, you are right I do not know why I constantly saw his comments as interference. Funny, it does not seem to be like that now.

Sunil: I think the fact that you have been very patient with us encouraged us all the way have really helped all of us. I felt that at some point, we were getting nowhere. Everybody was on each others throat. There was no breathing space. Nobody seemed to respect each other anymore.

worker may also make a wrong judgement and initiate early termination of treatment. The family members may recognize this and tell the social worker that they are not unrealistic with their worries. In this case, give more sessions and see if you have really gone through every aspect of the case. Retrace your steps and see if you have really clarified the presenting problem and the individual problems and addressed all maladaptive patterns. Find out if somebody is actively blocking the change.

Accept family initiative to terminate

One should recognize when the family members want to terminate therapy. Explore the reasons why they have initiated the termination. Perhaps the family could not cope with the crises; in the event that such crisis subsides, the family may wish to return to the sessions. This option can be given to the family. When the social worker's commitment to continue therapy is stronger than the family, chances are that behaviour change may not be too successful. Realize that the social worker's input may persist to have a therapeutic impact even after sessions have stopped. Be ready with an assignment schedule for the family members but share it at the appropriate time.

Initiate termination when necessary

Clarify the basis for the social worker's initiative to terminate the sessions.

Recognize persistence to adaptive change in some families. One could for example point out that family members could become more receptive to change later on. One could also talk about the cost effectiveness of continuing therapeutic efforts. Recognize when on going sessions are covertly undermining family member's initiative to seek more appropriate natural support; confront the family on the appropriateness of using professional resources for general support. Social worker is needed to work rationally and judiciously and inform them that prolonged therapy may foster dependency.

Recognize when the efforts in the therapeutic process is counter productive: for example family members continue to use confrontation to achieve revenge.

Conclude treatment constructively

Recognize that when therapy ends constructively family member will be more receptive to professional help that may be required later. Ending the process on a negative note could leave the family with unfinished business and build up resistance to further therapy. The importance of the closure as part of the fulfillment of the therapeutic contract should be realized. Summarize for the benefit of the individual and the family all prioritized problems, identify successes and improvements, as well as failures to observe a solid basis for future problem management.

Remember, when the family is ready for leaving the sessions, changes in the family behaviour are no longer easily reversible. The phenomenon of 'scapegoating' becomes minimal. They deal with their stresses in a more effective manner. The family can manage their impulses like anger in an appropriate way. Family handles leisure time more constructively. Family members are more perceptive and on minded and can accurately observe themselves as well as others. As termination proceeds there might be a tendency to 'mourn the loss' of the catalyst of conflict resolution. This should be recognized as a process in transference which may gradually lessen in time.

Finally, the social worker should say how he/she appreciated the fact he/she was allowed to come into their private lives in finding solutions for their problems. Appreciate the positive steps taken during the process and recognize the contribution of all the family members. Assign some responsibilities to them according to their role in the family. It will help in giving a positive note on the part of the social worker.

Help through Self Help Group 'Alcoholic Anonymous'

One of the most successful examples of the treatment and recovery of alcoholics is 'Alcoholic Anonymous' popularity known as 'AA'. 'Alcoholic Anonymous' (AA) is a practical experience of Bill W. in 1935, a resident of New York who was successfully sober for the first time in years, sought out another alcoholic who was also referred to a local doctor with a problem of heavy drinking. During his two months of sobriety, Bill W. noticed that his desire to drink lessened when he tried to help other alcoholic to get out of it. Working together, Bill W. and the doctor found that their ability to stay sober seemed closely related to the amount of help and encouragement they were able to give to other alcoholics. With continuous work for four years a new movement started slowly without any name and organization. More groups started developing in Akron, New York, Cleveland, and in a few other cities. In 1939 a book named *Alcoholic Anonymous* was published from which the name of this organization is derived and as a result of the shared help of a number of friends a movement named 'Alcoholic Anonymous' began to attract national and international attention.

It is based on the small groups formed by peers who come together for mutual assistance in finding out the ways and means to come out from the problem of alcoholism and problem drinking which disrupted their personal as well as family life. All the members in these groups have almost same type of problems arising due to alcohol.

For which the members come together to assist each other to help themselves. Their disturbed family atmosphere, lack of faith in each other, loss of personal status and always directed what to do and what not, the alcoholic in his/her own family becomes a person with no identity. He/she fight at many fronts such as with himself/herself to come out from the problem and with the outside atmosphere in which he/she is continuously rejected and the problems become more and more complex. In AA he/she seeks support from the group members and also give support to them who understand each other in more personal manner than less directive or commanding. In this approach the individual get self-support and power from the group members who were also like him/her at one time. The 12 steps of recovery are self-supporting and help the individual through his/her own efforts and contributions. Through active participation in one or the other activity and regular discussions with others who have similar problems, the alcoholic realize that his or her problem is not unique and it can be handled and solved successfully like other members of the group.

Twelve suggested steps of 'alcoholic anonymous'

AA is a way of life for the non-practicing alcoholic; a club or fraternity like atmosphere develops and most social activities of AA members revolve around that group. Members become dedicated to helping other remain sober, and like this by helping others they help themselves.

1. We admit we were powerless over alcohol – that our lives had become unmanageable.
2. Come to believe that a power greater than ourselves could restore us to sanity.
3. Make a decision to turn our wills and our lives over to the care of God as we understand Him.
4. Make a searching and fearless moral inventory of ourselves.
5. Admit to God, to ourselves and to another human being the exact nature of our wrongs.
6. Are entirely ready to have God remove all the defects of character.
7. Humbly ask Him to remove our shortcomings.
8. Make a list of all persons we have harmed, and become willing to make amends to them all.
9. Make direct amends to such people wherever possible, except when to do so will injure them, or others.
10. Continue to take personal inventory and when we were wrong promptly admit it.
11. Seek through prayer and meditation to improve our conscious contact with God: *As we understand Him*, praying only for knowledge of his will for us and the power to carry it out.
12. Have has a spiritual awakening as the result of these steps, we try to carry this message to alcoholics and to practice these principles in all our affairs.

Families suffering with alcohol problems can be helped through 'AA' in their local areas or nearby places. The social worker can also help such families in tracing out and associating with groups of 'AA' which are successfully working. By this the families can also get a moral support and a ray of hope for their valuable family members who unfortunately become the victim of alcohol related problems and lost the hope for life.

Some Myths and Misconceptions About Alcohol*

There are various myths and misconceptions prevailing in our society about alcohol and its use. The ignorant family members and the alcohol users become victim due to these myths and misconceptions because they do not know the real facts about alcohol and its effects. Here are some common myths and misconceptions about alcohol and its effects popular among people, which are explained with real facts so that the family members can understand, work and help the sufferer with more confidence and authority:

1. *Myth:* Alcohol stimulates a person to become more lively.
   Fact: Alcohol is actually a depressant of the brain and its functions. There is a common belief that it removes (depresses) inhibitions. Careful observation has shown that 'removing inhibitions' happens before alcohol levels in blood reaches a noticeable threshold. Thus, the real reason for 'removing inhibition' appears to be anticipatory learned behaviour.
2. *Myth:* Alcohol promotes good sleep.
   Fact: It is not true, but the reality is that people dependent on alcohol cannot sleep well without alcohol. Those who do not use alcohol regularly may have disturbed sleep after alcohol consumption.
3. *Myth:* Alcohol helps people to forget their problems.
   Fact: This has become a 'truth' because regular and heavy alcohol users often say this is the reason why they drink alcohol. But it is not true. It is only a short time and temporary effect of intoxication. Very often the opposite is found to be true-people bring up forgotten problems only when they are intoxicated.

---

* *Source:* Desai, G. Nimsh et al., Prevention of harm from alcohol use, WHO, New Delhi, 2003.

4. *Myth:* Alcohol is a good way to cope with cold weather.
   Fact: Alcohol makes blood vessels of the skin dilate and the skin feels warm. But in a cold environment, the body tries to save heat by cutting down the blood supply to the skin. Thus alcohol is not a good way to 'warm up' in the cold. If a person is exposed to the cold after consuming alcohol, there can be significant heat loss from the body. This can be dangerous for health.
5. *Myth:* Alcohol enhances sexual performance and desire.
   Fact: It is not correct. The reality is that alcohol interferes with achieving erections. In research studies, it is proved that alcohol reduces sexual desire and continuous use leads to impotence. Shakespeare's quote that alcohol 'provokes the desire but inhibit the performance' is well known.
6. *Myth:* People who become aggressive and violent after alcohol use cannot control their behaviour because it is caused by alcohol's action on the brain.
   Fact: Many people learn to associate certain moods and behaviours with the alcohol effect and behave in a manner in which they wish to behave. The behaviour then becomes 'conditioned'. People can learn to change the conditioning. Thus people, not alcohol, is to blame.
7. *Myth:* 'He is really a good man, it is the alcohol which makes him abuse me'.
   Fact: It is not true, take an example that when a woman is beaten by a husband while he is sober, she may consider this as unacceptable. However, if he behaves in exactly the same manner after drinking, she may forgive him and blame alcohol. Society's view of intoxicated people makes it less risky to behave deviantly while intoxicated. However, projects and researches on prevention of harm from alcohol have shown that if society will not tolerate unacceptable behaviour with or without alcohol, such behaviour ceases. An unacceptable behaviour is unacceptable, with or without alcohol.
8. *Myth:* Alcohol has been shown to be 'good for heart', so one should drink alcohol everyday.
   Fact: There is some research which has shown the potential protective effect of alcohol on the heart. This research has been based on consumption of small amount of alcohol, with medical advice (such as wine on a daily basis) with limited

quantity. Consumption of alcohol on a daily basis is a matter of concern as some people cannot control the quantity of alcohol consumed. Consumption can gradually increase to dangerous levels. Heavy alcohol consumption is certainly bad for the heart and the body.

9. *Myth:* Beer is not 'hard liquor', so it can be consumed safely.
   Fact: Beer is an alcoholic beverage, although it contains lesser amount of alcohol than 'hard liquor' like whisky or rum. Beer does contain 4 to 8 per cent alcohol. One 12-ounce bottle of beer is equal to one peg of whiskey. Thus, if somebody drinks six bottles of beer in an evening, he/she has consumed the equivalent of six pegs of whisky.
10. *Myth:* In our society, alcohol 'loosens up' people, so they enjoy themselves.
    Fact: Most societies have set the norms for uninhibited behaviour while intoxicated. People appear to adhere strictly to these norms and rules. The uncontrolled impulses appear to be controlled by society's instructions about the effects of alcohol upon behaviour. Thus, people learn about drunkenness from what their society 'knows' about drunkenness.

7

Case Studies

This chapter explains some case studies based on about 10 years continuous interaction of the author with the affected families which came into contact during his practice with the people suffering from alcohol related problems. The case studies presented are self-explanatory and they support some of the findings of the preceding chapters such as:

1. Alcohol use is deeply associated with status symbol and very common in all the social ceremonies/functions/events and in all the sections of society irrespective of region, religion, caste, and class.
2. The use of alcohol by most users is looked at as a source of pleasure, relaxation, relief and escape from the miseries and frustration of life. Of course, some of them, if can't afford it, indulge in it even at the cost of their family and consequent marital disharmony.
3. The beginning of alcohol use is normally as social drinking under the influence of friends, relatives, occupational group, co-workers or religious group.
4. The habit of alcohol is continued by users in the absence of an effective social control; and in some cases taking alcohol is a family or social custom.
5. There are various myths and misconceptions about alcohol due to which the use of alcohol is increasing from social drinking to problematic drinking and in such situations family of the alcoholic suffers a lot to the extent that many families

are ruined. Females and children in such families are the main sufferers.

6. Alcohol use in the family is one of the most important reasons for various problems in the family but neither the family nor the individual recognize it as a source of problem in initial stage. When they recognize, it has already got too late.

The names of the cases have been changed and their villages/cities are not mentioned in the case studies to protect identities. It was also requested by the cases interviewed under study and the families.

Case Study 1

Zile Singh belongs to a village in Kaithal district of Haryana. He is 47 years old and works as a caterer (locally known as *Halwai*), in marriage parties and other social functions in nearby villages as well as in the city of Kaithal and other nearby small towns. He takes work on contract basis and employ workers as per the requirement. He is a famous caterer for such functions in this area and working for last 12–14 years. He learned this job from another expert caterer of Kaithal city where he started working 26 years back as a helper. He worked with this caterer for sometime and then started his own work and became a well accepted contractor in this field. His income is good and he has his own house in his village.

He has four children – two sons and two daughters who are studying in a school in his native village. But his children are not doing well in their studies. They face problems in their studies such as academic failure, lying, running away from school, excessive indulgence in TV viewing etc. During discussions it was found that the family is not giving any attention to children because their mother (the wife of Zile Singh) is illiterate and do not have concern for education of her children. Zile Singh also do not bother much because he believes that education is not going to help his children in any way ultimately the boys will join his work as a cook or helper and indulge in their traditional work and the girls will be married therefore, there is no need of much education for them.

Zile Singh does not have good marital relations, he usually came across hot exchanges with his wife and many a times it happens in front of children. Maximum time he remains out of home because of the nature of his work and other reasons as he said that his wife is very non cooperative and always argue with him. The disturbed marital relations are also confirmed by neighbours and other close kins of Zile Singh. When asked that why his wife fight and argue with him, Zile Singh tried to avoid discussing on this point and expressed his ignorance.

When first asked about his drinking Zile Singh refused to own that he drinks alcohol. However, when he was confronted and explained that many a times when he met the researcher he was drunk, he accepted but still adamant that he was not a regular drinker and takes alcohol occasionally when others offer. During interview he became angry very frequently and tried to skip away. The researcher tried hard to contact him at his home, and or at his place of work. His work place was shifting frequently from one place to another. Zile Singh appeared tense and disturbed when discussion started and he could not stay for long. After a long interaction of three to four sessions when he was convinced about the motive of research work, he admitted that he used alcohol daily, but it is because of the nature of work. He told that he started drinking when he was 13–14 years of age, started working in this field and now continuously drinking for last 10–12 years. Though he has not revealed the extent and magnitude of his drinking honestly but the researcher confirmed it from co-workers, his employees, family members, neighbours, a local doctor and other kiths and kins that now Zile Singh is a chronic drinker. He drinks throughout the day and this situation is for about last six years since 2000. At present the situation is that sometimes he never cares about his professional responsibility and seriousness of his contract work as a caterer, after drink king alcohol he becomes unconscious and the work is done by his subordinate workers, who work on daily wages. This resulted to deterioration in his work which also affected his income.

His wife told that during last one year (in 2001) he was hospitalized three times for heavy drinking, which was confirmed from his daily wage workers. But Zile Singh denied about it. He claimed that he can give up the use of alcohol any moment, he only drinks alcohol because the nature of his work is like that otherwise he is not habitual. He was asked by the worker that if that was the case why he dose not give it up, he became angry and said I have already told that my nature of work is like that where one cannot work without drinking alcohol and also he has to provide it to others those who are linked to this work. However, with a constant probing that why should he use a substance which he neither like nor is habitual unless it serves some purpose he came out with the reasons that it is mainly to ease his depression, ward off loneliness and also to give company to his friends, co-workers who offer it and also want it from him in return.

Observations

The accommodation he has is a small semi-constructed house with two rooms which were constructed 3–4 years back and still without plaster. There is a half constructed bathroom with a hand pump in the open courtyard of house. The house does not have toilet and all go for toilet in open. Wife of Zile Singh seems disturbed and children were also not properly dressed. When researcher started talking there was a gathering around and it was really very difficult to talk in privacy in the first meeting. Anyhow in subsequent meetings some efforts were made in which his wife was cooperative but Zile Singh was not helping and extremely unwilling to share information. Marital relations of Zile Singh are disturbed, but neither Zile Singh nor his wife accept it. The researcher observed their tense relations during discussion with them jointly and separately. The relations with near and dear, relatives and friends are also not cordial for sometime. Zile Singh as well as his wife have various myths and misconceptions about alcohol and its use.

The financial position of his family seems poor though his earning is good. He has taken a loan of ₹ 40,000 out of which he repaid ₹ 15,000 but now he is not paying regular installments as a result of which it is now increasing to more financial burden on him. He has started spending a big amount of money on alcohol, which he never accepted in discussion but it was confirmed from his present condition, family responses and increasing financial liability.

Analysis

His extreme non-cooperation, tense and disturbed state in which he was, pointed to the fact that he had some fear and disturbing problem. His refusal to discuss much about his married life and criticizing his wife gave an impression that he had disturbed relations with her and that is because of his drinking habit, which started 4–5 years back when he started ignoring his responsibilities. His expression of utter ignorance about his family problems specially becoming aggressive on these issues gave the impression that he was hiding facts. His contradictory statements also point to the same. To the worker's mind the main reason for his disturbed family, carelessness towards children, and ignoring his work could be his addiction to alcohol, which he is always vehement to prove wrong. As a result of which his work as a famous caterer is going down day by day and his financial position is also deteriorating leading to more and more complications in his personal and family life.

Case Study 2

'Ram Chander', a young man of 30 years, is working in a factory at Faridabad as a mechanic and earns about ₹ 5,000 per month. He originally belongs to Ropar district of Punjab where his early childhood was spent till the age of five years. Later on he came to Faridabad since his father had started a business here. Ram Chander has four brothers and one sister of whom two are married except the youngest two brothers who are studying in college. Even though Ram Chander himself is non-matriculate, all his brothers and sisters are better educated and well placed. His father is a businessman and has good income.

As Ram Chander had been a protected child, he received much more attention from his parents, as compared to his other siblings. His overprotection hampered his studies. When he was in class VI, he fell in a bad company. His friends had little interest in studies and as a group they started playing truant. They started from home to the school but went for playing cricket or cinema. Being a pampered child Ram Chander was never checked by his parents. But when he failed in matriculation, he was severely scolded by his mother and his maternal uncle, due to this he realized his mistake to some extent. His maternal uncle put him in three years ITI training course. Due to busy schedule of this technical course he left his old friends, his company was changed and he completed the training in time. After this he got a job in the factory where he has been working ever since.

Ram Chander got married in 1990. His wife belongs to Delhi. They don't have any child till now (2005). His wife stays with her parents for past sometime. She being the only child had to attend to her parents due to their old age and consequent sickness. Ram Chander too often stays with them but frequently goes to meet his parents. His wife has taken up a school teacher's job near her parent's house to keep herself gainfully occupied. Ram Chander claims that he leads a happy and contented married life. He has taken a loan of ₹ 25,000 from the company in worker's welfare loan scheme to contribute in his father's business. He is repaying this loan through monthly installment of ₹ 700 p.m.

As far as alcohol use is concerned, Ram Chander uses alcohol for last 15 years (since 1989). Initially he used it casually but later he started using regularly with his co-workers and now for last six years (since 1998) he is a regular drinker. His frequency of using alcohol has also increased and now he drinks many times a day. He drinks not only the expensive foreign liquor, but also the cheap local brands available locally. Now he has his own circle of friends with whom he drinks alcohol. He spends ₹ 2,000 to more than ₹ 3,000 on alcohol and smoking in a month. Earlier his parents did not know about it, later when his father came to know about his drinking alcohol he ignored it, probably due to unawareness of its consequences. His elder brother also takes alcohol but moderately. However, his wife also knows about it but Ram Chander justifies it by saying that he takes it only occasionally and is not an addict so she does not mind it. This was confirmed by his wife in a separate interview with her at her parent's place. She expressed her unconcernedness and insouciance towards this problem of her husband because she does not need his help and moreover she spends her maximum time in her parents family. When asked that now the problem of his drinking alcohol is increasing day by day she ignored the question.

Whatever Ram Chander earns, he spends mostly on himself and gives a very small part of income for the household expenditure. Nobody is economically dependent on him, therefore, he is uninterested and mindless on the matter and overspending. His carelessness and non-cooperation with his family and spouse is increasing day by day, but nobody is concerned.

Observations

From the family lifestyle of Ram Chander and the way it is kept, it is observed that their standard of living is much higher than what is normally of the people in this class. All the adults in family are earning members and are not much concerned about anybody. His wife is also self-dependent and not much concerned for him because she is more involved with her parents moreover being an only child of her parents she prefers it. She expressed her concern for not having any child till now, but not seriously and ignored the point whenever came in discussion.

Analysis

Ram Chander was initiated to taking alcohol by his friends and co-workers among whom it is considered a status symbol and a means of celebrations. There are two main reasons for his continuing this habit: (i) He can afford it financially, and (ii) There is no strong opposition from his wife and other members of the family. His wife is not much concerned about this and Ram Chander is indulged in using alcohol more and more because he misses his wife at the time of need but he never disclosed it to anyone. In an informal discussion this was revealed by one of his friend.

Case Study 3

Atma Ram about 42 years of age, educated upto primary level, and a native of a village near Shamli in Mujaffar Nagar district, UP. He works as a casual labour and draws a salary about ₹ 2,500 pm.

Atma Ram is the eldest of three brothers and his two brothers stay in their native village and look after the small cultivation they have. His mother, wife and children stay with him at Sonepat in Haryana. His father had been an employee as a carpenter in a cart making shop at Shamli a small town and at that time they had a nice and comfortable life. When Atma Ram was 17 years of age his father, after being afflicted by paralysis lost his job and expired after some time. After the death of father the small family property was divided among the brothers and till then there was a continuous family dispute many times leading to fight specially among ladies. Mother of Atma Ram was also very upset with this.

Under these circumstances, Atma Ram was forced to come to Sonepat in search of a job where he started working as a casual labour. He is still very fond of his mother and brothers and frequently visits his village. He got married at the age of 22 and has three children – one daughter and two sons, all go to a government school for studies. Atma Ram wants to provide good education to his children for which he is willing to sacrifice his own comfort and undergo economic hardships. With this in mind he has also taken a life insurance policy for 20 years. In order to help him and overcome the economic constraint his wife has taken up a job of maid servant in some houses at ₹ 125 pm per house and works in 4–5 houses and earn average ₹ 500 pm. Her daily routine is to get up early in the morning, cook food for home and leave for work. On return from work in afternoon, she again attends to her household duties and cooks meal. Atma Ram admits that his wife's health is deteriorating but attributes it to the water and weather of place where they live rather than overwork. When asked whether or not his wife objects to his drinking and smoking 'Bidi' he replied with authority, 'What would she say? The fact is, she doesn't even ask me what do I do with my pay. She manage household expenses with whatever money I give in her hand'.

Atma Ram is drinking alcohol since last 12 years which he started with his co-workers. Atma Ram was very disturbed with the behaviour of his brothers and their wives because of them he had to leave his native village. He very much love his mother but is forced to live here in Sonepat where he feels uncomfortable and lives under stress and tension. He started drinking with some friends and co-workers. Now the frequency of use has also increased and his wife is very much concerned about it. A good part of his income is spent on alcohol and smoking which he cannot resist even if he wishes to do so. For this he was admitted to De-Addiction Centre, tried to stop drinking for sometime but could not stop. Now the family life is very disturbed. He wants to give it up but finds it extremely difficult. If he skips it any day he feels very restless and uneasy, doesn't get satisfaction in any job that he does. His expenditure on it is about ₹ 800 pm and even more.

When Atma Ram's wife was being interviewed, she was trying to pacify her youngest son, who appeared to be a case of malnutrition. She is fully aware that her husband is a regular drinker and spends a lot of money on it which could be utilized for family's basic needs. But she finds herself helpless about it since he doesn't pay any heed to her pleadings or suggestions. She and her children are scared of him as he loses his temper very soon and become violent. But in her opinion, in spite of all this he loves her and the children.

Observations

Atma Ram and his family lives in one roomed rented accommodation. The place is cluttered up with all kinds of things and lack in cleanliness and hygiene. Atma Ram gives the impression of being very authoritarian head of the family. This is confirmed by his wife too who says his words are final in family matters. Atma Ram very much love his wife and care for his family. He was also attached to his mother and brothers and their families but he was seriously shocked by the incidence of unfair property division and behaviour of sisters-in-law (wives of his brothers). Because of this he suffered with continuous stress and tension resulting to start drinking in the company of co-workers and friends. Now the problem of drinking alcohol reached to serious levels and the family is suffering with multifarious problems. He want to get rid of this problem but failed.

Analysis

Atma Ram was introduced to alcohol due to his association with friends and co-workers because he suffered with continuous stress due to family disputes and property. His friends also encouraged him to enjoy alcohol and get rid to continuous stress. He also enjoyed taking alcohol and feels relaxed when drinks alcohol. This resulted to continuous drinking and now in spite of his efforts to stop drinking alcohol he could not stop. His wife is also very much worried and disturbed. The position of family is deteriorating seriously.

Case Study 4

Babu Ram is a man of about 48 years of age, has been working as labourer and earns ₹ 2,500 pm. He originally belongs to a village in district Rewari, Haryana. Babu Ram has three sons and he lives with his wife and two younger children at Delhi. His elder son lives at his native village with his grandmother. He is barber by caste and his family was traditionally doing this profession. But because of inadequate income and financial hardship he chose to shift to Delhi. Here too it is extremely difficult for him to maintain the whole family. That is why he has left his older sons in the village so that they could look after the small piece of agriculture land they have there and help their uncle. He and his younger brother are the only two children in their family, though economically their family was not very sound but their childhood was very satisfied and contented with enough love and affection. After shifting to Delhi and experiencing a totally different lifestyle Babu Ram is completely dissatisfied with his life here and is seriously contemplating to return to his native village but could not decide due to his experiences he faced in village earlier. Because of this he always remains under stress which is precipitated by the financial and other problems he and his family faces in the city.

Babu Ram is very attached to and fond of his children. He suffer emotionally in keeping the older son in the village, but he is forced to be so due to his economic condition. The children also in their letters keep writing to him that they miss their parents and brothers and want them to return to the village. Babu Ram says that he has left his children at their destiny and God's will because he has no plans for their education or training in any work. He do not want to engage his children in his traditional occupation as barber because there is no income in this profession. Moreover, this profession does not have any respect in the community. He recalls his experiences which he suffered during his childhood days when his father and grandfather worked as barbers in their village.

His initiation to drinking alcohol was with his neighbours in a slum in Delhi where he is living. The locally brewed alcohol was available there on cheap rate and even on loan basis for which he only pays when he has money. Because he was not forced to pay regularly for drinking he started drinking very frequently. He says that he is not aware when he became regular drinker. Now he drinks throughout the day, his work is also seriously suffered. His wife and children live in a very difficult situation. Babu Ram is not giving any money to family because the whole money he earns goes to the alcohol suppliers who give him alcohol on loan basis. When more discussions were held with Babu Ram he explained that he realizes the hazards his family faces and wants to give up drinking completely. But his dependency on alcohol has increased so much and reached to the stage that he is unable to give it up, though he tried to reduce intake but failed. His monthly expenditure on alcohol is about ₹ 1,000 to 2,000 pm which he finds extremely difficult to afford. Out of his total income of ₹ 3,000 pm he gives only ₹ 500 for his family which is also not given regularly and now almost stopped giving any money. Major part of income goes as re-payment of loan which he had taken for his drinking. He has also stopped sending money to his mother and children living at their village. His mother was very much disturbed and unable to do anything. His grown up child engaged in casual labour in his village. When asked whether his wife objects to his drinking or not Babu Ram replied with a lower head that she does but he cannot help in coming out of his drinking. When her opinion was taken on Babu Ram's use of alcohol she said that she was very much opposed to his alcohol use because she knew that it was the main cause of their poverty. Further when he drinks Babu Ram becomes a changed man and become quite aggressive and irritable even though by nature he is not so. His wife works in some houses as maid servant and earns to take care of her family needs. When asked about the reasons for this she only said that it is because of their fate and ignore talking about their problems.

Observations

By his appearance Babu Ram looked a miserable and disappointed man who had lost all hopes in life. He was in very torn clothes and looked as if he had not attended to himself for quite sometime. Through-out his conversation he was in very low spirits. The most obvious fact in him is that he is well aware of the ill effects of alcohol and how it is disrupting his normal life, but finds himself helpless. Alcohol seems to have made him more careless about his personal appearance, family needs and his own profession. He also started ignoring his mother and children living at his native village. His married life was very smooth initially but is now disturbed and it also seemed to be greatly affected since they were talking very less to each other. This was not so earlier but since Babu Ram started drinking alcohol regularly and sometimes even whole day and ignored his family, their married life is seriously disturbed but his wife exercises too much restraint even if Babu Ram becomes violent after drinking.

Analysis

Babu Ram's case can be a typical one to show how alcohol addiction can ruin a person's life. From every available evidence he had been a nice husband and father, being fond of his family and looking after them. He feels the absence of his older son who lives in his native village. But ever since he got into the addiction of alcohol he and his family are affected in every way. Even though he still loves his family and in fact his conscience seems to be pricking him yet he finds himself helpless in the situation. He has lost all his self-confidence which leads him to leave everything in God's hands and is very depressed. His zeal or enthusiasm to do something better for his family or to be hopeful in life is completely lost and he tends to avoid even thinking about the problems and responsibilities facing him.

Case Study 5

Suraj Bhan belongs to a village in Karnal district in Haryana. He is at number three out of the four brothers and two sisters in his family. His all brothers and sisters are married who initially belong to a joint family but now all the brothers are living separately with their own families. All the brothers look after their agriculture land, which they got from their ancestors. He belongs to upper caste family in which using alcohol is considered as a social prestige. In his family use of alcohol is common among all male members. His father had been the Sarpanch of the village and the family has good respect in village and neighbouring areas, his father died about 15 years back and since then his frequency and quantity of alcohol intake is increased considerably. Suraj Bhan has studied upto 8th class and his brothers have also attended school upto 9th or 10th class and left in between. His childhood life has been quite full of love and affection and still there is a harmonious relationship between siblings. But his own marriage has been an unsuccessful one. He got married in 1970s, and they have three children, two sons and one daughter. He reacted very hard when the social worker and his team discussed his marital life and proved non-cooperative. But with the interviewer's (social worker) persistence he replied that his wife is always non-cooperative. When the interviewer (social worker) questioned him what were his role in care and love to his family he ignored it by saying that I am giving everything what they need.

When asked about his drinking habits, first of all Suraj Bhan refused to own that he uses alcohol. However, when with much persuasion and clarifications the researcher and his team was able to assure him that the information given by him would not be misused, he admitted that he takes alcohol occasionally when others offer it to him. He was very vehement that he does not spend any money from his own pocket which is contradictory to the information gathered in the first interview that he spends about ₹ 2,000 pm. When told about the contradiction, he said that the interviewer (social worker) must have written it wrong.

About the smoking which too was recorded in the previous interview he took it very lightly and said what is wrong in it, I smoke Hooka since childhood because it is a part of our culture and social life. As far as the effects of alcohol on him is concerned Suraj Bhan says that it makes no difference to him whatsoever. He claims that he can give it up any moment, because for that only a strong will power is needed. When the worker asked that if it is so then why he doesn't give it up, he said with a shrug, how he can do so in this society and village life where everything is linked with alcohol. He cited many examples such as serving alcohol in marriage parties, offering alcohol in government and public offices to get work etc. Moreover, he said that he would take it everyday if it was available without costing him anything and helpful in the present social system. However, with the constant probing that why should he use a thing which he neither likes nor is an addict to unless it serves some purpose, he came out with the reasons that it is mainly to ease his depression, enjoy social life and also to give company to his friends and relatives who offer it and also need or as a matter of social status and custom.

At present the real condition of Suraj Bhan's family is very critical. He takes alcohol through out the day and also indulge in neighbourhood fights and street brawls, makes noise after drinking alcohol and disturbs his whole family. His elder son who looks after his agriculture land also stated of drinking alcohol though not regularly. It effected the family income and condition of family is very pitiful. His wife seemed helpless and depressed, daughter who was married two years back also seemed worried about the family and health of her father. Suraj Bhan is suffering from financial crisis and has taken a loan of ₹ 1,50,000 from a local financer, which was confirmed by his family members. The family is worried about repayment of the loan which is increasing day by day. When asked about repayment of the loan, Suraj Bhan ignored it.

Observations

The accommodation Suraj Bhan has is a two rooms house with small kitchen, bathroom and big courtyard. As per usual practice wooden sticks and cowdung fuel is used in kitchen due to which the walls of house were not good looking. The house was white washed 3–4 years back at the time of marriage of his daughter. Courtyard is partly *kacha* and partly covered with bricks. His excessive drinking is characterized by verbal and physical abuse of his wife, children and also sometimes younger brothers, grandiose behaviour, dishonesty, irresponsibility, anger, impatience, irritability and strained relationship with children and immediate relatives. This also resulted in social alienation like loss of good friends, non-cooperation from kins and relatives and rejection from social functions/events. There were incidences of street fights leading to police case. In his interview he was non-cooperative and extremely unwilling to give information.

Analysis

His extreme non-cooperation and the tense and disturbed state in which he was pointed to the fact that he had some fear and disturbing problem. His refusal to discuss his married life or make any specific statements regarding it, gave the feeling that his fears were particularly occurring in regard to this area of his life which he do not want to discuss. His expression of utter ignorance as to what could be the reasons for his family problems, gave the impression that he was hiding facts. His contradictory statements also point to the same. To the interviewer's mind, the reason could be his addiction to alcohol (which he is so vehement to prove is all wrong) as a result of which he might have been ill treating his wife. The health of Suraj Bhan also deteriorating with stomach problems for which he only consults local doctors who are not qualified. More importantly he started suffering from confusion, apprehension, altered sense of perception and hallucination, and distorted memory.

Case Study 6

Ganpat Ram is a farmer of 47 years of age. He lives in a village in Ambala district and owns 62 acres of land. He is the only son of his father and his father was also the only son in his family. Ganpat Ram is having good family property which was looked after by his grandfather. The father of Ganpat Ram was illiterate and a simple man who could not look after his property, he only helps his father (grandfather of Ganpat Ram) in agricultural work and looks after the livestock. The childhood of Ganpat Ram was not very smooth because his father was an opium addict and also use alcohol occasionally. His mother was illiterate and a simple village lady. Because of the habit of taking opium the father of Ganpat Ram was not able to work in his farm and spends his time with some of his village friends who also use opium and always search for easy way to live, their main concern was to arrange the continuous supply of opium, because of which there had been continuous differences between the father and grandfather of Ganpat Ram.

The grandfather of Ganpat Ram wanted to give good education to him so he was admitted in a good school in nearby city with hostel facility. But Ganpat Ram fell into a bad company in school and started playing truant, spending time outside hostel, going to cinema hall for watching movies with his friends. Ganpat got a good amount of money from his grandfather who loved him a lot. He also started smoking and using alcohol. The matter was also reported to his parents, his grandfather took it very seriously and put restrictions on giving money to him. His academic performance was also very poor and he failed in 7th class. His grandfather again admitted him in the same school with arrangement of extra tuitions, but Ganpat could not change his company. He continued with his smoking and enjoying alcohol with his friends. Because of this he could not pass even middle standard and his grandfather took him back to village.

In village also Ganpat Ram continued using alcohol and due to this there had been a dispute between him and his grandfather. Because of good agriculture property the family has good economic condition but poor intrapersonal relations. The father of Ganpat Ram was not at all concerned about family affairs except for using opium which was also arranged by his grandfather. The problem of grandfather became more serious when his grandson (Ganpat) also started using alcohol almost everyday. The effort of his grandfather to engage him in farming and agriculture work failed and Ganpat started spending his maximum time outside home. The intake of alcohol also increased both in quality and frequency. All these problems increased the worries of his grandfather who arranged for his marriage to find out a solution for this problem and got him married in a good agricultural family who also have big land holding. But use of alcohol could not be controlled. Now Ganpat has two sons and one daughter, and the problem of alcohol use has become more serious.

Ganpat accused his father and grandmother who died some years back for this situation of his family. He does not accept using alcohol as a big problem and blame his grandfather for using his property for his personal interests and satisfaction. The educational performance of the children of Ganpat is also not good, because of which the wife of Ganpat is also worried but not serious. In 1997 grandfather of Ganpat died and his father also died two years back in 2002. The property is now under the control of his wife who gives it on contract basis to other villagers and gets a good amount of money.

Ganpat's wife is educated upto primary level. she never objected initially to the use of alcohol by Ganpat rather silently supported it because she accepted it as a symbol of social status and prestige of family. Now the intake of alcohol is increased to serious levels and Ganpat takes alcohol all the time, continues it for months and for many days he even do not eat food. His wife tried her best to stop his alcohol use and visited traditional faith healers such as *Maulvis/Ojhas* etc. for *jhadphoonk*. She also consulted quacks for this but nothing proved successful. Ganpat stops using alcohol for some days and some times upto two/three months but again starts using it with more intensity. He was admitted to hospital 3–4 times during last two years and after some days of treatment he ran away from the hospital and again started using alcohol.

Now Ganpat is going through very serious health problems. Doctors declared that his liver is damaged causing liver cirrhosis and advised total stop of alcohol with proper treatment.

Observations

Ganpat had a parental history of drug addiction and alcohol use. His father was an opium addict and never cared for family. His grandfather was the authority figure in family who had a good respect in village and he controlled the whole family. Because of good financial condition Ganpat never faced any hardships rather he misused it and started using alcohol during his school days which continued till date. His wife is semi-literate but very egoistic and never care for advise/help from other family members and try herself for the treatment but proved unsuccessful. She believes in traditional faith healing and also tried many times for it and still continue even after regular failure. She also tried treatment from quacks, where she spent a lot of money.

The family have good accommodation in the village but it is of old style. Being an agricultural family they also have livestock and do not have any financial problem. The control of property and agriculture work started suffering after the death of grandfather of Ganpat but now it is under the control of his wife.

Analysis

Ganpat was initiated to alcohol because of his family history of drugs and after this in the company of friends in hostel. There seems to be two main reasons for his continuous use of alcohol: (i) he can afford it financially, (ii) there is no proper and strong efforts to control this problem. He has lost all his self-confidence, not able to control his self, always remains crazy for alcohol due to which the symptoms of alcohol psychosis started appearing. He suffered from jaundice and doctors declared that his liver is seriously damaged. According to Ganpat, his father and grandmother were responsible for this stage but he never appreciate the role of his grandfather who tried his best to help Ganpat and saved the family property. His wife wanted to help him but she is also a very egoistic lady, always doubting that other people may grab the property of Ganpat, therefore, she seemed to be more concerned about the property than Ganpat Ram.

Case Study 7

Jasbir Singh aged 49 years, a native of a village in Jind district in Haryana. He belongs to a farmers family, has three brothers and two sisters. He is at number two among siblings. He lived in a joint family with his parents, brothers and two sisters all of whom are now married. Jointly they had 80 acres of land and were living comfortably but later on subsequent to the division of joint family into nuclear families and division of land he got 20 acres of land in his share.

Jasbir Singh was never comfortable in his school life because of which he could not pass middle standard. During childhood he was a very mischievous boy and he started using alcohol in adolescence in the company of his friends from his village and a nearby city. In spite of a strong opposition from his father about the company of his friends and use of alcohol he continued enjoying the company and use of alcohol. Usually he spends his day in city and comes in the night, sometimes late night after totally drunk. Many a times he also misbehaved with his father, mother and elder brother. He never attended to any of agriculture or domestic work of his family and always engaged in street disputes/fights/brawls for which sometimes complaints in police station were filed against him. Because of his father's reputation and intervention the matter was resolved but he never realized his mistake. He always demands money because his expenses were very high. Nobody in family could oppose because he always threatened his family members for separation. After the death of his father the family was divided and now he is a free bird.

He got married at the age of 21. His wife doesn't like his taking alcohol, but he doesn't listen to her and often quarrels with her when drunk. The couple after the marriage of more than 20 years has no child till now. He along with his wife consulted doctors and traditional faith healers, all suggested him to leave alcohol but he ignores it. He claims that in spite of his taking alcohol, he is able to look after his family well, and as far as taking alcohol is concerned, he wants to enjoy his life because he can afford to do so. When asked why he drinks alcohol he very proudly said that he drinks of his own with his personal money why others object to it. He enjoys good respect in his family but now gradually his brother started ignoring him and only intervenes when something serious happens. He links use of alcohol with his family status and always remain in search of occasion to serve alcohol to guests/relatives to boost his status and reputation of family in spite of the opposition of his mother and other family members. He always tries to purchase costly brands of alcohol which resulted into heavy expenses on alcohol and allied things. Because of heavy expenditure on alcohol etc. his financial position is also not good but he does not care for it and takes loan from local financers/grain market agents, or other acquaintances.

His father died of heart attack and at the time of illness of his father he was also in the company of his friends enjoying a cocktail party. Now after the death of his father he continued enjoying alcohol and the company of his friends more freely and frequently. This resulted to serious disputes among brothers and other family members. He started borrowing money from various sources and his debt has mounted up. His consumption of alcohol has also increased. Now he drinks throughout the day and could not avoid drinking due to physical and psychological dependence on alcohol and problems such as pain in stomach and body, becomes irritated very frequently, changes in his voice, speech and gait are clearly visible. His health is deteriorating day by day, to avoid physical and psychological problems he takes more alcohol, avoids consulting doctors and do not care of family concern for him.

Observations

The economic condition of Jasbir Singh is much better than an average farmer. His house is a typical that of an agricultural family, with a good infrastructure available for a good lifestyle in the village. His relationship with his wife was so because she initially obstructed to his drinking but now started ignoring it because of fear. He has no guilt feeling of his alcohol use and loss to his family's reputation.

Analysis

Jasbir Singh was initiated to taking alcohol during his adolescence age by his friends. Some of his close relatives also use alcohol whenever they visited his house, it also precipitated the problem and use of alcohol for Jasbir Singh become a common practice. He take it as a status symbol for his family and himself and very often involved in verbal and physical abuse of his wife, grandiose behaviour, anger, irritability and strained relations with brothers and some immediate relatives. His father could not bear the burden of problems continuously created by Jasbir Singh, suffered heart attack and died. Villagers and some relatives accused Jasbir Singh for the death of his father but he does not care and continued with drinking alcohol.

The health of Jasbir Singh was deteriorating, he complained for stomach pain but avoids consulting doctor and takes alcohol to get relief. Some psychosomatic symptoms such as skin rashes, diarrhoea, respiratory problems with confusion, apprehension and altered sense of perception are also clearly visible. He wants to do something for his family but only thinks of it and do not cooperate with anybody in family.

Case Study 8

Roshan Lal aged 43 years studied upto 6th class native of a village in Hissar district of Haryana is earning ₹ 3,500 pm in a textile mill in Hissar. At present he is living in Hissar with his wife and three children – a boy of eight years and 2 girls of 5 and 2 years.

Originally in his native village he had a joint family with his parents, four brothers, one sister, two uncles, and their families. Jointly they had 60 acres of land cultivating it together and living a comfortable life. But after the marriage of other younger members of the family and increasing needs and aspirations the joint family divided into nuclear families as per the common practice in rural families in Haryana and in traditional Indian family life. This division of family and land among his father and uncle and further among brothers lead to financial strains on the family. Roshan Lal found it difficult to meet with increasing needs of his own family in the village and usual family disputes specially among ladies in the family created more problems for him. He went to Panipat at the age of 20 years in search of work and took up manual jobs in some factory on daily wages. He worked there for three and half years and shifted to another factory after his dispute with his supervisor. After 8–9 months working at this new factory he again shifted to a textile mill at Hissar where he got a job to his satisfaction with initial salary of ₹ 1,500 pm and working in the same factory till now.

After shifting from Panipat to Hissar he developed his own circle of friends with co-workers and others who work in nearby factories. He started joining small get-togethers and evening parties arranged by the friends or co-workers on one or the other pretext.

In these feasts alcohol was served and Roshan Lal enjoyed these feasts. He said that it was not only helpful in getting relief from the day long tiredness and fatigue, but also forgetting the family problems and tension.

He worked hard and got good reputation among the factory staff due to which his salary was also increased time to time. As his income increased, his company with the friends and frequency of get-together and evening parties also increased and his frequency of taking alcohol also went up from occasional to regular and at present he takes alcohol throughout the day. In spite of this he also paid attention to constantly improving his financial position from other sources. He purchased a house in which he lives with his family and also gets about ₹ 800 per month as house rent from two rooms which he has given on rent.

He got married at the age of 24 years to a girl of 16 years. His wife does not like his drinking alcohol, but he does not listen to her and often quarrels with her when drunk. His wife silently complain for his violent behaviour and increasing carelessness toward family due to alcohol use. Many times she objected to the evening parties in which his friends serve alcohol but he never cared and he comes late night after severely drunk. When the researcher asked about his drinking alcohol and related problems he claims that in spite of his taking alcohol, he is able to look after his family well, and so far as his drinking alcohol is concerned, he wants to enjoy his life now when he can afford after a long struggle in his life.

He also maintains relations with his family at village, help his parents and brothers financially. His intake of alcohol is now increasing day by day which cause health problems also. His children are studying in a private school in nearby colony but not doing well in studies. He never give time and rarely attend to the academic needs of his children. When asked about it he said that he is not much educated so he cannot help them, and ignored the question by saying that he do not have much time now and went away.

Observations

The financial condition of Roshan Lal is much better than an average industrial worker. It is because of his hard work in his early days and help from his village property by way of supply of food items etc. The physical condition of his house was typical of a rural based resident. He do not care for maintaining the house, such as furniture etc. He believes in earning for enjoying the life and the needs of wife and children are always last in his priorities. His children are not doing well in their studies but he does not care for it. With the increase in use of alcohol his family problems and social relations also started changing from poor to worse but he is careless and do not agree that alcohol is responsible for it. Relations with wife are also poor. Due to regular use of alcohol with increase in quantity and frequency his health is also deteriorating for which he does not care.

Analysis

Roshan Lal is not able to forget the economic hardships and other problems of his early life at village after the division of family property and working as a labourer in Panipat and Hissar. Now he is financially good but suffers from continuous stress and tension which has no basis and it appears that he uses it only as an excuse to use alcohol. He started using alcohol as social drinking with friends but now he considers it as a source of relaxation and entertainment. To a great extent his circle of friends and co-workers is responsible for exposing Roshan Lal to the use of alcohol on which he has now become dependent. His family condition and future of his children is also very uncertain and he is very careless for this and do not agree that alcohol use is responsible for this situation.

8

Conclusions and Recommendations

The customs of drinking alcohol and the problems related to alcohol abuse are very complex and diverse in nature. Drinking alcohol may never have been problem free for traditional societies, but in the modern world, problems from drinking have taken new dimensions. As alcohol became more easily obtainable, therefore, the consumption increased to alarming levels. In a country like India where illiteracy, ignorance and unawareness for health are common, the increase in use of alcohol is not surprising. There are many social, religious, economic and political grounds, which precipitate the use and abuse of alcohol. These are clearly visible if we go through the records of alcohol sale and data available with the excise departments of the sate governments.

The fast and competitive life has changed the lifestyle, values and thinking of people. Hence, drinking alcohol today cannot be understood easily. Alcohol abuse, heavy and inappropriate drinking leads to serious individual, family, community, and social problems. The ill-effect of alcohol drinking and drinking behaviour affect the whole family in many ways. Drinking impairs the role performance, disturbs social relationships and destroys the financial condition of the family. In terms of traditional problems, it has entered into the new forms, resulting into changes in social circumstances and leading to many serious consequences.

Therefore, on the basis of the analyses of the facts, observation and explanations, analysis of the case studies and experiences shared by the affected families one can conclude that:

- There is a substantial increase in the consumption of alcohol in India as well as in Haryana State. India in general and Haryana in particular is emerging as a rapidly growing market for alcohol production, sale and marketing over the last decade.
- Alcohol use/abuse is increasing in all societies irrespective of region, religion, caste, class, occupation, sex and age considerations.
- Family is the worst sufferer due to alcohol use and the incidences of family violence, child neglect and abuse, broken homes, divorce, separation, accidents show an upward trend which has serious implications on the family.
- The use and abuse of alcohol has seriously disturbed the family relations and the worst affected relationship is the martial relations.
- Violence against women is one of the important consequences of heavy and continuous drinking. Women family members such as mother, sister, daughter, and wife of the alcoholics/problem drinkers face violence ranging from verbal aggression, misbehaviour and physical injuries. The risk of violence increases many times when the male partner drinks alcohol everyday.
- The children of alcoholics/problem drinking parents were found at risk and suffer from various forms of neglect such as improper schooling or even no education, role changes and burdened with responsibilities not suitable to the age, physical and mental torture and violence.
- Families with alcohol problems suffer with serious financial problems. The basic family needs and essential personal requirements of the family members were not fulfilled because one or more family members consume large share of family income in the use of alcohol.
- The use of alcohol starts from social and casual drinking which gradually develops as heavy or problem drinking. This tendency is increasing which is responsible for increasing family problems.
- Because of continuous use of alcohol children in such families suffer from many types of emotional problems, verbal aggression and violence. Children were found suffering with

psychosomatic problems, self-blame, negative attitudes to their parents and themselves, guilt feeling, anxiety-related disorders, plebeians, depression, and disturbed behaviour patterns.

- Children in the families with alcohol use/misuse were involved in illegal activities. Sexual abuse of children (specially girls) was also a serious problem in alcohol using families. Some cases of incest were also reported in the severely affected families.
- Alcohol problems tend to be seen in families and through generations. It is form of 'social contagion' because alcohol drinking/problem drinking is a learned behaviour and because of many reasons, children and other family members imitate the behaviour of alcoholics/problem drinkers.
- The use and abuse of alcohol causes wide range of health problems to the users as well as to other family members. A number of health problems such as pancreatitis, cirrhosis, mal-absorption syndrome, loss of appetite were common among the users. Continuous use of alcohol leads to more complications, which adds to the financial problems because of increasing medical expenses.
- Health status of spouse and children in the families with alcohol use/abuse is very poor. In some families chronic and relapsed cases of TB were also found. Carelessness in medical care and treatment is very common. Children were found suffering with malnutrition, which results to more serious and complicated health problems.
- The family members tried their best to stop the use of alcohol. At one point of time alcoholics/problem drinkers also tried to stop the use of alcohol. But in the absence of proper knowledge and services for treatment they could not succeed. In many cases the families were exploited by some quacks and religious faith healers such as *ojjhas, sufis, sadhus, moulvis* etc. In the absence of proper treatment services, the efforts to stop the use of alcohol usually failed. The services of counseling and de-addiction centres were not found appropriate. These centres do not have proper resources, trained and experienced staff, infrastructure and required support from administration.
- The continuous and problem drinking causes serious damage to the family's social status and reputation. Neighbours, family

friends, relatives and co-workers who initially feel sympathetic to the family gradually start feeling unconcerned, after some-time start alienation and reaches to total dissociation. At one point of time they want to get rid of the suffering family.

- Celebration of social functions, religious ceremonies and family functions were seriously affected by the continuous problem drinking. The family members always suffer with a fear of any miss happening during the function either in their own function or while participating in the other's function. Thus, these families suffer social ostracism which seriously affects the growth of children.
- The continuous use/abuse of alcohol leads to serious financial problems in the family. Family assets such as agriculture land, jewellery, shops, plots, own house, livestock and even small savings of the family members are at stake. Most of the families were suffering from the problem of indebtedness.
- Because of continuous and heavy use of alcohol family suffer social ostracism. The neighbours, family friends, relatives and other acquaintances start ignoring the family of alcoholics/problem drinkers from social functions, marriages, religious, common festivals, and community gatherings.

Recommendations

It is clear from the findings that alcohol use/abuse/misuse is a very serious problem in the society, which affects family in many ways. Fighting with this problem requires serious efforts from all sections in which government has a very important role. There is a need to formulate and implement national policy, which should focus on reducing alcohol related problems. This policy should make clear reference to family alcohol problems.

Central government/state governments must have a commitment to tackle the alcohol problem and not to denounce it on the one hand and promote on the other. Prohibition is enshrined in the Constitution of India under Directive Principles of State Policy. How far prohibition is the answer to the alcohol problems is a serious question but the prohibition introduced in the states of Andhra Pradesh, Gujarat and Haryana has not proved effective and had to reverse the prohibition policy in Andhra Pradesh and Haryana. In the changing situations prohibition may not be the answer to alcohol problems, but a serious attempt on the part of the national government is required which should be based on scientific approach, ways and means to deal with the problem.

The alcohol problem must be addressed in accordance with the international situation because alcohol market is now expanding to developing countries also, which was earlier restricted only to the boundaries of the country. Therefore, the active participation of international organizations such as World Health Drug Control Programme and other agencies involved in this area should be ensured. The study led to the following recommendations for central and state governments:

Policy Strategies

- Experiences show that total prohibition of alcohol is an unachievable goal. It has no impact on the consumption of alcohol, rather it promotes many other problems such as illicit brewing, cross border smuggling and organized crime, involvement of youth in sale, trafficking and distributing of alcohol, etc. More than a national prohibition policy there is a need to introduce effective regulatory measures and preventive steps for controlling the use/misuse/abuse of alcohol. At present, the steps taken for the production sale, purchase and distribution of alcohol are not effectively enforced leading to misuse of the existing laws and bluffing the enforcement agencies. This leads to increase in the consumption of alcohol as a result of which the alcohol problems increase in the families. Strict regulatory mechanisms should be introduced for production, sale, purchase, and distribution of alcohol.
- Production of liquor should be made more strict with implementation of regulations and quality and quantity control measures. The cost of production and profits made thereof are the main attractions for the manufacturers. It should be under very strict control and should not be an attractive business.
- There should be a total ban on all forms of advertising (direct or indirect) and promotional activities of alcohol companies. There is a ban on advertising in India but the indirect advertising is still going on. It should be completely banned and strict punishments should be given to those who violate the ban.

- Licensing system that limits the number and location for sale, time of availability and the size are introduced in one or the other form but these are very loosely implemented. Rampant corruption is a hindrance in proper implementation. It leads to increase in the harmful use of alcohol, which affects the individual, community and the family. Therefore, all the rules related to licensing system for sale of alcoholic products, location for sale, time of availability and the size should be strictly implemented throughout the country. A high level control and monitoring system should be developed to check the corruption involved in implementation of such rules and laws. Small size bottles such as 100 ml or less should be banned and packing in pouch must be stopped.
- Age limit for sale and purchase of alcoholic products, which is 25 years and 18 years respectively, should be strictly enforced. Sale to persons under age should be prohibited and strict punishments should be prescribed for those who violate the rules.
- A range of punishments and penalties increasing at every repeated violation should be introduced against the producers, sellers and distributors such as temporary or permanent closure, cancellation of license, withdrawal of license and black listing should be implemented in order to ensure compliance with the necessary measures.
- Adequate policing and enforcement of alcohol sales and licensing laws should be implemented while focusing at premises associated with a higher level of harm.
- A high-powered independent constitutional body on alcohol and drug abuse should be constituted by bringing a legislation in the Vidhan Sabha.

Education and Public Awareness

- An educational programme focusing on client, suffering family, community to make aware with the features of alcohol, addictive process, social and problem drinking is required to be developed and introduced.
- Such educational programmes should be introduced with policy measures with a focus to reinforce awareness of the problems created by alcohol and to prepare the ground for specific intervention and policy changes.

- Public awareness on the health risks including the intoxicating and addictive characteristics of alcohol consumption and on the benefits of reducing harmful alcohol use should be introduced. This should be done with the help, cooperation and coordination of health department, public relation department and local administration.
- Extensive educational programmes should be introduced to inform children and youth about the consequences of alcohol consumption on health, family and society and of the effective measures that can be taken to prevent and minimize harm from alcohol.
- Sufficient funds should be provided to monitor and evaluate the impact of programmes introduced for education, prevention and public awareness.
- Regular consultations should be made with the neighbouring countries and other countries of world to bring effective changes in the educational and control programmes. The programmes of other countries should be properly evaluated and changed as per the culture, social needs and local requirements before introducing in the new setting.
- Media campaigns should be used to inform and raise awareness among masses about the harm of alcohol use/abuse/misuse. A wide publicity should be made on regular basis for implementation of policy measures and programmes for minimizing the alcohol use.
- Provisions should be made for free telephone helpline for children and women suffering from the alcohol problems so that timely help can be provided by the concerned agencies.

Health and Treatment

- The existing health services do not have any programme to help the individuals and families suffering from alcohol problems. It is important to make necessary changes in the health programmes to introduce special wards, in and out patient services for alcoholics/problem drinkers. In every hospital at district level five to ten beds should be reserved for alcohol patients. Trained and qualified doctors, social workers, para-medical staff should be appointed to extend services to the affected population.

- Community approach for the treatment of alcoholics/problem drinkers, which is cost effective to be promoted in rural areas and small towns. Initial information about the problems of alcohol use and treatment through PHCs (Primary Health Centres) should be provided at the village and city level. The government should provide required manpower and infrastructure.
- To help the families suffering from serious alcohol problems specialized and flexible treatment modalities should be provided to suit individual needs. This can be introduced by networking with other NGOs/Civil Society Organizations. Longer treatment for patients with psychiatric problems, poor social support, lack of employment is very much required. Longer retention in treatment through short-term treatment by admitting in hospital and care followed up by outpatient care in the community.
- Relapse is very common in the treatment of alcohol related problems. It is important to incorporate relapse prevention and long term after care services into existing programmes.
- Government of India has funded detoxification and counseling centres under the auspices of National Drug De-addiction Programme to provide treatment to the people suffering with addiction and alcoholism. In Haryana these Drug De-addiction centre's and counseling centres are also working in all the districts but the working of these centres is far from satisfactory as they receive one time grant. The required political will and administrative help is totally missing. Hence, either the centres are not working properly or defunct. The agencies running these centres are not showing interest in the activities required to help the needy population. Therefore, the government should take urgent steps to run these centres with proper care and attention so that the problem of addiction to alcohol and its effect on family can be properly handled.

Intervention and Assistance for Family Members Affected by Alcoholism/Alcohol Dependence/Problem Drinking

- Drinking of alcohol and harmful use of alcohol is linked with various myths and misconceptions in India. It is a big hurdle in recognizing that harmful alcohol use and alcohol dependence can harm the physical condition, development and well-being of the family members. Hence, efforts should be made to educate the family members in general and the effected people in particular about the pharmacology, characteristics and effects of alcohol consumption.

- Effective legislative, executive, administrative, and other measures necessary to promote the delivery of support and help for the family members of people with harmful alcohol consumption and alcohol dependence should be implemented.
- A comprehensive community based system, which includes close cooperation between the police, social workers, the courts, and judicial system, NGOs and professional diagnostic and counseling services should be developed for family members who suffer from alcohol related problems.
- Children of parents with harmful alcohol consumption and alcohol dependence should be given proper care, help and psychosocial assistance. Programmes to provide support to prevent social neglect because of harmful alcohol use should be developed and introduced to help such families and their children.
- Programmes for diagnosing and counseling adult family members of the alcoholics/alcohol dependents/problem drinkers should be introduced in hospitals. De-addiction centres, counseling centres and rehabilitation centres to help the families with emotional and psychological problems should be established/re-established. The existing arrangement of mental health services in the state run hospitals is insufficient and ineffective.
- Training and support programmes should be developed to expand skills of health workers, primary care providers, volunteers working with support groups for initial intervention for the hazardous and harmful alcohol use and the families affected.

References

Advani, G.B., H.K. Sharma and D. Mohan (1980). 'Alcohol Abuse in Rural Areas of Ajmer District', in D. Mohan et al. (eds), *Observations of Preliminary Research Project in Current Research on Drug Abuse*, New Delhi: Gemini, 169–174.

Ahlstrom-Laakso, S. (1975). *Drinking Habits among Alcoholics*, Helsinki: The Finnish Foundation for Alcohol Studies.

Alwan, Ala (2011). 'Action Needed to Reduce Health Impact of Harmful Alcohol Use', *The Globe*, 1: 3–4.

Balakrishna, N. (1967). 'Road Accidents in India', quoted in chapter 4, 'Alcohol in Machine Age', in *Liquor Menace in India* by Tek Chand, New Delhi: Gandhi Peace Foundation, 1972.

Bang, A.T. and R.A. Bang (1991). 'Community Participation in Research and Action against Alcoholism', *World Health Forum*, 12: 104–109.

Bejarano, J. et al. (2000). 'Consumo de drugs en casta rica ... 1995', in Marva Dixon, 'The Impact of Alcohol in Latin American Countries', *The Globe: Towards a Global Alcohol Policy*, special edition, August: 58–62.

Bejarano, J., H. Carvojal and L. San Lee (1996). 'Consummate de drogas en Costa Rica. Resultados de la encuesta nacional de 1995'. quoted in The Impact of Alcohol in Latin American Countries by Marva Dixon, *The Globe* (special edition), August 2000, London: Institute of Alcohol Studies, 59.

Bhagwat, A.G. and M. Islam (1980). 'Alcoholic Liver Diseases in Man (1911–1979): A Probing Review – Part II', *Indian Journal of Pathology and Microbiology*, 23: 73–88.

Bower, C.D. (1992). 'Physical Effects of Alcohol', *Psychiatry in Practice*, 6–7.

Breeze, E. (1985). *Women and Drinking*, London: HMSO.

Broderick, C.B. and S.S. Schrader (1991). 'The History of Professional Marriage and Family Therapy', in A.S. Gurman and D.P. Kniskern (eds), *Handbook of Family Therapy*, Vol. 2, New York: Brunner.

Bryan, K.J. (2010). 'Alcohol, HIV and Public Health', *The Globe*, Issue 3: 3–4, London: Institute of Alcohol Studies.

Burgess, E.W. and H.J. Locke (1945). *The Family*, New York: American Book Company, 26–27.

Chakravarthy, C. (1990). 'Community Workers Estimate of Drinking and Alcohol-Related Problems in Rural Areas'. *Indian Journal of Psychological Medicine*, 13: 49–56.

Chand, Tek (1972). *Liquor Menace in India*, New Delhi: Gandhi Peace Foundation.

Coleman, (1969). 'Association of Socio-economic Factors, with Drug Use Among College Youth', in *An Indian Town* by M.Z. Khan et al., UNODC.

Cooke, D.J. and C.A. Allan (1984). 'Stressful Life Events and Alcohol Abuse in Women: A General Population Study', *British Journal of Addiction*, 79: 425–433.

Cooper, M.L. (1994). 'Motivations for Alcohol Use among Adolescents', *Psychological Assessment*, 6: 117–128.

Cox, G.B., L. Meijer, D.I. Carr and S.A. Freng (1993). 'Systems Alliance and Support (SAS): A Programme for Intensive Case Management for Chronic Public Inabriates', *Alcoholism Treatment Quarterly*, 3(4): 125–38.

De Boer, N.C. et al. (1993). 'Alcohol and Social Anxiety in Women and Men: Pharmacological and Expectancy Effects', *Addictive Behaviors*, 18: 117–126.

Deb, P.C. and R.B. Jindal (1974). 'Drinking in Rural Areas: A Study in Selected Villages of Punjab', Ludhiana: Punjab Agriculture University.

Desai, N.G. and R. Ray (1989). 'Treatment and Outcome of Alcohol Dependence', in R. Ray and R.W. Pickens (eds), *Proceedings of the Indo-US Symposium on Alcohol and Drug Abuse*, NIMHANS Publication No. 20, Bangalore: National Institute of Public Health and Neuro Sciences (NIMHANS), 109–116.

Desai, N.G. et al. (2003). *Prevention of Harm from Alcohol Use*, New Delhi: WHO.

Detrick, A. and V. Stiepock (1992). 'Treating Persons with Mental Illness, Substance Abuse and Legal Problems: The Rhode Island Experience', *New Directions for Mental Health Services*, 56: 65–77.

Dixon, Marva (2000). 'The Impact of Alcohol in Latin American Countries', *The Globe: Towards a Global Alcohol Policy*, special edition, August: 58–62.

Downs, W.R. and B.A. Miller (1996). 'Inter-generational Links between Childhood Abuse and Alcohol-related Problems in the Community', in Larry Harrison (ed.), *Alcohol Problems in the Community*, London: Routledge.

Dube, K.C. (1972). 'Drug Abuse in Northern India: Observations Concerning Delhi and Agra Regions', *Bulletin on Narcotics*, 24 (1): 49–53.

Dube, K.C. and S.K. Handa (1969). 'Drug Habits in Health and Mental Disorders', *Indian Journal of Psychiatry*, 11: 23.

Edwards, G. (1989). 'Social Background to the Use and Abuse of Alcohol and Drugs: Professional Aspects', *Alcohol and Drug Dependence*, 78–92.

Edwards, G. et al. (1994). *Alcohol Policy and the Public Good*, Oxford: Oxford University Press.

Eurocare (1995). *A Summary of Alcohol Policy and the Public Good: A Guide for Action*, England: WHO.

Eurocare and Coface (1998). *Alcohol Problems in the Family: A Report to the European Union*, Cambridgeshire.

Excise and Taxation Department, Haryana (2007–08). *Haryana Excise Policy*, Chandigarh: Government of Haryana.

Fagan, J. (1993). 'Interactions among Drugs, Alcohol and Violence: Dilemmas and Frameworks of Public Health Policy', *Health Affairs*, 12 (4): 65–79.

Famularo, R. et al. (1992a). 'Parental Substance Abuse and the Nature of Child Maltreatment', *Child Abuse and Neglect*, 16: 475–83.

Famularo, R. et al. (1992b). 'Psychiatric Diagnosis of Abusive Mothers: A Preliminary Report', *Journal of Nervous and Mental Disease*, 180 (10): 681–61.

Fillmore, K. (1988). *Alcohol Use across the Life Course: A Critical Review of Seventy Years of International Longitudinal Research*, Toronto: Addiction Research Foundation.

Finkelhor, D. (1979). *Sexually Victimized Children*, New York: Free Press.

Frazer, J. (1950). *The Golden Bough*, New York: Macmillan.

Friedlander, W.A. and R.Z. Apte (1982). *Introduction to Social Welfare*, New Delhi: Prentice Hall of India.

Goddard, E. (1991). *Drinking in England and Wales in the Late 1980s*, London: HMSD.

Goode, W.J. (1989). *The Family*, New Delhi: Prentice Hall of India.

Grant, M. and R. Hodgson (eds) (1991). *Responding to Drug and Alcohol Problems in the Community: A Manual for Primary Health Workers with Guidelines for Trainers*, Geneva: WHO.

Green, Arnold W. (1972). *Sociology*, New York: McGraw Hill Inc., 449.

Greenfield, T. (1986). 'Quantity Per Occasion and Consequences of Drinking: A Reconsideration and Recommendation'. *International Journal of the Addictions*, 21: 1059–1079.

Gronbeek, M. et al. (1994). 'Influence of Sex, Age, Body Mass Index and Smoking on Alcohol Intake and Mortality', *British Medical Journal*, 308: 302–306.

Gunasekera, O. (2000). 'Curbing the Alcohol Epidemic in Asia', *The Globe: Towards a Global Alcohol Policy*, special edition, August: 63–67.

Gururaj, G. et al. (2011). *Alcohol-related Harm: Implications for Public Health and Policy in India*, Bangalore: National Institute of Public Health and Neuro Sciences (NIMHANS).

Harrison, Larry and Hugo Luck (1996). 'Drinking and Homelessness in UK', in Larry Harrison (ed.), *Alcohol Problems in the Community*, Chapter-5, London: Routledge, 115–140.

Harz, C., M.A. Plant and M. Watts (1990). *Alcohol and Health: A Hand Book of Nurses, Midwives, and Health Visitors*, London: Medical Council on Alcoholism.

Heather, Nick (1995). *Treatment Approaches to Alcohol Problems*, WHO Regional Publications, European Series No. 65, Copenhagen: Regional Office for Europe.

Homan, S. et al. (1993). 'Reaching Beyond Crisis Management: Design and Implementation of Extended Shelter Based Services for Chemically Dependent Homeless Women and their Children', quoted in *Alcohol Problems in the Community* by Larry Harrison (ed.), New York: Routledge: 115–140.

Hurlock, E.B. (1991). *Developmental Psychology: A Life-span Approach*, New Delhi: Tata McGraw Hill Publishing Company Ltd.

ICMR (1977). 'Collaborative Study on the Effects of Intervention Programme on Non-medicinal Use of Drugs in the Country', Preliminary Base Line Survey Report: Summary and Conclusions.

Jernigan, David (2000). 'Alcohol: Bigger Health Threat than Tobacco', *The Globe*, London: Institute of Alcohol Studies.

Johnson, L.C. and S.J. Yanca (2011). *Social Work Practice: A Generalist Approach*, New Delhi: PHI Learning Pvt. Ltd.

Johnson, N.B. (1982). 'Sex Differences, Women's Roles and Alcohol Use: Preliminary National Data', *Journal of Social Issues*, 38: 93–116.

Kantor, G.K. (1996). 'Violent Families and Alcohol-Abusing Families: Examining the Consequences for Children', paper presented at the Annual Meeting of the American Society of Criminology, quoted in *Alcohol Problems in the Community* by Larry Harrison (ed.), London: Routlege, 15–16.

Kantor, G.K. and M.A. Straus (1990). 'Parental Drinking, Violence and Child Aggression', Paper presented at the Annual Meeting of the American Psychological Association, Boston, MA, August.

Knupher, G. (1984). 'The Risks of Drunkenness (or, Ebrietos Resurrleta): A Comparison of Frequent Intoxication Indices and of Population Sub-groups as to Problem Risks', *British Journal of Addiction*, 79: 185–196.

Laticia G. et al. (1996). Manual on Family Therapy, A Project Supported by Europian Union.

Lehto, J. (1995). *The Economics of Alcohol Policy*, WHO Regional Publications, European Series No. 61, Copenhagen: Regional Office for Europe.

Macdanell, A.A. (1951). *A Vedic Reader for Students*, London: Geoffrey Cumberlege, 152–164.

Madrigal, E. (2000). 'Latin America'. Chapter 9, quoted in The Impact of Alcohol in Latin American Countries' by Marva Dixon, *The Globe* (special edition), August, London: Institute of Alcohol Studies, 59.

Mann, Marty (1952). *Primer on Alcoholism*, London: Victor Gollancz Ltd.

Mathrubootham, N. (1989). *Epidemiological Study of Drinking Behaviour in a Rural Population*, Ph.D. Dissertation, University of Madras.

McGlothline, W.H. (1975). 'Drug Use and Abuse: A Research Paper', Washington: National Institute of Mental Health.

McNeil, Andrew (1998). 'Alcohol Problems in the Family: A Report to the European Union', *Health in France*, (1994) French High Committee on Public Health (1996), London, Institute of Alcohol Studies.

Mellibruda, Jerzy (2001). 'Alcohol-related Problems in Poland', *The Globe International: Alcohol and Drug Problems*, Israel: 13–15.

Merikangas, K.R. et al. (1998). 'Comorbidity of Substance Use Disorders with Mood and Anxiety Disorders: Results of the International Consortium of Psychiatric Epidemiology', *Addictive Behaviors*, 23: 893–907.

Mills-Hopper (1992). *Alcohol Concern: Women and Alcohol – A Research-based Evaluation*, London: Mills-Hopper Associates for Alcohol Concern.

Mohan, D. et al. (1980). 'Patterns of Alcohol Consumption of Rural Punjab', *Indian Journal of Medical Research*, 73: 702–711.

Mouly, G. (1968). *Psychology for Effective Teaching*, New York: Holt, Reinhart and Winston.

Murray, C. and A. Lopez (1996). *The Global Burden of Disease*, New York: Oxford University Press.

Murthy, Pratima and M.C. Nirmala (2005). 'Working with Families of Alcohol Dependents', Developing Community Alcohol Rehabilitation and Work Place Prevention Programme, UNODC Regional Office, South Asia.

Natera, G. et al. (1996). 'Marital Violence in Maxico and Its Relation to Excessive Drinking'. paper presented at an International Conference on Intoxication and Aggressive Behavior: Understanding and Preventing Alcohol Related Violence, Toronto.

Neff, J.A. and B.A. Husaini (1985). 'Stress-buffer Properties of Alcohol Consumption: The Role of Urbanicity and Religious Identification', *Journal of Health and Social Behavior*, 26: 207–222.

Nirmala, M.C. and P. Murthy (2005). 'Family Counseling in Drug Addiction', published in Developing Community Drug Rehabilitation and Work Place Prevention Programme, Regional Office for South Asia, New Delhi.

Obot, I.S. (1993). *Drinking Behavior and Attitudes in Nigeria: A General Population Survey (in the Middlebelt Region)*, CDS Monographic Series No. 1193, Jos: University of Jos.

Office of Population Censuses and Surveys (OPCS) (1992). *General Household Survey 1990*, London: HMSO.

Orme, T.C. and J. Rimmer (1981). 'Alcoholism and Child Abuse: A Review', *Journal of Studies on Alcohol*, 42: 73–87.

Pan-American Health Organization (PAHO), Special Report (1990). 'Epidemiological Report on Use and Abuse of Psychoactive Substances in 16 Countries of Latin America and the Caribbean', *Bulletin of PAHO*, 24 (I): 93–139.

Paonaskar, V. (1994). *The Drug Trap*, Bombay: Mejda Marketing Pvt. Ltd.

Pierson, J. and M. Thomas (2010). *Dictionary of Social Work: The Definitive A to Z of Social Work and Social Care*, London: McGraw Hill Open University Press.

Plant, M.A. (1994). 'Reducing Alcohol-related Harm: A Balanced and Disaggregated Perspective', Paper presented at the 5th International Conference on Drug-related Harm, Toronto, Canada.

Plant, M.A. et al. (1985). *Alcohol, Drugs and School Leavers*, London: Tavistock.

Ponnudurai, R. et al. (1991). 'An Epidemiological Study of Alcoholism', *Indian Journal of Psychiatry*, 33: 176–179.

Radomosky, N.A. (1991). 'The Association of Parental Alcoholism and Rigidity with Chronic Illness and Abuse among Women' *Journal of Family Practice*, 35: 54–60.

Rajwanshi, A. et al. (1985). 'Alcoholic Liver Diseases in North India', *Indian Journal of Pathology and Microbiology*, 28: 129–136.

Ranganathan, Shanthi (1989). *Alcoholism and Drug Dependency: The Professional's Master Guide*, New Delhi: Ministry of Welfare, Government of India.

Richardson, D. (1981). 'The Effect of Alcohol on Male Aggression Towards Female Targets', *Motivation and Emotions*, 5: 335–344.

Riley, L. and Mac Marshall (eds) (1999). *Alcohol and Public Health in 8 Developing Countries*, Geneva: WHO.

Room, R. et al. (1995). *Problems Related to Drinking Alcohol in Developing Societies: A Public Health Approach*, Geneva: WHO Publication, 115–164.

Room, Robin et al. (2002). *Alcohol in Developing Societies: A Public Health Approach*, Geneva: WHO.

Rosovosky H. and G. Borges (1992). quoted in 'The Impact of Alcohol in Latin American Countries', by Marva Dixon, *The Globe* (special edition) August 2000: 58–62, London: Institute of Alcohol Studies.

Royal College of General Practitioners (1986). 'Alcohol: A Balanced View', quoted in chapter 7 by Jan Waterson, 'Gender Divisions and Drinking Problems', *Alcohol Problems in the Community* by Larry Harrison (ed.), London: Routledge, 1996: 170–199.

Rutherford, D. (1997). *A Lot of Bottle,* New York: The Institute of Alcohol Studies.

Saxena, S. (1999). 'Memorandum to World Health Organization, Geneva, 14 January 1997', Quoted in Global Status Report on Alcohol 1999, Geneva: WHO.

Saxena, Shekhar (2002). 'Country Profile on Alcohol in India', in L. Riley and Mac Marshall (eds), *Alcohol and Public Health in 8 Developing Countries*, Geneva: WHO, 37–60.

Schuckit, M.A. (1995). 'A Long-term Study of Sins of Alcoholics', *Alcohol Health & Research World,* 19 (3): 172–175.

Sethi, B.B. and J.K. Trivedi (1979). 'Drug Abuse in Rural Population'. *Indian Journal of Psychiatry,* 21: 211–216.

Sgroi, S.M. (1982). *Hand Book of Clinical Intervention in Child Sexual Abuse*, Lexington, M.A: Lexington Books.

Sharma, A. and R.S. Murthy (1988). 'A 4–5 Years of Follow Up Study of Male Alcoholism', *NIMHANS Journal*, 6: 111–113.

Sholevar, G.P. (2003). 'Family Theory and Therapy', in G.P. Sholevar and L.D. Schwoeri (eds), *Textbook of Family and Couples Therapy: Clinical Applications*, Washington, DC: American Psychiatric Publishing Inc.

Singh, Chandra Paul (2000). *Alcohol and Drug Dependence among the Industrial Workers*, Delhi: Shipra Publications, 19–20.

Singh, G. and B. Lal (1979). 'Alcohol in India', *Indian Journal of Psychiatry*, 21: 39–45.

Single, E. and S. Wortley (1993). 'Drinking in Various Settings as it Relates to Demographic Variables and Level of Consumption: Findings from a National Survey in Canada', *Jaurnal of Studies on Alcohol*, 54: 590–599.

Smith, L. (1992). 'Help-seeking in Alcohol-dependent Families', *Alcohol and Alcoholism*, 27 (1): 3–9.

Southern Health Board, Ireland (1997). 'Smoking, Alcohol and Drug Use in Cork and Kerry'.

Statistical Abstract Haryana (2010–11). Publication No. 997, Department of Economic and Statistical Analysis, Government of Haryana, Chandigarh.

Stephens, C.J. (1985). 'Perception of Pregnancy and Social Support as Predictors of Alcohol Consumption during Pregnancy', *Alcoholism: Clinical Experimental Research*, 9: 344–348.

Straton, Peele and Marcus Grant (eds) (1999). *Alcohol and Pleasure: A Health Perspective*, Philadelphia, USA: Brumer Mazel.

Sundaram, K.R. (1981). 'Epidemiological Techniques in Drug Abuse', in Mohan D. et al., *Current Research in Drug Abuse in India*, New Delhi: Gemini, 8–17.

Sundaram, K.R., D. Mohan, G. Advani (1984). 'Alcohol Abuse in a Rural Community in India', Part I: Epidemiological Study. *Drug and Alcohol Dependence*, 14: 27–36.

Taylor, E. (1930). *Anthropology*, London: Watts & Company.

Upadhyay, R.K. (2003). *Social Case Work*, Jaipur and New Delhi: Rawat Publications, 116.

Verma, V.K. et al. (1980). 'Extent and Pattern of Alcohol Use and Alcohol-related Problems in North India', *Indian Journal of Psychiatry*, 22: 331–337.

Waterson, Jan (1996). 'Gender Divisions and Drinking Problems', in Larry Harrison (ed.), *Alcohol Problems in the Community*, Chapter-7, London: Routledge.

West, M.O. and R.J. Prinz (1987). 'Parental Alcoholism and Childhood Psychopathology', *Psychological Bulletin*, 102 (2): 204–218.

World Health Organization (1990). *Drug Dependence and Alcohol-related Problems: A Manual for Community Health Workers with Guidelines for Trainers*, Geneva.

World Health Organization (1993). *International Classification of Diseases-10 (ICD-10)*, Geneva.

World Health Organization (1999). Global Status Report on Alcohol, Geneva.

World Health Organization (2004). 'Global Status Report: Alcohol Policy', Geneva.

Newspapers

The Hindustan Times (1990). 'Haryana Racing Ahead in Liquor Consumptions', 1 January.

——. (1998). 'Faridabad: Wettest in Wet Haryana', 25 August.

——. (1997). 'Village that Ignited Prohibition Spark Repents', 22 December.

——. (1999). 'Serious Health Problems among Indian Women', 12 February.

——. (2002). 'Illicit Liquor Claims Yet Another Life in Tarn Taran', 8 February.

The Times of India (2004). 'Drunk Driving Darkness Festivities', 7 March.

——. (2004a). 'Whisky Still a Big Draw in North India', 24 November.

——. (2005). 'Study Shows Drinking can Boost Brainpower', 5 August.

——. (2007). 'Drunk Man 'Kills' Father-in-Law', 12 December.

The Tribune (2006). 'Illicit Distillation Source of Livelihood', 10 January.

दैनिक भास्कर, (2003), 'धुएं की धुंध में डूबता हरियाणा का किशोर', 20 जनवरी।

हरि भूमि, (2003), 'पंचायत में पुलिस कर्मियों ने माफी मांगी', 4 अगस्त।

दैनिक भास्कर, (2004), 'बच्ची का हत्यारा 14 दिन की हिरासत में', 13 जून।

दैनिक जागरण, (2004), 'धड़ल्ले से हो रहा है शराब का कारोबार', 17 जून।

अमर उजाला, (2004), 'लाहन बरामद', 22 अगस्त।

दैनिक भास्कर, (2004), 'शराब पीकर पुरूषों से अधिक संयमित रहती हैं महिलायें', 27 अक्टूबर।

दैनिक भास्कर, (2004), 'शराब तस्करी में महिला सहित तीन गिरफ्तार', 30 नवम्बर।

दैनिक भास्कर, (2004), 'गूंगी बच्ची से दुष्कर्म', 15 नवम्बर।

दैनिक भास्कर, (2004), 'शराब तस्करी में तीन लोग गिरफ्तार', 18 नवम्बर।

अमर उजाला, (2004), 'दो रूपये में शराब का पैग पीना है तो झबीरण आइये', 3 दिसम्बर।

दैनिक भास्कर, (2004), 'शराब के ठेकों के खिलाफ उतरी महिलाएं', 28 दिसम्बर।

दैनिक भास्कर, (2004), 'बच्ची की पटक-पटक कर हत्या', 9 जनवरी।

दैनिक भास्कर, (2005), 'जहरीला द्रव्य पीने से युवक की मौत', 10 जनवरी।

दैनिक जागरण, (2005), 'धुत वकीलों ने साथी को धुना', 22 जनवरी।

दैनिक जागरण, (2005), 'पहली से होंगी शराब की दुकानें बंद', 30 जनवरी।

दैनिक जागरण, (2005), 'आलू की आड़ में शराब तस्करी', 30 जनवरी।

दैनिक जागरण, (2005), 'भारी मात्रा में शराब बरामद', 6 फरवरी।

दैनिक जागरण, (2005), 'जहरीली शराब से हुई मौत या हृदयघात! मामला गहराया', 7 फरवरी।

दैनिक जागरण, (2005), 'शराब पकड़ने गई पुलिस पार्टी पर हमला', 7 मार्च।

दैनिक भास्कर, (2005), 'लालपरी को लेकर दोस्त ने की थी दोस्त की हत्या', 4 जून।

दैनिक जागरण, (2005), 'नशे में धुत व्यक्ति ने बेटे को मार डाला', 6 जुलाई।

दैनिक जागरण, (2005), 'शराब में जहर मिलाकर पति की हत्या', 13 अगस्त।

दैनिक जागरण, (2005), 'परीक्षा में फेल होने पर बेटे को गोली से उड़ाया', 11 सितम्बर।

दैनिक जागरण, (2005), 'शराबियों ने फोड़ी बोतलें, एक घायल', 12 सितम्बर।

दैनिक जागरण, (2005), 'शींद में दो युवकों ने बेरहमी से की शराबी पिता की हत्या', 12 सितम्बर।

दैनिक जागरण, (2005), 'पत्नी को पीट-पीटकर मार डाला', 8 अक्टूबर।

दैनिक जागरण, (2007), 'अपनों का बहाया खून', 12 अप्रैल।

पंजाब केसरी, (2007), 'जवान बेटी के आगे नंगा नाचा सिरफिरा', 11 सितम्बर।

Index